BLUE GUIDE

CW01509224

AEGEAN TURKEY: FROM TROY TO BODRUM

PAOLA PUGSLEY

BLUE GUIDE AEGEAN TURKEY:
FROM TROY TO BODRUM

Published by Blue Guides Limited, a Somerset Books Company
Unit 2, Old Brewery Road, Wiveliscombe, Somerset TA4 2PW
blueguides.com
'Blue Guide' is a registered trademark.

Text © Paola Pugsley/Blue Guides 2018
The right of Paola Pugsley to be identified as author of this work have been asserted
by her in accordance with the Copyright Designs and Patents Act, 1988.

All rights reserved. No part of this publication may be reproduced or used in
any form or by any means—photographic, electronic or mechanical—without
permission of the publisher.

ISBN 978-1-916568-00-6

The author and publisher have made reasonable efforts to ensure the accuracy
of all the information in this ebook; however, they can accept no responsibility
for any loss, injury or inconvenience sustained by any traveller as a result of
information or advice contained in the guide.

Every effort has been made to trace the copyright owners of material reproduced in
this guide. We would be pleased to hear from any copyright owners we have been
unable to reach.

Statement of editorial independence: Blue Guides, their authors and editors, are
prohibited from accepting payment from any restaurant, hotel, gallery or other
establishment for its inclusion in this guide or on www.blueguides.com, or for a
more favourable mention than would otherwise have been made.

Series editor: Annabel Barber
Maps, plans and graphics by Blue Guides and Imre Bába © Blue Guides
Digitised by Zsolt Átányi with Anikó Kuzmich.

Cover image: Poppies at Hierapolis. Photo taken by the author
This image and the photo on p. 7 © Paola Pugsley.

blueguides.com
'Blue Guide' is a registered trademark.
We welcome reader comments, questions and feedback:
editorial@blueguides.com

About the author
Paola Pugsley is a professional archaeologist with an interest in the
Mediterranean and particularly in the eastern part of it. She first visited Turkey in
1970 as a tourist, driving all the way to the Nemrut Dağ, which she climbed on a
most uncomfortable donkey. She vowed to return—but had to wait until
the early 1990s. From then on she has worked every summer on excavations,
moving steadily east. Her interest lies in bringing to life the visible and invisible
past and in encouraging visitors and armchair travellers alike to engage in and see
the sites both in their long-term development and physical setting.
Other volumes in this series are *Blue Guide Eastern Turkey*,
Blue Guide Southeastern Turkey, *Blue Guide Central Anatolia*,
Blue Guide The Black Sea Coast and *Blue Guide Mediterranean Turkey*.

CONTENTS

INTRODUCTION

When Freya Stark came here in the early autumn of 1952, she was on a quest (the very word she used in the title of the book detailing her adventures: *Ionia: A Quest*). Armed with her Classics, she was looking for the material reality underpinning the narratives of the likes of Herodotus and Pindar. As far as she was concerned, she was in Ionia (the other component of the title), sometimes in Aeolia, occasionally in Caria. She never doubted that she, like the antiquarian travellers before her, was in an extension of ancient Greece. Her experience remains unique: travelling as a woman, a foreigner and on her own, she aroused curiosity and a sort of protective sympathy. She had a novelty value that made her feel occasionally like an animal in a zoo but which at times secured VIP treatment from the local people. Archaeologically the region was not ready for her (hence her disparaging comments on the state of the theatre at Pergamon). Transportation was not easy; the crossing of the Meander Delta, some 8km wide, entailed the use of a lorry, a tractor, a ferry and an overnight stay. She came across only one visitor on the same quest as hers, and yet she toured 55 sites.

Seventy years on, things have changed in many respects. Today, for a start, you will certainly not be alone, probably not even in the depths of winter (the climate on the coast can be benign and Turkish pensioners use timeshares for a week in the sun when the tourists are away). And in the high season, tourists come not in units but in millions. Despite the efforts of the Turkish government to rebalance and diversify tourism away from the coast and direct it more to the interior (set out in a document detailing the strategy for 2023, the centenary of the Republic), it may prove difficult to persuade holiday-makers to eschew the beaches. As far as archaeology is concerned, the region has been made ready for mass consumption. When I was here in 1969, it was still possible to photograph, not far from the main road, a couple of marble Ionian columns topped with an architrave. They stood sprouting from an overgrown field like an improbable weed. Now archaeological remains have either been obliterated by development, neglect, stone robbing or ploughing or they are fenced off, restored, reconstructed and signposted. They come with a *bekçi* (custodian), an entry ticket and a visitor centre. Bodrum and İzmir have major airports, which means you can bypass Istanbul altogether, and the roads have improved enormously—though the topography still makes for some interesting driving. Crossing the Meander, at any rate, is no longer a challenge.

This volume, which follows the coast from Troy to Bodrum, must necessarily start, before getting into detail, with a little geography. The topographical constraints that almost no longer exist have nevertheless been a reality for thousands of years and have impinged on the human development of the area. They cannot be ignored or brushed aside. Moreover, politically, the shores of Aegean Turkey are where Greece took off, where Greece met Anatolia. For millennia this was one world and the flow of people and ideas across the Aegean is another reality that has only recently been halted—in this case by an intrusive border.

Geographically, 'Troy to Bodrum' is a hilly region, subject to frequent earth tremors and landslides, very much like of the rest of Turkey. It is crossed by two mountain ranges running east–west. One extends into the Çeşme peninsula; the other, to the south, runs along the north bank of the Meander and ends at the Aegean in the Samsun Dağı, the ancient Mycale. These hard schist ridges are high enough to be a barrier to movement. They are separated by depressions into which the main rivers run. From the north (with the ancient names in brackets) they are the Bakır Çay (Caecus/Kaikos), the Gediz Çay (Hermus), the Küçük

Half-hidden in the undergrowth: the state of play in 1969.

Menderes (Cayster) and the Büyük Menderes (Meander). The last three run not along valleys cut by running water but in grabens, flat-bottomed depressions caused by the collapse of the sea floor. As a consequence, their valleys are wide and U-shaped and because of the shallow gradient, the waters move slowly, with plenty of time and space to shed silt and anything else they are carrying. Land is constantly created at the mouth of the rivers while recurrent flooding and alluviation ensure a continual renewal of the surfaces under cultivation (though this might be less true today, with dams and other mechanisms to control the flow of water). Agriculture (vines, olives, cereal crops and animal rearing) has always been strong but it developed in pockets, separated by areas of scrub, maquis, swamp and forest (the last two now much depleted).

On the coast, the sea provided a means of communication. Although it is not very deep, it is prone to treacherous currents and storms. The horst geology (i.e. the presence of raised ridges between the grabens) has not been favourable to the formation of good harbours. Even the most famous anchorage, İzmir, is not free of problems. Up until very recently these ecological constraints weighed heavily on the development of the area. While rivers were navigable in antiquity and were the main route for inland penetration, the immediate hinterland remained difficult to cross north–south, affording plenty of pockets where unruly nomadic Türkmen could defy an Ottoman government which as late as the 19th century still wished to turn them into settled taxpayers. Bandits also occupied the sparsely populated mountains. Çakırcalı Mehmet Efe, whose headquarters were at Ödemiş southeast of İzmir, was able to terrorise the area (a thousand murders were attributed to him) until he was killed by police at Muğla in 1912. Even so, he managed to construct for himself a reputation as a sort of Robin Hood and his life was celebrated in a work by the Ankara State Ballet in 2010.

Historically, occupation has been dense in the valleys and on the coast. Urbanisation has been part of the landscape since ancient times, shrinking only with the Byzantines, who maintained few towns inland and those mainly for strategic purposes, to stem the flow of nomads down the Meander Valley.

THE PURPOSE OF THIS TRAVEL GUIDE

The purpose of this guide, like the others in this series, is both to entice and explain. The Aegean coast of Turkey probably needs no introduction as it has been a popular destination since mass tourism developed. Before that it figured prominently in antiquarians' lists of 'places to see'. It is already covered by a multitude of travel guides. This one begs to be different. Remains of the past do not just stand in isolation in time and space. The painstaking work of archaeologists and historians goes well beyond the here and now that you can experience when visiting. Monuments have a long history. Earlier developments can explain why they are where they are and account for their appearance; later events cover the period of degradation, the inevitable result of neglect when a structure has lost its *raison d'être*. Today these signs can be read in the archaeological and historical records: piecing them together enriches the experience of any visitor.

In these troubled times, when the number of tourists to popular Turkish destinations has plummeted because of perceived insecurity and a tricky political situation, this guide offers a chance for the armchair tourist to experience and explore in absolute safety. A later actual visit will then be enhanced by solid background knowledge.

This short volume does not aim at a complete write-up of the history of the area but enough information will be on hand when needed, site by site, rather than in a lump at the end labelled 'Background Information', in small print that no one will ever read. Additionally, to keep everything in context, there is a rough timeline at the end of this book, together with a glossary. In order to keep the text light and readable, italics have been kept to a minimum and commonly-used Turkish words in the plural have been given an ungrammatical 's' ending (e.g. otogars, Turkish coach stations). The pronunciation guide is no more than what it says: a guide, with the aim of helping travellers to read and say place names correctly so that they can ask for directions.

AEOLIA, IONIA AND ANCIENT MIGRATION

The idea that the east coast of the Aegean was systematically colonised by mainland Greeks, i.e. by would-be colonists under the leadership of a hero, is deeply engrained. Travellers, including Freya Stark, and archaeologists working on location, have all taken it as a fact. The ancient sources, albeit with a number of variants, agree that the Aeolians, a few years after the Trojan War, set out from Thessaly (or was it Boeotia?) under the leadership of Orestes, son of Agamemnon, to settle in Lesbos and on the coast north of the Gulf of İzmir. Four generations later the Ionians, fleeing the invading Dorians, occupied the coast south of İzmir as well as the islands of Chios and Samos. They had strong support in Athens and the enterprise was eventually presented as an Athenian triumph. Each ethnic group was organised into a federation of twelve cities. The Aeolian League had its seat at the Temple of Apollo at Gryneum; and the Ionian League had theirs at the Temple of Poseidon on the Mycale peninsula.

All this accorded well with the colonial attitudes of the late 19th century, when excavations began. After the Bronze Age, it was reckoned, progress could only have come from the West. However, as archaeological research continued, the evidence to back up this narrative failed to materialise. There is no trace in the Archaic material of a single dominant group either north or south of İzmir; no trace of new arrivals; no changes in the pottery. Archaeologically speaking, an Iron-Age Greek migration into western Asia remains invisible.

A re-evaluation of the sources was thus long overdue. It is interesting that Homer (7th century BC), who was well placed in İzmir, at the supposed junction of the two ethnicities, has nothing to say on the matter. No Aeolia, no migrations. The information comes later, and the later it is, the more detailed and complete. Strabo, in the 1st century AD, gives the fullest account. On the ground, however, archaeology for the 7th century BC shows a very reduced Greek presence on the coast, with Phrygians and Lydians dominant in the hinterland. The leagues, it has been suggested, were not an expression of 'being Greek' but a way to cope with the patchwork of diverse ethnic groups that had occupied the space left by the demise of the Hittite Empire. About the same time, the expansionist policy of Miletus, up the coast and into the Black Sea, encouraged Athens to do likewise and set up a colony at Sigeum in the Troad, as close as possible to Troy, which was taking off as a cult centre celebrating Homeric heroes. Identities were being established with the assistance of made-up genealogies; new identities were forged as a reaction. The climax came with the Persian Wars at the end of the 5th century BC, when Athens was able to establish its primacy. It is then that Ionia (Aeolia had by then faded) looked west for leadership and the migration myth was crystallised. In the Hellenistic period Troy, Priene, Pergamon and Sardis all organised games in imitation of the Athenian *Panathenaica*. Architectural styles converge and Athens emerges as the mother of them all. The triumph of Ionia lives on today in the Turkish word for Greece: Yunanistan.

TROY & THE TROAD

Troy, by the village of Truva (in the Biga Peninsula, c. 16km south of Çanakkale, signposted; *map A, 5; open daily 8–7.30, shorter hours in winter, charge*) is a small place with an immense aura, so big that over half a million visitors come here every year to see it—although the visible remains amount, quite honestly, to not much more than some derelict stone walls and the odd ruin. Nevertheless, after 2,500 years the 'Troy effect' remains undiminished (*see below*). On the ground, the identity of Troy, its *raison d'être*, its development and eventual demise as a functioning settlement, are still hotly debated but as excavations progress and past work is reassessed, the picture is becoming clearer.

THE TROY EFFECT AND THE GREAT IDENTITY MUDDLE

It has been said that if Homer visited Troy today he would not recognise the place because its environment has changed so much. That is certainly true but other forces have been at work and even the Trojans themselves, or at least those who were alive during the Trojan War, would, if they came back, suffer a major identity crisis. Identity is the mainstay of archaeology these days and Troy is a good example of how it can alter with the twists and turns of fate.

It can be said with some certainty that Troy began as a native settlement of Anatolians, a people about whom we know very little. Whatever the reason for the Trojan War of c. 1200 BC, it was fought between the native Trojans and their allies on the one hand, and outsiders, the Mycenaean Greeks, on the other. After their defeat the Trojans dispersed. The victors went home to their various native cities and the site of Troy was eventually deserted. That said, some form of ritual celebration of heroic ancestors had been taking place there for a while by the time that Xerxes, the Persian king, came by in 480 BC, the Temple of Athena and the treasury had been set up. The place was certainly not empty: Greeks and other migrants from the West had occupied the space vacated by the Trojans. Later, in 334 BC, Alexander the Great arrived on the same quest as Xerxes (although he was ultimately heading east). He also boasted an ancestor's claim in that, apparently, his mother was a descendant of Achilles. He bestowed the status of *polis* on the site and encouraged the cult of ancestors and heroes. The Homeric myths of which Troy was the physical manifestation became the glue uniting the region's disparate communities. Besides Hisarlık and its temple to Athena, other features in the landscape were pressed into service to reinforce the aura. Various humps and bumps in the surrounding terrain were promoted to the status of heroes' graves. Thus, for instance, the mound at the south of the Sigeon Ridge to the west, originally a Neolithic settlement, was monumentalised in the 3rd century BC as the 'Achilleion' or resting place of Achilles.

Round about this time, the myth of Aeneas was taking shape, the story of the gallant Trojan who had fled the doomed city in flames, heading west with his father on his back and leading his young son Ascanius (also known as Iulus). His piety and bravery had made him a suitable ancestor for an up-and-coming Mediterranean power looking for credentials: Rome. As an added bonus, Aeneas was related to King Priam and Venus was his mother. Wrapped up in beautiful hexameters by Virgil, the saga became the bedrock of the legitimacy of the Julio-Claudian dynasty and its successors. Yet although rooted in the Homeric classical tradition (the mainstay of any form of education and culture, the essence of things Greek that Rome so much admired and wished to appropriate), the story, if one thinks about it, actually celebrates a bunch of losers. The Trojans—albeit bravely—had lost the war and it is strange that the martial Romans should have chosen the vanquished, however pious, as ancestors (Dio Chrysostom, the 1st-century AD writer and orator, had spotted the incongruity and suggested in his *Oration to the Trojans* that in reality it was the Greeks who had lost the war and that Aeneas had set forth not as a fugitive but as a conquering coloniser).

The beautification of Troy reached its peak under the Romans, who poured vast resources into it and encouraged its cult. Distinguished visitors like Caesar and Germanicus made an appearance. Later, Hadrian rebuilt the tumulus of Ajax by the Hellespont, a little bit inland so that the sea would not damage it. Caracalla erected a tumulus (today's Uvecik Tepe) for his freedman Festus, mimicking Achilles and the funerary monument he built for Patroclus. A statue to Achilles was also erected. And so it continued. Emperor Julian in the 4th century found the Temple of Athena in good shape (much to his surprise; it appeared that Christianity was no threat). By the 5th century, however, pilgrims had ceased to come. Times were hard and the pilgrims' map had altered.

The pull of Troy, however, had not vanished. For the European ruling houses from Charlemagne onwards, legitimacy meant being able to establish a connection with the defunct Roman Empire. In Britain, Brutus (great-grandson of Aeneas) was chosen by Geoffrey of Monmouth in the mid-12th century to act as founding father, uniting the Normans and the Anglo Saxons. Antenor, a relation of Priam, became the founder of Padua and also the ancestor of the Danes. As late as 1714, Jean Lévesque de Burigny enjoyed a spell in the Bastille for daring to suggest that the Franks were not Trojans but migrants from Germany.

Back in Asia Minor, after the 15th-century historian Michael Critobulus compared the sack of Byzantium by Mehmet II to the sack of Troy (the sacred locus of East-West rivalry), Mehmet himself made an appearance at the site, in August 1462. He did not come expressly to visit Troy (he was on his way to attack Lesbos), but while here he found time to address the local population and to inform them that they had been avenged, since he had toppled the Byzantine Greeks. He addressed his audience as Teucri, a reference to the mythical founder of Troy thousands years before but also a word that happened to chime usefully with 'Turchi', as these latest arrivals on the western Asian scene were called by Venetian merchants. It was they who had been the first (in 1337) to use the word 'Turchia' to designate the new ethnic status of the land the Byzantines had been forced to vacate, when referring to the Menteşe emir as '*dominus Turquiae*'. Mehmet II had classical ambitions; it is rumoured that he even had a codex of the *Iliad* in his library. His courtiers probably spotted the pleasing assonance. The idea was not original; it was current in Europe at the time as one of the explanations proffered to make sense of historical developments. What Mehmet's Trojan audience made of it one does not know.

Troy is a UNESCO site within a national park (Troya Milli Tarihi Parkı), set up in the 1970s to protect the area's culture and ecology. With minimal park administration, however, no rangers, rampant urbanisation and the intensification of agriculture and road building, it is no surprise that ecological damage continues unabated. It is true that the dam on the Karamenderes Çay, the ancient Scamander, is outside the park, but its effect will nevertheless be felt well within it. The floodplain of the Scamander, Troy's home ground, is a favourite place for migrant birds. But Troy is used to ecological changes. The study of deep cores has enabled a reconstruction of the evolution of the past environment showing that 10,000 years ago the sea lapped the edges of the high plateau (250m) to the south, creating a bay on whose east coast, according to some, a settlement developed in the mid-4th millennium BC (known as Troy 0). This was on a hillock (Hisarlık; *see below*) overlooking the plain which by that time was already silting up, filling in bays to the west, the estuary of the Dümrek Su (the ancient Simois) and eventually reaching the present coastline, which is unlikely to progress further. The mighty currents of the Hellespont, here only 2km wide, which are known to reach a speed of one metre per second, as well as the strong northeasterly winds and the waves, will see to that.

The development of the settlement, now studied in painstaking detail, has proved to be unique. Urban conglomerations normally wax and wane according to economic, commercial or physical factors. Pompeii is a prime example. Troy has added a new dimension to this rule in that it has existed and sometimes prospered for 2,500 years, purely as a place of memory of the heroes and gods central to Graeco-Roman civilisation. And the cult shows no signs of abating: if anything, with tourism, it has extended its appeal well beyond its original Mediterranean sphere.

NINE OR TEN CITIES: THE PHASES OF TROY

The history of Troy is condensed within 47 layers that belong to nine or ten superimposed cities and settlements starting in the Middle Bronze Age (mid-4th millennium BC). The Homeric Troy is Troy VII. A map of the site and the building layers is given below, with descriptions of the various phases of the city.

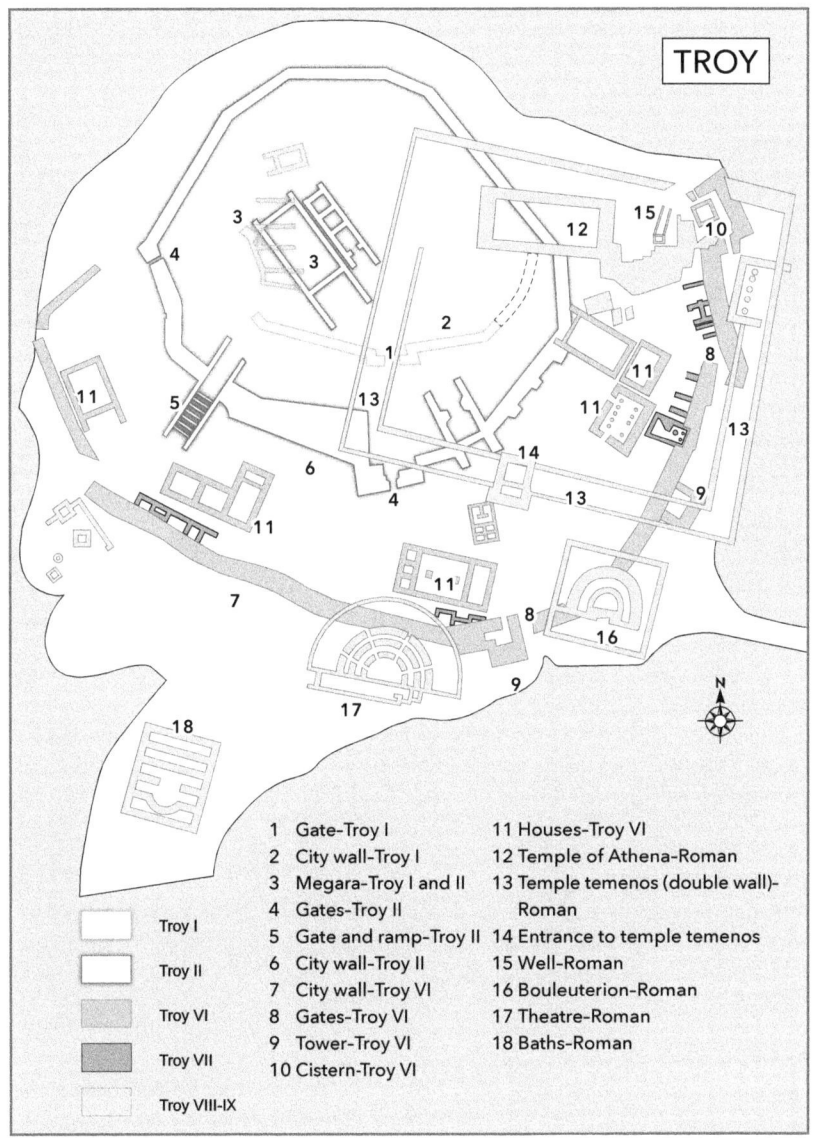

1 Gate-Troy I	11 Houses-Troy VI
2 City wall-Troy I	12 Temple of Athena-Roman
3 Megara-Troy I and II	13 Temple temenos (double wall)-
4 Gates-Troy II	Roman
5 Gate and ramp-Troy II	14 Entrance to temple temenos
6 City wall-Troy II	15 Well-Roman
7 City wall-Troy VI	16 Bouleuterion-Roman
8 Gates-Troy VI	17 Theatre-Roman
9 Tower-Troy VI	18 Baths-Roman
10 Cistern-Troy VI	

Troy I
Troy II
Troy VI
Troy VII
Troy VIII-IX

TROY 0

Not much is known about Troy 0 and even less why that particular spot was chosen. It is a vantage point with a steep drop to the west, but there is a higher vantage point immediately to the south. The choice is thought to have been linked to maritime trade and to access to the Black Sea, but how much maritime trade was there in those early days? Moreover, if ships needed a place to shelter while waiting for favourable winds to enter the Dardanelles, the waters in the bay, shallow and prone to silting up as they are, would not have been much use. Later, ships used Beşik Bay to the west, directly overlooking the Aegean, for that purpose.

TROY I

Troy I (early 3rd millennium BC) was probably just a fishing community. It may have had a harbour, though harbours in this shifting topography are not much of a certainty. Troy I's mudbrick housing was strictly egalitarian and utilitarian—and not very comfortable because of lack of light and of communal spaces. It consisted of a row of long rooms fronting the street. In this it differed from the Aegean set-up, where dwellings are typically clustered around a central court, as well as from Eastern and Central Anatolia's totally unplanned housing. The site was defended. Remains of a defensive wall built in a characteristic herringbone pattern can be seen in the middle of the mound at the bottom of the so-called 'Schliemann Trench', where the German excavator went down to bedrock looking for Homer and his heroes and, in so doing, revealed the depth of the settlement deposits. Troy I was destroyed by a conflagration.

TROY II

Troy I was followed by Troy II (2600–2400 BC) and a change of scene. We now see an elite emerging, with a spacious megaron as the ruler's dwelling. The walled site, still small (110m across) and featuring a spectacular ramp (now restored), has far-flung connections. It would seem, from the finds, to have been able to control the movement of a small amount of luxury items, either as a gate to Anatolia or as part of the Aegean–Black Sea route. The so-called Priam's Treasure found in this context (*see p. 17*) fits well into the picture. One is reminded of Alaca Hüyük and Horoztepe's spectacular finds (*for Alaca Hüyük, see Blue Guide Central Anatolia; for Horoztepe, see Blue Guide Turkey: the Black Sea Coast*).

TROY III, IV AND V

After destruction by fire, Troy III and IV and V, which cover the period to 1800 BC, are of lesser importance, just farming communities it would seem. However, the evidence of Minoan contacts provided by the presence of Linear A writing is quite spectacular.

TROY VI AND VII

The tail end of the Bronze Age, to c. 1200 BC, is the period when Troy comes into its own. Tablets from Boğazköy identify it as Wilusa (a denomination thought by some to be the origin of Ilium, an alternative name for Troy), the capital of a petty kingdom covering the Biga peninsula, part of Arzawa, a loose confederation of tribes, possibly a Hittite vassal, in a constant war of attrition with the Myceneans. Resources included wool, timber and agricultural produce; trade, and income also came from horse breeding, piracy, slave raids and harbour dues. Miletus had returned to Hittite hands in 1250 BC, though the event had not deterred the Mycenaeans from conducting an aggressive policy. Their slave raids on the Anatolian coast had angered the Hittite king, Hattusilis III. This is Troy VI. Its walled acropolis, with five gates in a 3m thick and 9m high wall made of well-fitted limestone blocks topped by a mud brick superstructure, was certainly made to impress. Its high-status buildings were obliterated by later constructions. The lower town, with an estimated population of 10,000, was defended by a wall and a ditch. After earthquake damage, Troy VI was succeeded by Troy VII, which by almost general consensus was the Homeric Troy destroyed by human agency c. 1200 BC. Arrowheads, slingshots and spear points have been found in the charred debris. For about 500 years after the destruction the city lay low. It was eventually reoccupied by people apparently from the north; their knobbed pottery says that much at least. Their houses were small and mean.

Homer's *Iliad*, which was to propel Troy to stardom, dates from the second half of the 8th century BC. It was certainly preceded by much oral transmission, with bards singing of the 'wrath of Achilles' and the 'rosy-fingered dawn' at banquets and other public gatherings. The legend grew and grew, attaining cult status. By Homer's time, Priam's Troy was no more but its ruins could still be seen, especially a stretch of the Troy VII acropolis wall just south of the later Temple of Athena. Here, by the outer face of the wall, a high platform with 28 stone circles has been excavated. Drinking vessels dated to c. 8th/7th century BC and traces of burning suggested a funerary ritual with ancestor worship, as found on the Greek islands, Naxos being but one example. This is the time of population movements; the pottery is proto-Geometric, a style which is not Anatolian and may be linked to a Greek presence along the coast. The next we know about the area is that Xerxes, on his way west to attack Athens, stopped here in 480 BC and performed a king's sacrifice involving a thousand oxen (*Herodotus, 7:43*). Was he an admirer of Homer or did he think that starving the locals would make them more malleable? By then the stone circles were out of use and the only temple was apparently dedicated to a local goddess or to Cybele. Troy became Persian for a while and declined even further. It was revived by Alexander the Great, on his way east to conquer the world. He had certainly read his *Iliad* and was inspired to confer the status of *polis* on the ruins. Among the ruins, however, there was a small temple dedicated to Athena and in the temple a treasury with 'original' weapons from the Trojan War, by then an event a thousand years old. Alexander left his own armour in exchange for some of the antiquities. Then he made sacrifices to entreat the spirit of Priam and ran naked all the way to the Achilleion, the presumed tomb of Achilles on the Sigeon Ridge.

TROY VIII

Troy was by now a Greek city, unwalled at first, until the Galatians struck in 270 BC. It was taken under the protective wing of Athens and elevated to the status of capital of the Athena Koinon, a loose federation of coastal Greek cities. A new temple to Athena Ilias went up, an ambitious project with an immense temenos, the building of which accounts for the obliteration of much of the preceding levels. The treasury of the league was kept here. With amazing attention to detail, Athens incorporated into the design of the building the legend of the Locris maidens. It runs like this: to atone for the misdeeds of their ancestor Ajax (he had raped Cassandra in full view of the statue of Athena where she had sought protection), the people of Locris would send two maidens to the temple every year to do menial tasks. The maidens had to avoid being seen by the goddess (or at least by her statue) and were advised not to venture outside as the locals were allowed to stone them to death on sight. An underground passage between the north edge of the temenos and a well kept them out of sight of the irascible goddess. The temple, the propylon and the access ramp were all modelled on the Athenian acropolis. The festivities were the same: Panathenaica games were celebrated here and in other poleis of the newly-created Ionia, except that here they included performances of the Homeric poems with the remains of the Troy VII wall as a backdrop. The city was now called Ilium, a homage to Priam's grandfather.

TROY IX AND TROY X

Troy IX marks the advent of the Romans and the reconstruction after damage inflicted by the Roman rebel Fimbria in 85 BC. The renovation began with a visit by Augustus, who claimed Trojan ancestry, in 20 BC. Whether he contributed personally or used his elevated status to encourage others, is not clear but it certainly worked, then and later on. Ilium received in due course a stoa, an aqueduct, a nymphaeum, baths, a theatre to complement the Hellenistic odeion (repaired after earthquake damage and beautified with coloured marble by Hadrian in AD 124), a collection of statues for the agora and other buildings of unknown purpose. Whenever there was an earth tremor, Rome was ready to proffer help, and there was peace for 300 years. Ilium then minted its own coins and rivalled Aphrodisias as a recipient of imperial favour.

Late Antiquity is kind to Ilium, but decline sets in nevertheless. By AD 500, the agora was being used as a cemetery, the lower town was abandoned and people sought refuge in the citadel. Bishops are attested but no recognisable Christian buildings have been identified; they could have been in the lower town, of which barely two percent has been excavated (the bulk of information about it comes from geophysics), or it could simply be that the cult of Ilium was regarded as timeless and was thus not considered unacceptably pagan.

Troy X (Byzantine Troy) is little known. It was the first to suffer from the arrival of the Turks in 1309.

HISTORY OF THE EXCAVATIONS

Troy is the site of the Trojan War as codified by Homer, a native of Smyrna, in the first extensive works in the Greek language that were destined to become, until comparatively recently, a cornerstone of Western education. It comes as no surprise, therefore, that the quest for the place where it all happened had been in motion from early on. The Romans, and before them the Greeks, seem to have known where to look: the ritual complexes they built were exactly on top of the Troy of the Trojan War. But in the Middle Ages the memories faded and were lost, buildings crumbled, doubts crept in and alternative sites were proposed on the basis of topographical details provided by Homer. The Biga peninsula has other ancient settlements and ruins are not an uncommon occurrence in the wider area.

A thorough investigation on the spot was rightly thought to provide proof, and, as archaeology developed in the second half of the 19th century, the quest for Troy intensified. Heinrich Schliemann, who is credited with discovering Homeric Troy, was not the first to believe firmly in the potential of the hill of Hisarlık (the place of the fort), though all he could see at the time was rubble on the mound and some Hellenistic remains lower down. Frank Calvert, among others, shared the belief. Indeed Calvert, an English gentleman farmer living in the vicinity and with a long association with the area, had discovered the Temple of Athena on Hisarlık and had purchased part of the mound. The German-born Schliemann, however, had more of the requisites for such an ambitious project: a larger than life personality, a driving enthusiasm, his own money, experience of the world beyond the cossetted reaches of academia and a generous helping of ruthlessness. His work, which brought him fame and recognition, was criticised by his contemporaries and by the archaeologists who later had to make sense of his notes, his muddled recording, his unorthodox procedures and his sometimes hasty conclusions. But he found what he thought at the time was the proof: Priam's treasure (*see box below*). That he got it wrong by a thousand years is almost immaterial. Subsequent work, mainly by German and American archaeologists, has proven conclusively that Hisarlık was the site of Homer's Troy.

Excavations are ongoing to this day. They have extended to the area below the mound to the south, the site of the lower city discovered by Franz Kauffer, an engineer doing survey work in 1793 for the French ambassador to the Ottoman Court. The lower town was laid out on a grid and was particularly extensive in the Roman period, featuring houses with mosaic floors. It was defended by a wall and a ditch. It is not open to the public.

PRIAM'S TREASURE

On 27th May 1873, the Ottoman government representative Amin Efendi was alerted by workers that important finds had come to light in the so-called Schliemann Trench, a north–south excavation, 40m wide and 17m deep, intended to reach bedrock and establish a stratigraphy. Schliemann had been there on his own or with his wife Sophia, and it is not quite clear exactly what he found. The findspot itself is controversial. The level is Troy II and the discovery of treasure deep down in a burnt layer convinced him that he had hit Priam's palace, though in fact he was out by about 1000 years.

Given the outstanding nature of the material, his main concern was to move it abroad as quickly as possible. In that he was successful as, while Amin Efendi went to the Dardanelles for further instructions, the finds were packed and taken to Frank Calvert's farm. At that point they consisted of six crates and a bag. By June 6th they had reached the Greek island of Syros, where there were no customs, and proceeded to Athens. Here Schliemann made a new inventory and it seems that other objects were added to the original hoard of gold and silver jewellery and vessels, bronze daggers, axes and chisels. The Turks were understandably upset since the permit that they had granted to Schliemann contained a clause whereby finds were to be split 50/50.

Schliemann himself, however, was not too worried. He was well aware of the bargaining power that such an extraordinary find conferred. European museums would vie to lay their hands on it and officialdom could be counted upon to pacify the Ottomans and assist him in getting a new excavation permit. The Ottoman government sued in the Greek courts but the Greeks found that they had no authority to judge a case between two parties of whom neither was a Greek citizen. When the decision was reversed by the Royal Court and the treasure was to be seized, it disappeared. An out of court settlement was reached, money changed hands, though it is not clear exactly what was agreed. There was no paper trail. The hoard resurfaced in London and was on display at the Victoria & Albert Museum in December 1877. Possible sales to the British Museum, the Hermitage and the Smithsonian fell through and a few years later the objects were on the move again, this time to Germany. The original 'six crates and a bag' had become 40 crates. It is thought that Schliemann had been adding material from other parts of the site—or from other sites altogether—to make the collection more appealing. He eventually decided to donate it to the German people, much to the chagrin of his wife, who would have preferred to use it to decorate their mansion in Athens.

At the time of WWII, the basement of the Arts Museum in Berlin was deemed sufficiently safe but later another move was planned, to the Flakturm, an anti-aircraft tower in the city-centre zoo. Here the treasure and other invaluable pieces such as the head of Nefertiti and the Pergamon marbles were stored. In 1945, however, the Russian Trophy Brigades, specifically designed to target artworks to move them to the USSR, seized it and took it to the Pushkin Museum in Moscow, where it sank beneath the western radar. With Glasnost, things opened up a bit and crucial evidence was supplied by the museum cleaners, who came across some relevant paperwork. Eventually, in 1990, the museum acknowledged that it had the collection, which is currently on display there. It is still not quite clear what it consists of.

Because of Schliemann's reckless behaviour, a lot of information has been lost. Moreover, it seems that before WWII, the Berlin Museum had made identical electrotype copies of a number of items and donated them to the Pushkin Museum, a circumstance which can only confuse matters further.

Visiting Troy

Visiting the site can be hard work: there are a lot of ups and downs and uneven surfaces and in the summer it can be scorching. People coming from Ephesus or Pergamon are bound to be disappointed, as in spite of its very long occupation, the site does not lend itself to spectacular reconstructions. It is a case of 'all in the mind', rather than 'all set out before you'. The excavators have made a valiant effort, with a steady supply of well thought-out explanatory panels, but they still have to be read and digested while other fanciful exhibits are of dubious value (*see below*). There are guides, and a lot will depend on how good your guide is. Troy remains a place of memory, where the scant remains act as prompts to one's imagination.

WHEN IS A HORSE NOT A HORSE

Nowhere in the *Iliad* is it mentioned that the Greeks brought the ten-year siege to a successful conclusion by tricking the Trojans into towing into their city a large wooden horse in which sufficient Greek warriors had been hidden to create havoc and set fire to the town. Nevertheless, the Trojan Horse lives on as an established fact. Visitors to the site are provided with one to climb into, with improbably large windows (excellent for photo opportunities). There is another one in Çanakkale by the harbour. It was made for the 2004 movie and is beginning to show its age.

Artistic representations of the famous artefact are known from the 8/7th century BC. The tale crops up in the *Odyssey*, in a couple of later Greek tragedies and in Virgil at the end of the 1st millennium BC. By then doubts were being voiced. In his Natural History (7:202), Pliny the Elder clearly speaks of a battering ram and he is echoed later on by Pausanias (23:8–10). Battering rams and other siege engines were known in the Middle East from the 2nd millennium BC, though there is no evidence that the Mycenaeans ever used them. The Hittites did in the 17th century BC. Excavators have identified, in the relevant level of Troy VII (the Troy of the Trojan War), a stretch of wall damaged and hastily repaired. Battering rams could have a skeleton crew hidden under a cover of skins, ready to jump into the breach and scale the wall. In the Homeric story, though, we get much more than just a sense of brute force. It is a tale of ruse and deceit, in which the Trojans are shown as hopelessly gullible victims of an inescapable fate. This has led to theories that involve no battering rams or huge constructions, but simply the smuggling of warriors into the besieged city by a ruse. At the siege of Joppa (now Jaffa) in the 15th century BC, the Egyptians managed to smuggle soldiers in pithoi, huge clay jars supposedly full of grain (the same trick used by Ali Baba and his 40 thieves). But this does not explain the horse. Animal-shaped vessels are common in Bronze-Age Anatolia, where they were used for libations. Sometimes they are on wheels. The late Bronze Age relief at the Alaca Hüyük entrance gate (the original is in the Museum of Civilisations in Ankara) shows a horse on wheels with a spout on its back. Unfortunately, neither size nor purpose are clear. It remains to be seen whether the Trojan horse was a real object or a poetic invention conflating various traditions.

EXPLORING THE TROAD

The Troad (*map A, 5*) is a large area bounded to the south by the Kaz Dağı, the old Mount Ida, wherefrom the Homeric gods watched the unfolding of the siege of Troy. They have now vacated it and the place is the home of a Muslim legend. Classical ruins are close by at Neandria, Alexandria Troas and at Assos. All of them are worth a visit, with the proviso that—certainly in the case of the last two—much has been lost because of their proximity to the sea and to Istanbul. Both sites have been quarried for building material.

Bozca island (Bozcaada) is an inviting destination for a day trip. This is the ancient Tenedos, where the Greeks hid to trick the Trojans into believing that they had abandoned the siege and gone home. The island's castle, whose existence stretches from the Byzantines to the Ottomans, has been restored to a full complement of crenellations and is open to the public. The shaded alleyways and the fine beaches, especially on the east side of the island, are also an attraction.

NEANDRIA

Of the city Neandria (*map A, 5*), signposted southwest of Ezine and dated to the 7th century BC, nothing much is left or indeed known; it was already a thing of the past in the early 1st century AD when Pliny the Elder (*5:122*) listed it among the cities that no longer existed. It has, however, its place in history as the findspot of the first Aeolian capital in 1882. Apart from the fine views and the remains of the city walls, it is worth visiting to ponder the origin and the demise of the Aeolian (or Aeolic) Order. A typical Aeolian capital (*illustrated*) has vertical volutes with palmettes and leaves between and below them. According to Philippe Bettancourt, it originated in the Bronze Age as a combination of the Mesopotamian Tree of Life design and the Egyptian lotus and lily capitals, as seen on tablets and reliefs. The transition to

Aeolian capital

monumentalisation may have happened in Syria-Palestine, where stone versions are found at a number of sites dated to the 10th–9th centuries BC. The Aeolian style, as identified in Archaic cities on the eastern Aegean coast down to Bodrum, as well as on the islands of Lesbos and Chios, is a variant of that. One can chart the transition from an emphasis on decoration and elegance to functionality as buildings become bigger and tiled roofs heavier. Eventually, while delicate vertical volutes with leaf decoration remain a feature of furniture and of non-load-bearing building elements such as balustrades, bigger structures use the Ionian Order, which is broader, sturdier and structurally stronger. So it is that Athens, which used the Aeolian Order in the mid-6th century BC, gives it up in the 5th. The Order had become obsolete by Classical times, except in the minor decorative arts.

ALEXANDRIA TROAS

Alexandria Troas (*map A, 5*) was founded by Antigonus I Monophthalmus, one of Alexander's generals who ruled over the section of the dismembered empire that stretched from Macedonia to the Indus. The purpose of the foundation was to provide the region with a harbour. Although not favoured by topography (an artificial harbour, 400m in diameter, had to be created with a second smaller basin and a jetty), the new foundation was successful. According to Plutarch's *Life of Caesar*, in the 1st century BC the great man contemplated moving his headquarters here, close to the supposed birthplace of his divine ancestors, basking in the (however-tenuous) connection with Alexander the Great and far away from troublesome Rome. Later, Constantine had it on his list of possible sites for the new Rome (in the end he chose Byzantium, better placed both strategically and commercially).

But Alexandria Troas had something to offer that Byzantium lacked: good building stone. This accounts for its unimpressive appearance today, since it has been mercilessly plundered for buildings in Istanbul (the Blue Mosque being one example) or more utilitarian structures like city walls. The Ottoman navy found that column shafts could be turned into excellent cannon balls. These were in very high demand, even in peacetime, as ambassadors would require as many as 30 for a salute, a practice that was still ongoing in the 19th century. One column could make six cannon balls; statue heads could also be pressed into service. Thus Alexandria Troas lost most of its walls, its stadium, nymphaeum, baths, theatre and aqueduct: what was not rolled down to the shore and loaded onto ships was left for the local people to use as building stone, to make mortars and olive presses and to burn for lime. The persistent belief that there was treasure somewhere and that frequent Western visitors were looking for it, encouraged more plundering. European visitors have been comparatively frequent because of Alexandria Troas' convenient location on the coast. There is a continuous tale of varnishing structures until the mid-19th century, when the site was practically exhausted and the harbour was silting up. Banditry was rife. Today one can see some abandoned columns in the harbours, view ruins of the baths and visit the hot sulphur springs, said to cure a number of ailments from leprosy to rheumatism.

THE QUARRIES
The quarries of the famous '*granito violetto*' are 7km inland on the Cığrı Dağ between Ezine and Ayvacık. The stone, so named by the 16th-century Roman stoneworkers, has an attractive grey-purple tinge due to feldspar intrusions in the granite. Exploitation of this surface quarry began in the Archaic Period to supply Neandria, increased with the foundation of Alexandria Troas and peaked in Roman times when

the beautiful stone was also exported, as the AD 313 inscription from Lepcis Magna testifies. Deeper beds were tapped for monumental columns. Later the quarry was under imperial administration supplying mainly the east Mediterranean. It was still exploited in Byzantine times, when Bishop Sylvanus was summoned to exorcise a demon that was preventing a loaded ship from taking to water. The number of abandoned, finished and unfinished columns, among them Charles Newton's 'Seven Sleepers', seven huge monolithic columns damaged by later attempts to make olive oil presses out of them, which can be seen in the Yedi Taşlar quarry 13km west of Koçalı, has caused people to question the pattern of exploitation. It may become clearer when Alexandria Troas and its quarries are more fully investigated.

MY TOWER IS MY HOME

Ayda Arel has identified a number of tower dwellings in western Anatolia. Some of them were originally defensive and it is here that their genesis lies. Towers as a mark of ownership or control of the landscape are a feature well known around the Mediterranean (think of the Mani, or medieval Italy). It is thought that when the Latins came in force to western Anatolia, they encouraged the local families to adopt a feudal system; tower dwellings would then have been both defensive and prestigious. Unless it goes further back to the time of the Persian occupation, when Xenophon, at the end of his Mesopotamian adventure, conducted a raid on Asidates's dwelling which he describes as a 'fortified tower' (*Anabasis*, 7:8) with an outer wall eight mud bricks thick (at least two metres).

The power of a number of local families, some running their own armies, did not abate with the Ottoman conquest. Old ties to the land, supported not by paperwork but by oral tradition, were reinforced by the erection of impressive buildings including mausolea. Ottoman land law did not apply in these areas; the local chiefs were able to appropriate what the Ottomans considered state or common land. A number of local chiefs were able to claim prior ownership of the land and of city districts through long tribal lineages connecting them to the original Türkmen settlers. The Ottomans were complaisant; the settlement pattern was not disrupted. Some families left their mark on the land, such as the Karamanoğlu in the east and the Cihanoğlu in the İzmir area and around Aydın. The Cihanoğlu Kule at Koçarlı southwest of Aydın (the large windows are 19th-century alterations) and Arpaz Kalesi at Esenköy south of Nazilli (*map B, 4*), belonging to another local important family, the Arpazlı, are good examples. Further south on the Bodrum peninsula at Müsgebi near Ortakent, a few tower houses have survived amid the urban sprawl.

A TOWER HOUSE AT YERKESİĞİ

Hasan Kalesi (*map A, 5*), near the village of Yerkesiği ('the place of the cut', so named because of the canal diverting water from Pınarbaşı to the Aegean), overlooking

Beşik Bay between Üvecik and Yeniköy, was in the 18th century at the centre of a large estate, part of the appanage of the great admiral Hasan Paşa (the very same that features on the façade of Çeşme Castle with his lion on a leash; he had bought a cub in Algiers when he was serving there). Here the admiral had his retreat and a place where he could suitably entertain the sultan. Choiseul Gouffier, the French ambassador to the Ottoman court, made a fine engraving of the domicile in 1783. Today only the tower remains. The two-storey house, with two entrances so that the sultan would never have to retrace his steps, is no more. The 12m high tower with lookout turrets and crenellations, now just a masonry shell (the interior was of wood), was not defensive but a prestige building, as the plastering and stucco decoration suggest. Just look at the size of the windows, which are original. The three-storey building, with vaulted cisterns underground and stabling for animals on the ground floor, had an entrance on the first floor with an exterior staircase, a drawbridge and a terraced roof.

GÜLPINAR

On your way to Assos, take the road south hugging the coast and at Gülpınar (*map A, 5*) ask for the Bahçelerici area. Here, in a fine rural setting, is the **Temple of Apollo Smintheus**—or what is left of it. Its remains have been traced in the surrounding villages as far as 25km away. The proximity to the sea suggests that some blocks may have ended up in Istanbul. The physical setting, however, could not be purloined, so you can still enjoy that and it is well worth the detour.

The present remains belong to a late Hellenistic temple but the cult of Apollo Smintheus apparently goes back a long way, to the time of the Trojan War. At the beginning of the *Iliad* there is a mention of a certain Chryses, a priest in the temple of Apollo in the vicinity. Furious at the abduction of his daughter by Agamemnon, the old man enlisted divine assistance and Apollo duly used his arrows to shoot a variety of plagues at the Greeks until they released the young lady. That is one of the meanings of Smintheus, the sender of plagues (but also healer of plagues). However, around the 18th century a separate strand, namely the 'mouse motif', took on a life of its own after the discovery that '*sminthos*' meant mouse in the local Mysian language and in some Greek-Cretan dialects. Miniature mice in metal or pottery were a recurrent find across the Empire; the first documented find, in a drain in Paris, goes back to the 6th century according to Gregory of Tours. According to a recent study by Philip Kiernan, though, the wide distribution of these miniature mice does not point to an empire-wide cult of Apollo with a mouse connection. Little mice were commonly added to household objects as ornaments. A mouse, being a nocturnal animal, was a natural natural way to ornament a lamp, a nocturnal object. But the same animal would nibble the wick and drink the oil. Perhaps the representation had some apotropaic meaning. None of this sheds much light on what manifestation of Apollo was worshipped here. Certainly during excavations (starting with the Società dei Dilettanti in 1866), no mouse has come to light. Strabo (*13.1.48*) does mention a statue by the Greek sculptor Skopas which was in the temple and where the god was represented with a mouse. But we do not have the statue nor a copy. It may be the one that is represented on local coinage.

ASSOS

All around the village of Behramkale, a corruption of the Byzantine *Makhram*, are the ruins of Assos (*map A, 5*), in a beautiful setting overlooking the Gulf of Edremit and its fine beaches. On the whole Assos has suffered from its proximity to the sea and to Istanbul: much has been lost by plundering, described as systematic from the mid-19th century. What could not be transported fed the lime kilns. In addition, the commanding views that attract you here (a sheer, south-facing drop 235m above sea level) were not lost on the military, who covered the acropolis with installations in the 1880s and were back at the time of the Cyprus War in 1974, with anti-aircraft artillery erected in the Temple of Athena. The 'Pompeii of Asia Minor', in the words of an early 19th-century traveller, was destroyed before it could be studied. The University of Çanakkale is doing its best with what is left.

A BRIEF HISTORY

Assos, according to tradition, was founded by colonists from Lesbos, who endowed it with an artificial harbour in the late 6th century BC. The population was probably a mix of Greeks, Lydians and Phrygians. Under Lydian control at the time, it was minting its own coins by the late 5th century BC. It fell to the Persians and by 365 BC we know for certain that it had walls, as its Persian governor, having rebelled against central power, was unsuccessfully besieged within them. Persian power waned and Assos blossomed as a philosophical centre under the rule of Hermias of Atarneus, the freed slave of a Bithynian banker and actual ruler of the area. Not only had Hermias been well educated by his owner, studying in Athens at Plato's Academy, but he inherited the land after his master's death. As ruler, he turned Assos into a philosophical hub, welcoming Aristotle and Theophrastus there for a number of years. Later, after the death of Hermias, who was captured by the Persians and taken all the way to Susa to be tortured and killed, Assos produced its best-known native philosopher. Cleanthes of Assos, born in 331 to a poor family, was able to study at the Platonic Academy in Athens for three years, rising to become its head. A prolific author, he wrote on a variety of topics. Unfortunately, not much of his oeuvre survives. His division of philosophy into six branches (dialectics, rhetoric, ethics, physics, politics and theology) remains the cornerstone of the discipline. He was a Stoic and it is said that he died at a great age, by suicide. From then on it was a history of decline for Assos, as Alexandria Troas was on the ascendant. When Orhan, the Ottoman ruler, captured Assos in 1330, it was no more than a village and its population had fled to Lesbos.

Visiting Assos

Excavations at Assos started in 1881, led by Francis Bacon, an American architect who went on to marry a niece of Frank Calvert, which explains why the museum in

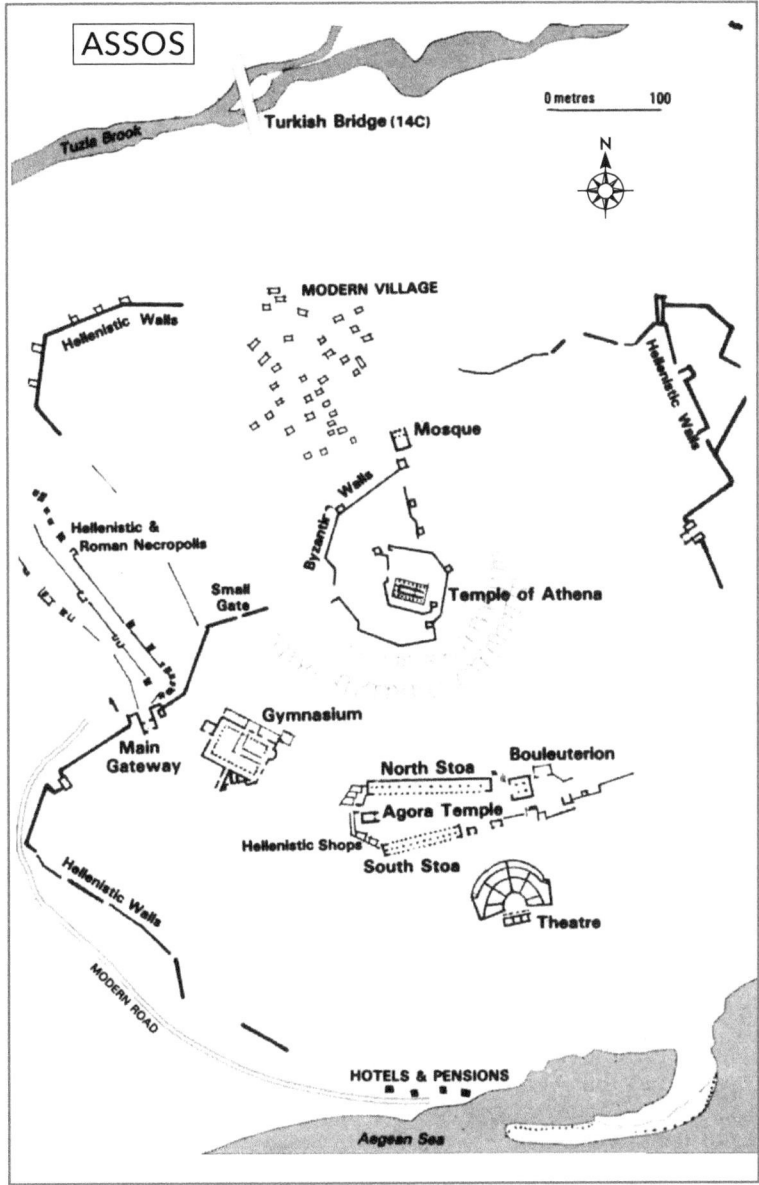

Worcester (Mass.) has some antiquities from Troy. Walls and some public structures are known but the domestic areas with the street plan are still elusive, probably buried under the present village.

The **city walls**, by far the most prominent feature, show different styles of masonry meaning that they cannot be precisely dated. We know, however, that they must have been present in the early 4th century BC. Eleven rectangular towers have been identified. To the north the semicircular tower facing the bridge on Tuzla Çay may, according to McNicoll, have housed a catapult. Little is known of the Byzantine acropolis wall systematically dismantled by the first American excavators in the 1880s. The transverse wall between the acropolis and the main gateway is dated to the 3rd century BC. Other prominent features include the Temple of Athena on the acropolis (dated late 6th century BC), the theatre to the south where the marble seats, spirited away to Istanbul, have recently been replaced, and remains of the agora and stoas in between.

In the **Temple of Athena** the columns have been re-erected. A rare Doric temple in Asia Minor, it failed at first to attract much attention as its sculptural programme did not conform to Vitruvius' diktat about what a Doric temple should look like and compared poorly with the shining examples on the Greek mainland. It did not help that after the Byzantines had used the stone to build the acropolis wall and its gates, the villagers treated it as a quarry to build their houses and industrial installations such as a windmill and an olive oil factory. Moreover what is left of the sculptural decoration is now dispersed between Boston, the Louvre and Istanbul museums. That did not deter Bonna Westcoat from making a thorough study of the structure. The temple, built directly on the bedrock with the local andesite, had a tiled roof supported by a wooden structure. The columns may be in the Doric style, but the decorative programme is unique. The pediment was left empty and the decoration, apart from the metopes, was apparently concentrated on the four sides in a frieze running along the architrave. The figures and the fantastic animals, including sphinxes, centaurs, fighting bulls, lions savaging their prey and tritons but also featuring Herakles and symposiasts betray Anatolian influences reaching to Mesopotamia, as well as connections to the Greek world, possibly via Ionia. According to Westcoat, they represent a liminal space where the civilised and the natural worlds meet, with Athena presiding over both. The style of the reliefs suggests a locally trained workforce. The combination of various styles: Doric with a touch of Aeolian and Anatolian, suggests that in the absence of any evidence for a strong Athenian connection, this was an independent development, possibly by a local architect busy experimenting.

The **Hudavendigar Camii** (the Mosque of the Lord of the World), between the temple and the village, is an early Ottoman mosque built by Murat I in 1369 after he conquered Edirne. At the entrance you will notice a Greek inscription with a Chi-Rho sign on the door frame, which deceived early visitors into believing that the mosque had been the Byzantine church of St Cornelius. But it is not so; it was simply built with its spolia.

A full plan of the 150m long **Hellenistic agora**, on a terrace south of the acropolis, was drawn by the very first excavator. It shows a two-storey Doric stoa to the north, a long building to the south and a small prostyle temple in between with the bouleuterion to the east; today there is really not much to see. Even the Hellenistic mosaic floor in the temple cella has vanished. The 2nd-century BC gymnasium to the west is also equally invisible. These buildings have been particularly targeted as they were made of marble, which was reused in the **Byzantine church** located not far from the gymnasium, while a fair amount went into lime kilns. One was in fact set up on the stylobate of the gymnasium. The marble seats of the **theatre**, with a fine view of the sea, did not end up in a lime kiln. The structure was in very good shape at the beginning of the 19th century, when the seats were either used in local housing or removed by the army to Istanbul. As the soldiers used sledges to take the stones to harbour, pieces of the agora were saved by being incorporated into the road they had built for the purpose.

THE KAZ DAĞLARI

The Kaz Dağları mountains to the south of the Troad are now a national park and the site of an annual pilgrimage. The location is quite elevated (1770m), exposed and dry. As the Greek gods have left, so their place has been taken by a maiden whose job, when she was alive, was to lead geese to pasture. Sarıkız (the 'yellow girl') was no simple goose girl though, being born to Fatima, the daughter of the Prophet. Her short life, of which there are a number of alternative versions, was full of woe. Her tomb is here, and to it come Alevi and Türkmen alike, towards the end of September, to celebrate her life or remember Fatima's grief at her death with singing and dancing. The rumoured 'secret ceremonies' remain secret, though an important element is the colour yellow, which traditionally brings good luck, beneficial and sacred at the same time. It is also, however, a reference to the Oğuz tribe of the Tahtacı, whose emblem are yellow goose feet and who originally settled around Balıkesir to the east. Here an unorthodox form of Islam fuses with the beliefs of the Türkmen.

PRACTICAL INFORMATION

GETTING AROUND

For dolmuşes and ferries to Bozcaada (Tenedos), ask the Tourist Office in Çanakkale, near the ferry on İskele Meydanı. The otogar is along Atatürk Cd. near the Town Hall (Belediye).

Organised tours can be booked in Çanakkale. Trips to Troy and Assos are also organised from further afield (Istanbul and the Aegean coast) but it can result in a very long and tiring day.

WHERE TO STAY

Çanakkale (*map A, 5*) is the main centre of the area, a strategic location as its twin Ottoman fortifications, the Çimenlik Kale (Meadow Castle) on the south side and the Kilitbahir Kalesi on the north make well clear. Indeed the place was originally called Kale-i-Sultaniye, when the castles were built by Memhet II after the fall of Byzantium. The name Çanakkale ('pot castle') dating from the end of the 19th century and made official in 1927, refers to the gaudy painted pottery that was sold to passing ships.

The area also caters for visitors to Gallipoli and one has to be careful in picking one's dates, especially towards late April, the time of the main celebrations at Gallipoli. The seaside promenade known as the Kordon is well provided. Try the Anzac Hotel (*grandanzachotel.com*) by the Clock Tower, on Demircioğlu Cd, or the nearby Helen Park Hotel (*helenparkhotel.com*). For something Ottoman (and to bask in the shadow of Schliemann, who spent a night here, so they say), try the Hotel des Etrangers (*hoteldesetrangers.com.tr*).

There is a good choice of **accommodation along the coast**, for example the İda Kale Resort Otel at Güzelyalı (*idakaleresort.com.tr*) or further south in the westernmost reaches of Turkey at Babakale, the Denizhan Hotel (*denizhanhotel.com*), which comes with a view of the much rebuilt Ottoman castle and a fish restaurant with a good reputation.

An alternative is to stay on the **island of Bozcaada** (ferry from Geyikli Feribot İskelesi opposite the island). Very different a few years back, as portrayed in Dmetri Kakmi's *Mother Land*, it is now fully devoted to tourism and packed full of pansiyons and hotels. Among them Rooms in Rum's at Atatürk Cd. 41 (*bozcaadatatili.com/tr/rooms-in-rums*) is a guesthouse with plenty of character.

At **Assos**, in the centre of the village where the dolmuş stops, the Dolunay Pansiyon (*T: 286 721 71 72*) and the Eris Pansiyon (*T: 286 721 70 80*) will do you very well.

Away from the coast, on the west edge of **Ezine** village, the inexpensive Ezine Geyikli Otel (*geyikliotel.com*) is an excellent alternative.

WHAT TO EAT

Like the rest of the Aegean coast the area is a popular tourist destination. This comes with a spread of fast food, of which there are some local variants that one should try at least once, such as the *Çanakkale bomba* (a bread pocket filled with *sucuk*, a spicy beef sausage, omelette, pickles, tomatoes and whatever else comes handy) or the *Ayvalık tost*, roughly the same thing but as a toasted sandwich; both come with a generous dollop of ketchup and mayonnaise.

In Çanakkale there is a good choice of eateries on the seafront promenade, the Kordon. The Kavala is good for fish. A local dessert is the *Çanakkale peynir helvası*, made of cheese from Ezine (originally a mix of sheep, goat and cow's milk) combined with semolina and egg.

At Assos go for *avcı böreği*, a spicy börek with mince, stuffed pumpkin flowers and *mantı* (sort of ravioli with tomato sauce and yoghurt) at the Mantı and Börek Evi in the main square.

WHAT TO DO

At **Göçebe El Sanatları** (Nomad Handicrafts), a centre for traditional woodworking 5km northeast of Edremit (*map A, 6*), various items are on offer including clogs. Mehmet Ali Tuzlu has revived his grandfather's occupation and manufactures clogs to meet the increasing demand from mosques, hotels and hamams. They are made of plane tree wood from the Kaz Mountains.

PERGAMON

The site of the ancient city of Pergamon is now partly under the modern city of Bergama, while its acropolis to the northeast has been left to the archaeologists. The site has now been extensively excavated, studied and documented, as well as partly reconstructed. Work by German archaeologists has been ongoing since 1878. Of late, the welcome addition of a cable car to the acropolis entrance has made visiting a less daunting and tiring experience. Even so, you should set aside a full day for Pergamon, bearing in mind that the site extends below the acropolis into town with the spectacular Kızıl Avlu, and across to the southwest at the Asclepieum.

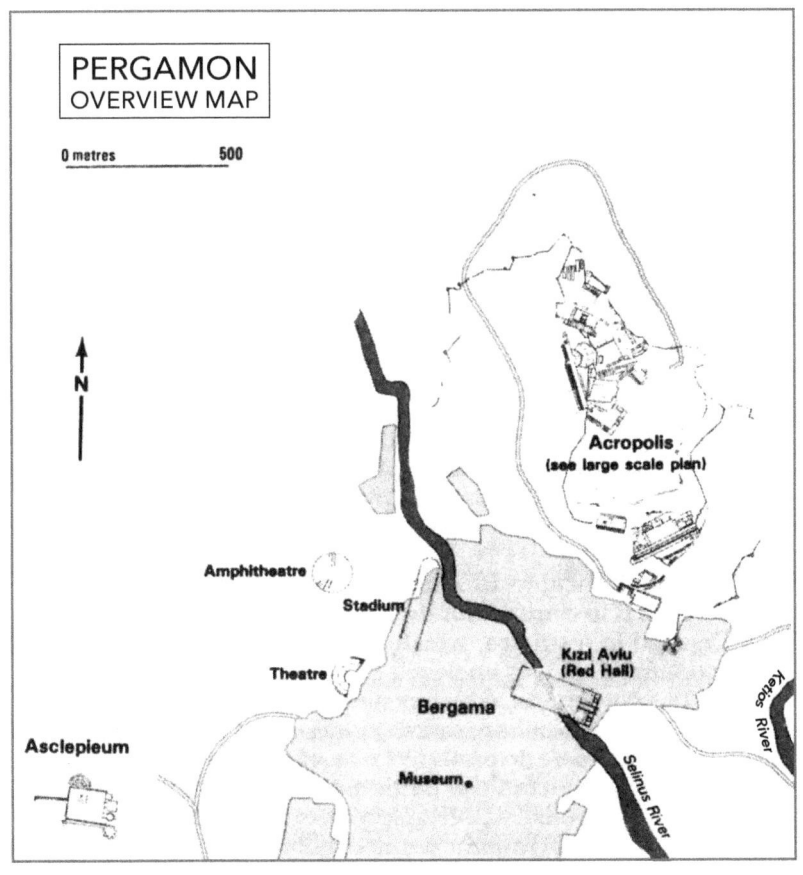

PERGAMON
OVERVIEW MAP

0 metres   500

N

Acropolis
(see large scale plan)

Amphitheatre

Stadium

Theatre

Kızıl Avlu
(Red Hall)

Bergama

Asclepieum

Museum

Selinus River

Ketios River

SETTING THE SCENE

The rock of Pergamon, almost 400m high, in the western reaches of the Pindasos range, running parallel to and south of the Kaz Dağları, is of volcanic origin. The elevation sits between two streams (the Bergama Çay, the ancient Selinus, and the Ilica Deresi, the ancient Ketios, to the east); it has been described aptly as a 'peninsula on dry land'; its sides are very steep except to the south where the slope is more gentle. The rock overlooks the plain crossed by the Bakır Çay (the ancient Caecus or Kaikos) that meanders in its graben; the sea now and possibly also in the past is some 30km away. Back in the mists of time the site would have been attractive as a defensive location, though the lack of water would have been a serious drawback; nothing permanent could be developed until that obstacle was solved, either with cisterns or an aqueduct. The location has never been on an obvious trade route, though it is not far from the known commercial axes. The presence of thermal springs down in the plain could have been an added attraction.

HISTORY OF PERGAMON

Traces of Chalcolithic occupation in the 4th millennium BC have been observed on the acropolis. Later in the Bronze Age, one can think of more sustained activity, with walls on the acropolis and prestige burials lower down, though the tumuli so far explored, including the immense Yığma Tepe downtown to the southeast, are known to be Hellenistic.

Early Pergamon may have been a settlement linked to the mythical Kingdom of Theutrania. The myth of Telephos, a descendant of that dynasty and credited with founding Pergamon, points in that direction. There may have been, in the 8th century BC, some Greek settlers' involvement, but they left no trace and anyway the place was certainly occupied; Archaic 6th-century BC tiles and sculpture remains suggest the presence of a sanctuary on the acropolis.

When Pergamon is first heard of in a sure context in 399 BC (*Anabasis* 7,8) there is a distinct whiff of violence and lawlessness about the place. The area was at that time ruled by Hellas, who had inherited the title to the land from her deceased husband, a local who had sided with the Persians, and although the place at the time was part of the Persian Empire, Hellas was in fact acting independently. Xenophon had intended to conclude his Mesopotamian adventure by incorporating the remains of his Ten Thousand into the Spartan army, but his stay takes an unexpected turn and soon he is embroiled in raiding a neighbouring fortified farm, doing well both by Hellas who had asked him for help, and by himself as, at the end of operations, he gets the pick of the booty.

Sixty years later Pergamon's time had come. Alexander the Great had defeated the Persians and at his death, his successors (the Diadochoi) carved up his realm amongst themselves. Pergamon fell to Lysimachus after the Battle of Ipsos in 301 BC. Lysimachus was then at the apogee of his power and had amassed considerable wealth. He entrusted part of it (nine talents, the equivalent of 225 tons of silver) to one of his strongmen, Philetaerus, of a Macedonian family from Tios in Paphlagonia on the Black Sea coast. These were turbulent times and Lysimachus was never able to recover his treasure: he was slain in the next conflict in 281 BC and the area fell to the Seleucids, whose power base was more to the east and south. Philetaerus was able to take advantage of the loose control of the new rulers and the impregnable position of the acropolis to carve himself a space in history. As for the nine talents, he hung on to his treasure and put it all to good use.

The Pergamon rock is not the best place to build but it certainly affords grandiose vistas and dramatic landscapes, lending itself to huge projects requiring an innovative approach. Philetaerus and his successors (the Attalids, so named after Philetaeros's father Attalus) clearly succumbed to the 'building bug' and invested a fortune in their artistic and architectural pursuits. Politically, as early allies of the Romans in the region, they became increasingly involved in Aegean affairs, extending their kingdom at the expense of the Seleucids.

In 133 BC it all came to a logical conclusion, at least in the eyes of the last of the Attalids, Attalus III, who bequeathed the kingdom to the Romans in his will. Whatever his motives, it can be said that Attalus III was a great realist, he knew what was coming and bowed to the inevitable. By going along with the up and coming Roman power, he hoped to secure their benevolence, and in the long run he was right.

The transition, however, was not smooth. For a start Pergamon was a *polis*, by definition a free city: it could not be bequeathed to anyone. Attalus III could pass on to the Romans the royal property, its revenues, the army and the demanial possessions i.e. land in public ownership. As we have very little information about the territory of Pergamon, we are in the dark about temple properties, territories of tribes and about the state of other settlements. Moreover Attalus' bastard son Eumenes III did not want to honour the deal and started a bitter civil war which only ended with his death. The newly set up Roman province turned out smaller than the Pergamene kingdom, which had reached as far as Konya, as Rome pacified some of its client kings with Pergamene land. Finally, with the imposition of taxation, Rome's heavy-handed approach became apparent. When Mithridates, King of Pontus, set about freeing the Aegean cities from the new conquerors, the Pergamenes welcomed him and took bloody revenge on the Romans and on the Italians that were living in the city; in vain the newcomers sought asylum in the Asclepieum.

From then on, with the occasional setback, times were prosperous as peace set in. Many locals did well by the Roman connection and climbed the social and political ladder, becoming Roman senators. Back in their birth city they spent lavishly on beautifying it. Pergamon was the first Asian city to become the seat of the imperial cult (the coveted neokorate). Roman emperors played the same game, making Pergamon a showcase of imperial power with new public buildings including a theatre, an amphitheatre (that could be used for mock naval battles by diverting the nearby stream) and a circus on the west slope of the acropolis. It all begs the question: what was Pergamon's economic base? So far, only the city has been investigated (bearing in mind that most of the lower town is under present-day Bergama). Archaeologists are now turning their sights to the countryside but very little is known about it. Agriculture was certainly a mainstay: one hears of large estates such as the one where Galen's father, an architect, lived (*De Methodo Medendi 17, 4*). Trade and commerce are something of a mystery. Pergamon was not on an obvious trade route, but it had a harbour at Elaia, now east of the mouth of the Bakır Çay (the ancient Kaikos), presently some 400m away from the sea. Geophysical investigations have shown a 1km long seafront with two harbours, possibly one commercial and one military, and two distinct walled urban areas. A fleet is mentioned in the sources. The cult of Asclepius and the miraculous cures that he bestowed were certainly a money spinner. Parchment, i.e. the production of treated animal skins used for writing, is another possibility. However, according to Herodotus (5,58), the process had been known to the Ionians well before Pergamon was even heard of. A monopoly seems out of the question. However, if Pergamon's parchment was particularly good, allowing, for instance, for writing on both sides; it would have been a profitable industry. Papyrus, the other standard writing medium, was only good for scrolls, whereas parchment could be bound into books, easier to consult. Moreover, the Egyptians, who had cornered the papyrus market, were known occasionally to enforce export bans for political reasons, as Varro tells us (according to Pliny, 13,70). Pergamon's finances remain to this day a bit of a mystery.

Decline appears to have set in by the 3rd century of the present era. An earthquake and the sack by the Goths in 262 did not help. The new fortifications that went up then only took in the acropolis, reaching midway down the slope. The enclosed area was not densely built-up, suggesting that it was used as a refuge. Churches were built outside the walls, where the population was; there was a bishop. While not politically or economically notable, the town was still an intellectual beacon in the 4th century. Aedesius the Neoplatonist philosopher had his school here, training sophists, magicians and fortune tellers (it was rumoured to be the best in western Anatolia); Oribasius continued in the medical tradition of Galen and was personal physician to Emperor Julian. Beyond the 4th century, things get more obscure; the acropolis appears to have been abandoned about that time.

In the mid-7th century the Byzantine wall enclosing only the acropolis served as a redoubt to face the Arab threat: the town was captured twice in 663 and again in 716. As the lower town emptied, wealthy Byzantines sought refuge in their fortified country estates. From then on came a lingering decline, punctuated by renewed fortification works to maintain control of the important strategic stronghold. Excavations have shown a dense network of streets as the population retreated to the heights, possibly under the protection of a garrison. When Theodoros II Laskaris, the Byzantine emperor ruling from

Nicaea, visited in the mid-13th century, he was dismayed. He compared the inhabitants to mice living in their holes amid the ruins of their past splendour. With the Ottoman conquest of 1336 Pergamon came back to life, gradually re-occupying the lower slope of the rock and eventually the plain. Today it is a very busy town with a serious traffic and parking problem.

Down by the coast Elaia, which had suffered with Pergamon's decline, survived into Byzantine times trading honey, oysters and oil. In the 10th century its most famous citizen was St Paul the Younger, a monk whose ambition was to settle as a stylite in Herakleia ad Latmos. It did not quite work and he ended up there as a hermit in a remote cave up in the mountains, occasionally spending time on Samos.

Visiting Pergamon: the Acropolis

First a word of caution: Pergamon (*open daily 8–7, closes at 5pm in winter; charge*) is on a steep slope and is very exposed: shade is rare. Although there is a wooden walkway, this does not give access to all the features that are signposted and some, like the House of Attalus, are not worth the trouble. Going cross country to follow the badly-marked trail can be hard work. Moreover, there is only one exit (at the cable car's departure and arrival points), meaning you may have to retrace your steps uphill under the blazing sun just to get out.

While there is a carriage road to the acropolis, you will be better off taking a five-minute ride in the cable car (*charge*), signposted along Akropol Cd. It will take you to the Zeus Café to the east of the Upper Agora, at the heart of the original Hellenistic settlement that Philetaerus protected with a wall in the early 3rd century BC; fittingly, Karl Humann is buried here (*see p. 35*). To the north were the ruler's palaces with grain stores and cisterns; the old town was immediately to the south. Here was the Hellenistic Temple of Zeus (Pergamon was yet another of his birthplaces), all in marble—quite a novelty for the time. The temple declined in importance as other focal points of the cult of Zeus, such as the great altar and the Trajaneum, were erected.

Site of the Great Altar

The Great Altar, immediately to the north of the site of the Temple of Zeus, was conceived by Attalus I (241–197 BC)—the first of the Attalids to style himself king while basking in his victory over the Galatians—as a monumental locus for the ruler's cult and completed by his son Eumenes II (197–159 BC). Excavations of the foundations and of the precinct suggest earlier activity reaching back to the Archaic Period. In early Hellenistic times the area was densely populated and had cisterns. To build the foundation of the terrace, buildings were demolished and the rock was cut away; However, a small apsidal structure partly cut in the rock and partly built in andesite ashlars was carefully integrated into the later altar's foundations, suggesting the presence of a previous focus of cult, possibly an earlier ruler's cult.

The foundation itself was a beehive structure filled with rubble. In order to negotiate the steep slope, the terrace was cut in the rock to the north and was supported by massive buttresses to the west and south. The precinct was accessed from the east and the altar opened to the west with a spectacular staircase. The altar itself, an impressive structure all in white marble, would have been visible on the slope from miles away.

THE GREAT ALTAR

Both Attalus I and his son Eumenes II styled themselves 'soter', the saviour, the preserver of civilisation, which in their case meant Greek against barbarian Galatian. For good measure, Eumenes II had also defeated the Macedonians. The time was ripe for a big celebration, which is exactly what the great altar represents. There is nothing comparable to it, either in antiquity or later. For a start, its highly visible position on a slope made it exceptional. The engineering skills required to place a structure of this magnitude (36m by 34m) in such a difficult topographical location were certainly considerable. The Pergamon altar is also unique in that it does not fit anywhere into the known development of the Ionian style. The structure was U-shaped, open to the west, with access via a grand staircase. All was in marble from Lesbos. A colonnade ran around the wings and the back. On the roof a wealth of centaurs, griffins, tritons and deities on quadrigas were variously arranged: between the columns were more statues.

A frieze decorated the base and another was barely visible beyond the colonnade. The two friezes are very different in character and theme and may hold a clue to the meaning of the monument. The lower frieze has all the exuberance and expressiveness that is typical of Hellenistic art. Its 63 panels, which extend for a total length of 60m, represent the battle between the gods and the giants, i.e. the triumph of order over chaos, mirroring the feelings of the two Attalids after they had defeated the Galatians. On the top of the staircase, the Telephos frieze (74 panels, 56m) could not be more different. The style is intimate, movement is subdued, action restrained, relief shallow. It has been suggested that the artistic approach was purposely old-fashioned as it harked back to the glorious origins of the Pergamene rulers. Telephos was their ancestor, the son of Herakles who had gained immortality by helping the gods against the giants. If, as has been suggested, the design of the altar was intended to represent the palace of the gods on Olympus (something like a grand peristyle house), then we see here the besieging giants fighting a losing battle below, while above, in perfect serenity, the victors, in this case the descendants of Herakles, bask in the glory.

The Great Altar has now been reconstructed in the Pergamon Museum in Berlin, at Bodenstrasse 1/3 (closed for renovation at the time of writing). A model is on display at the Bergama Museum on Cumhuriyet Cd. (open 8–7, shorter hours in winter; charge).

KARL HUMANN AND THE GREAT ALTAR

Karl Humann, a German-born railway engineer, ended up working around the Mediterranean almost by chance. He was in Istanbul when the Ottomans began busily building railways and roads. It was the time of the great Ottoman reforms and in the period 1867–73 he was given the task of supervising the construction of roads in Anatolia. Being in the area he visited Pergamon, whose ruins were more abundant than at present. There he saw a fragment of the Great Altar relief emerge from the mud after a storm. Although not an archaeologist by training, he had experience of antiquities and together with his brother had participated in excavations of the Heraion on the island of Samos. He realised how important it was to organise a rescue excavation. The Byzantine wall on the acropolis had been built by scavenging from the ruins of this unique monument. For a while the defensive structure had been left untouched, as it was used as a refuge by the population, but now it was being dismantled and fed to the lime kilns. Humann was able to reach high in the hierarchy of the German government to secure financial support and to obtain a firman from the Ottoman ruler. Excavations began in 1878. Moving the Great Altar to Berlin was not easy. Roads had to be built and in extreme cases buffalo carts came in handy.

Humann was to go on to conduct research into other Middle Eastern sites but he remains most famous for saving the Great Altar and for initiating the German involvement with Pergamon, which is still ongoing. He died in Smyrna in 1896 and was buried there. Later, in 1967, his remains were re-interred on the acropolis in the upper agora just south of the Great Altar.

Temple of Athena

Along the trail and beyond the citadel gate, turn left for the Temple of Athena and its precinct, passing the location of the two-storey propylon now reconstructed in the Pergamon Museum in Berlin.

The temple, a small marble peripteros of six by ten columns, is older than the altar which was aligned to it. It housed the important documents of city and copies of treaties. The famous *Dying Gaul*, a statue commissioned by the Pergamene rulers to celebrate their victory over the Galatians and a great favourite of the Romans, who made several replicas of the artwork (one can be seen in the Capitoline Museums in Rome), was housed here according to some. Unfortunately the area was used as a quarry for building material in later times. Inscriptions—and Pergamon does not have many of them—were lost. The temple maintained its pre-eminent role in city life until the building of the Trajaneum and of the Red Hall in the early 2nd century (*see below*); in due course, a Byzantine church was built with its spolia. The church incorporated the so-called round monument (a circular structure in Lesbos marble in the middle of the precinct, possibly a monumental statue base) as its apse.

The Library

Access to the celebrated Pergamon Library was through the second floor of the north stoa—or so it was thought until recently, when new research cast serious doubts on the identification. There is no doubt that there was a substantial library in Pergamon, set up by Eumenes II or earlier by Attalus I. Ancient sources, Strabo (*13,1,54*) for example, enthused about it and maintained that with its 17,000 books and scrolls it rivalled Alexandria's. That was the basis for the identification by early excavators, though we have no knowledge of the physical appearance of the Alexandria Library. The Pergamene complex has four rooms with mosaic floors, all cut into the cliff. The one to the north is the largest and best preserved. It has been suggested that it could equally have been a ceremonial or banqueting hall. The three-metre statue of Athena that used to be on the podium facing the entrance would equally fit in that context. As for the statue bases of ancient writers here, they are not in their primary location. They could have come from anywhere. At present it is thought that the library might have been in the royal district, the Basileia, at the top of the acropolis. The ultimate fate of the precious books was rather ignominious. After being transported to Alexandria in Egypt, a gift of Anthony to Cleopatra, they were, according to the 12th-century writer Abd al-Latif al-Baghdadi, fed to the furnaces of the city baths, on the order of the victorious Caliph Omar in the 7th century, on the grounds that books were incompatible with Islam as the whole truth was already encapsulated in the Qur'an.

The palaces (Basileia), Trajaneum and Arsenal

The Basileia, the location of various **rulers' palaces**, most of them peristyle houses with luxurious fittings of marble, painted plaster and mosaic (now under restoration), is further uphill. To the west the **Trajaneum**, a very ambitious project dedicated to the cult of Zeus and of the Roman emperors, stood on the highest point of the rock on a terrace measuring 60m by 70m, obliterating Hellenistic housing and supported by massive substructures covered with barrel vaults. The temple, a peripteros of six by nine, like the Temple of Athena but larger and on a marble podium, was in the Corinthian order with massive columns and was flanked by two colonnaded halls. In early Byzantine times the prevailing scarcity of metals prompted the removal of the metal clamps holding the foundation together, damaging the structure which was also mined for building material for the defensive walls and for marble to feed the kilns. This is a volcanic area and is short of limestone, indispensable for making mortar. Today a number of columns and architraves have been re-erected and the sight is quite impressive.

The area beyond, at the very top end of the acropolis, was never residential. Here the Hellenistic rulers had an **arsenal**, with stores of food and military supplies. Large ventilated structures for storing grain have been identified and, on the military side, the 3rd-century BC munitions depot containing 8,940 stone balls, some weighing over 500kg, to be used in a siege engine, shows that the garrison was well prepared. Water provisions, i.e. the cisterns containing enough water to withstand one year's siege at the time of Philetaerus, were equally impressive. Later, water supply became an issue and was solved by proving the city with aqueducts tapping the water from

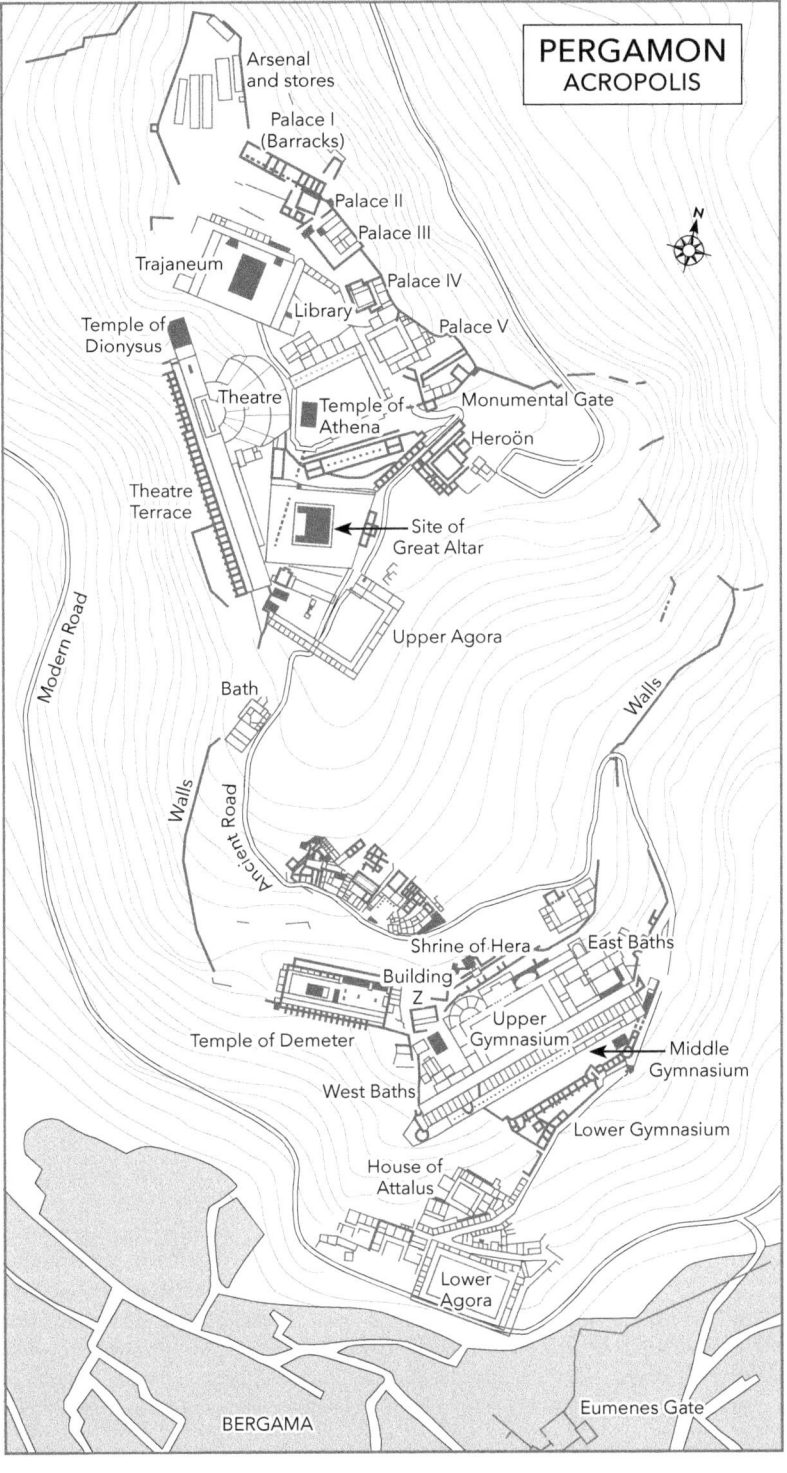

PERGAMON
ACROPOLIS

Arsenal and stores

Palace I (Barracks)

Palace II

Palace III

Trajaneum

Palace IV

Library

Palace V

Temple of Dionysus

Theatre

Temple of Athena

Monumental Gate

Heroön

Theatre Terrace

Site of Great Altar

Modern Road

Upper Agora

Bath

Walls

Walls

Ancient Road

Shrine of Hera

East Baths

Building Z

Temple of Demeter

Upper Gymnasium

Middle Gymnasium

West Baths

Lower Gymnasium

House of Attalus

Lower Agora

BERGAMA

Eumenes Gate

N

the Madradağ, 45km away, and bringing it in under pressure to the top of the acropolis. The substructures of the Hellenistic pressure pipelines can still be seen. A piped water supply was maintained up to the time of the Arab raids.

The Theatre and Temple of Dionysus

The **Hellenistic Theatre** sits on the precipitous slope west of the Temple of Athena; its remains were discovered in 1878 under the spoil of the excavation of the altar and of the Temple of Athena. To accommodate the steep topography, the cavea breaks all the rules of theatre building in ancient Greece. It is less than a semicircle and it has no fixed skene, allowing an unimpeded view of the surroundings. Holes to fix a temporary wooden backdrop have been identified. The structure, with a capacity of 10,000 spectators, was fronted by a terrace running north–south supported by huge retaining walls. In Hellenistic times the theatre, as a place of assembly and a venue for processions, was the most significant public building in the city. The west side of terrace was taken up by a stoa with shops. The complex Theatre Terrace was planned as a single structure at the time of Eumenes II.

At the north end of the terrace was the Ionic **Temple of Dionysus Kathegemon** ('the leader', another possible ancestor of the Attalids), a tall building on a high podium and accessed by an elaborate staircase, all in andesite. Its chief priest was traditionally a member of the royal family. It was rebuilt in Roman times after a fire, with lavish marble cladding. Its altar stood at the bottom of the stairs. In the middle of the terrace and south of the theatre, the niche building has been identified as a ceremonial structure with a banqueting hall-cum-cult room of Dionysus, partially hewn out of the bare rock to the east. Next to it, a Byzantine cemetery church with three naves is dated to the 10th–13th century.

Building Z and the Temple of Demeter

Retrace your steps to the Temple of Athena and head down the slope, crossing the upper agora. The trail takes you first to **Building Z**, a 1500m square peristyle house discovered in the 1990s and now restored and open to the public. Although the building was originally Hellenistic (actually built on top of the then-redundant Philetaerian wall) and may have started as an annexe to the Temple of Demeter (*see below*), what you can admire today is its northern section (the south end is badly eroded) in its Roman garb. The well-preserved mosaic pavements, suggesting that the owner was a devotee of the theatre, and the rare instances of mural stucco decoration reveal a high-status dwelling that had its own bath house. It was abandoned in the 3rd century and the Byzantines did not take much interest in it; it was possibly too far down the slope for safety and the water supply was unreliable.

The remains of the **Temple of Demeter** can be seen nearby to the west. As an earth mother, Demeter was very much in the tradition of the Anatolian Mother Goddess. The terracing of the site and other building activity are apparent from the 4th century BC. However, when Philetaerus built Pergamon's first defensive wall, he left the temple outside the circuit because Demeter was the goddess not only of fertility but also of death, and death could have no place in the city. That did not stymie the growth of the cult, which reached its apogee in the 2nd century

BC. At that time the temple was included within the new enceinte of city walls, built by Eumenes II. In Roman imperial times the buildings were renovated and a few more cults were added to the line-up, to include the Orphic mysteries. Female members of the imperial family were appointed as priestesses. What you see today are the massive terracing works required to establish a secure flat surface. You have to imagine a smallish temple fronted by two columns in the west, surrounded on three side by a two-storey stoa forming a precinct entered through a propylon to the east.

The Gymnasium

The gymnasium is entered along the trail via the Festival Gate (a modern name), in an area that was at some point buried under tons of debris from the excavations higher up. The Pergamenes attached great importance to the upbringing of the ephebes (generally 18 to 30-year-old males, though sometimes younger children were included in the term). In this they followed the Greeks, who were very aware of the benefits of physical activity and from the 6/5th century BC set aside open spaces outside the city walls for youngsters to exercise in. Purpose-built structures followed about a century later with the creation of open spaces (palaestrae) surrounded by rooms and the setting up of educational institutions. The focus was on education and on being a good, healthy citizen. Pergamon's gymnasium was built with those goals in mind. It was laid out over three terraces with the usual complement of a massive foundation and retaining walls. The two baths on either side are a Roman addition. The upper terrace (the trail will take you around it) had a central court, a palaestra (75m by 35m) surrounded by a stoa on three sides and a running track taking up the whole width of the terrace at the south edge. On the north side were an odeion for meetings and performances and a couple of ceremonial rooms (*see below*). To the east a temple of Dionysus with arrangements for ritual meals has been excavated. The two terraces below, connected by staircases, were smaller.

To quote the excavators, the gymnasium must have been a 'forest of statues' with a profusion of marble and bronze portraits either free-standing, with or without a base, or dowelled into the wall. The gymnasium is where young people were presented with their role models and were encouraged to be pious, hence a profusion of effigies of gods and demigods. Hercules was only a demigod yet he ranked highly here; together with Hermes he formed a duo symbolising physical prowess and intelligence. Attalid rulers featured extensively, larger than life and suitably martial. They eventually gave way to equally oversize and martial images of Roman emperors. From the 1st century BC other role models included benefactors, among them Pasparos. He was the former alumnus who successfully pleaded the Pergamene cause in Rome after the destruction wreaked by the Mithridatic wars in the early 1st century BC. He must have had a silver tongue to cause the Romans to forget the massacre of their compatriots at the time (*see above*). Winning athletes were also celebrated, together with philosophers and prominent citizens. Statue bases featured not only the name of the incumbent but also a complete *cursus honorum*. Some spots were necessarily favoured: the prime location was the central hall on the upper terrace.

The House of Attalus and Lower Agora

The **House of Attalus**, home of the Roman consul Gaius Claudius Attalus Paterklianos down the slope was built very much on the same two-storey peristyle plan as the palaces in the Basileia, but whereas the latter enjoyed safety and seclusion, Attalus had a better vista and multiple gardens: he knew that his mansion would have impressed anyone coming to see him. The lavishly decorated rooms with mosaic floors, opus sectile pavements and frescoes, have been reconstructed as banqueting rooms by the excavators. The building however was under restoration at the time of writing; until work is complete, it is not worth the detour.

The trail proceeds to the **Lower Agora**, an area which is little understood as it has not been completely excavated and a certain amount of material has been lost because of its proximity to the town. It may have been developed when the city wall was enlarged by Eumenes II, with a 4km wall circuit taking in a large part of the slope down to the river Selinus (Bergama Çay). At this point it is possible that the upper agora took on a different character, as a royal and sacred area, as commercial functions were shifted to the newly laid-out space, an area 90m by 45m surrounded by a two storey Doric portico with andesite columns.

Visiting Pergamon: the Kizil Avlu

The Kızıl Avlu (the Red Hall; *open daily 8.30–5.30; charge*) is located at the east end of a large terrace, 270m by 100m, in the lower town. It was at the time of writing shrouded in scaffolding for extensive restoration and reconstruction; this has scared the storks away. Its foundations include a double tunnel 196m long allowing the river Selinus to flow into the Bakır Çay to the southeast. The terrace was designed at the time of Hadrian for a temple with a temenos extending west. The location of the entrance through a propylon to the west along Dizdar Sk is known. The northwest corner has been located at the crossroads at the top end of Mermer Direkler Cd.

The Kızıl Avlu complex, large part of which is now overlaid by the Ottoman town, has had a difficult history. The southeast corner of the temenos was used industrially to the 1960s for olive oil production and pottery making. An advantage of this has been that the red bricks the structure was made of (and which gave it its name) ensured its survival: reused bricks do not make good building material, so it was not robbed. Additional protection was the work of the storks, who liked to nest on the tall walls. It is unlucky in Turkey to upset a stork, so the buildings were left largely alone while the Ottoman town developed around them.

In the temenos, the built structures to the east consist of a huge hall flanked by two round buildings. The building programme may have been initiated locally or it may have been yet another mark of imperial favour. One does not know. It now appears with some certainty that ten years or so into the project, changes were made to the plans giving the complex, in particular the hall, an Egyptian character. The date, first half of the 2nd century, points to Emperor Hadrian. Indeed his Villa Adriana at Tivoli has a famous feature in the same style, the Canopus. It is not clear what brought about the change of plan. Is it that Hadrian was fond of things Egyptian or was he grieving for his lover Antinous, drowned in the Nile in 130, and seeking to honour him? It could even be that he brought sculptors from Egypt to build the water features reminiscent of the Nile (pools mimicking the annual flood of the sacred river and bringing prosperity) and the huge caryatids with figures of Egyptian gods, some of which have now been restored. Look at them and you get an idea of the rampant megalomania of the times.

The Red Hall itself was accessed from the west past a monolithic marble door with an estimated weight of some 40 tons; the marble paved forecourt would have been used for processions. The cult area was in the eastern section. Here remains of the caryatids were found and have been reconstructed to a height of some 10m including plinth, statue, head dress and bell-shaped capital. They were placed back to back with the head dress uniting the two figures and ensuring stability. Since the walls are still standing to a height of 19m, there is plenty of scope for a second floor; in fact it is thought that the building originally had three storeys. Egyptian gods, including those with animal heads, are represented. The material is white marble, with black marble for the body parts, all fitted together with tenons. The nearest parallel is in the Hathor chapel of Hatshepsut's mortuary temple in the Valley of the Kings in Egypt (and her caryatids were only 5m tall). A modern replica has been erected outside the building. The Red Hall, covered in marble tiles and clad in coloured marble inside, was flanked by two round building looking very much like miniature pantheons. The one to the north is now a mosque. The one to the south, where the entrance now is, was used in the 1930s as a depot for finds which eventually caused the floor to collapse and the dome to crack. It will eventually become a museum and an information centre.

With the advent of Christianity, a church dedicated to St John the Evangelist was erected inside the building, on a raised floor; but when Charles Boileau Elliott visited in 1838 he found the nave being used as a cowyard. At some point the chancel housed a Greek school. But the storks kept coming back year after year, protecting the building.

Visiting Pergamon: the Asclepieum

The Asclepieum (on Prof. Dr Frieldhelm Korte Cd.; *open 8–5; longer hours in summer; charge*) is to the west past the location of the Roman theatre (*signposted from post office on Cumhuriyet Cd.*). Like all volcanic sites, Pergamon was blessed with thermal springs which amply made up for the lack of limestone. Pergamon's healing waters were located at the Asclepieum and were, according to the finds, a popular destination well before someone thought to replicate Epidaurus's success and introduced the cult of Asclepius here around the 4th century BC. Having been taught medicine by the legendary centaur Chiron, presumably after the latter had completed the education of Achilles, Asclepius went out into the world to practise his art, which included the raising the dead. His daughters were suitably called Hygeia and Panacea. A god by the 5th century BC, Asclepius, through his priests, had by then cornered the market of healing waters and his shrines were about the only place people could go for relief when sick. Help was always at hand. Priests were no mean psychologists and secular doctors could be called upon. It is useful also to remember that Hippocrates, the founder of modern medicine, lived at about the same time: medicine as we know it was taking off.

The cure could be complex and might require a prolonged stay at the springs. The god had to reveal himself to the sufferer, which he normally did in a dream, which would then be interpreted by the priests, who would prescribe the appropriate medicine. These could focus mainly on diet and exercise, or might be something absolutely extravagant. The sophist Hermocrates, for example, was prescribed a diet of partridge smoked in frankincense and was only able to start his cure when he had gained the favour of the emperor. The success rate of these prescriptions is a well-guarded secret. Reports are conflicting. Aelius Aristides, a 2nd-century AD orator and author and an inveterate hypochondriac based in Smyrna, thought the water excellent for asthma, chest infections and foot problems; unfortunately for him, he had trekked all the way to Pergamon to cure his bad stomach.

Thermal springs were a locus of pilgrimage and one would expect the Asclepieum to have had provisions for the accommodation of guests. However, these have not been found. All we have is the temple complex which was reached at the end of ceremonial way starting from the city theatre on the west slope of the acropolis. The Via Tecta, part of which has been cleared, was paved and had a colonnade with shops on either side leading up to a grand entrance, the Corinthian propylon, presented to the temple by the wealthy citizen Claudius Charax. Originally Hellenistic, the Via Tecta was remodelled in Roman times, as were the visible remains at the Asclepieum. These mainly date from around the end of the 2nd century, the combined efforts of Roman emperors and local euergetism after a disastrous earthquake. The original cult place was around springs issuing from a rocky ridge crossing the complex. Here traces of Bronze Age cultic structures and figurines have been found that suggest the worship of a female deity. The fountains and the pool were for patients to drink the water from or immerse themselves in. These days one can have a taste of the water (though do bear in mind that a recent study, while praising the healing quality of the waters, warned against drinking them because of the high arsenic content). Mud baths were also possible. All around was a stoa; in the southwest corner spacious, open-plan latrines with marble seats could accommodate 40 men at any one time. Ladies had a separate, smaller facility. Waste water from the springs was channelled there to keep everything clean. The circular building at the east end of the south stoa is dubbed the treatment centre, though the evidence for such an attribution is thin. Originally it was built on two floors with apses and recesses. Some have suggested a temple of Telephos, the mythical founder of Pergamon, but the presence of a tunnel connecting it to the springs suggests otherwise. The temple of Asclepius is next to it to the north. Gifted by the consul Lucius Rufinus, the round building fronted by a colonnade had an oculus; all built in andesite with a mosaic floor, the structure may have found its inspiration in the Pantheon in Rome. It housed statues of Asclepius and of other deities associated with healing. Although hospitality arrangements have not been identified, it is clear that people stayed here for a spell; otherwise there would have been no need for the library (the square building in the northeast corner) or the theatre (beyond the north stoa).

FROM PERGAMON TO MENEMEM

No longer an unspoilt stretch of coastline, the area offers a number of sites in the southern reaches of Aeolia, an intellectual construct of 19th-century historians who thought in terms of neat Greek migrations, all of it occurring in almost virgin land with limited local input—Aeolia to the north, Ionia to the south.

ÇANDARLI

Çandarlı (*map B, 1*), famous for its scented wines, is a pleasant seaside resort with long sandy beaches where you can swim in full view of the fully renovated Ottoman castle and its imposing towers and curtain wall enclosing an oblong court. It is not open to the public. It was built by Vizir Çandarlı Halil Paşa in the mid-15th century, on top of an earlier Venetian structure which itself incorporates Greek spolia, to control the coast at a time when Murat II used to spend time in Magnesia. Note the large, Ottoman, arched openings on the south side to accommodate guns. The long peninsula, offering obvious harbour facilities, had attracted settlers earlier on and indeed Çandarlı sits on the site of the ancient city of Pitane, a Greek foundation. However, evidence of occupation goes back further, to the 3rd millennium BC, and has been attributed to the Pelasgians, a convenient umbrella term for people connected with the sea but about whom one otherwise knows little.

Çandarlı was built with Pitane's stones. Therefore the two-and-a-half-metre thick defensive wall that protected the peninsula is no more, the harbour installations (Strabo credited it with two harbours) have vanished; the stadium at the tip of the peninsula is but a rumour. Pitane left little mark on history. In Hellenistic times it was absorbed by Pergamon, the up-and-coming power nearby. Its necropolis on the mainland shows oriental influences. The finds are in Pergamon Museum, where you can also admire the Archaic kouros found in the isthmus in 1958.

GRYNEUM

Gryneum, near the village of Yenişakran (*map B, 1*) on the small peninsula of Temaşalık Burnu, occupies a space that is too small for a city. One comes to the conclusion that the Apollo temple, about which Pausanias waxed lyrical in his *Description of Greece* (1:21), was on the headland and the city somewhere on the mainland. Not much is known about the latter apart from the fact it was traditionally one of the league of twelve Aeolian *poleis* falling in the 5th century BC into Persian hands, then conquered by the Macedonians and eventually absorbed by Myrina (*see below*). Gryneum lingered on into Roman times, as the finds of mosaics suggest. The white marble Temple of Apollo on the headland was famous for its oracle of great antiquity, apparently as old as the Trojan War. According to Aelius Aristides, it was still functioning in the 2nd century AD. The headland remains unexcavated. Traces of a precinct have been identified but the columns are not in white marble, so they may belong to a Byzantine structure. Gryneum is an excellent place for a break—and do not forget to take your picnic basket with you.

MYRINA

Myrina (*map B, 1*) is at the south end of the Çandarlı Körfezi. It seems to have an illustrious past, having been founded by no less than the Queen of the Amazons. As a Greek town it had some weight, at least going by the hefty contribution it made to the Delian League. Today there is little to see (with the added complication that there was more than one Myrina in the region—the island of Lemnos had one for instance—so written sources are of uncertain use). A couple of destructive earthquakes are recorded. In AD 17 in the wake of the damage, Emperor Tiberius awarded tax relief for five years to the whole region from Sardes to the Aegean and sent financial aid. The grateful cities, Myrina among them, had a colossal statue of the emperor surrounded by figures representing the cities erected in the forum in Rome. A copy can be seen to this day in Puteoli. Later, in 106, destruction was followed by rebuilding and obscurity.

Myrina has been little investigated, and what was done was carried out in the 19th century. It occupies two hills at the mouth of the Güzelhisar Çayı. To the east is Birki Tepe, which judging by the polygonal wall circuit was probably the acropolis. The Byzantines were busy here and they erected a defensive wall. The hollow at the foot of the west slope is thought to have been the theatre, though nothing else remains of it. The other hill was terraced, suggesting domestic occupation. Remains of the ancient harbour installations have been identified on the shore, including perforated blocks for mooring vessels. On the north slope of Birki Tepe, the vast necropolis dated to the late Hellenistic period was excavated in the late 19th century. The finds seem to show a rather impoverished community: apart from objects of daily use they include over a thousand mass-produced, moulded terracottas similar to those that made the Boeotian town of Tanagra famous. The geology of the area is also suitable for rock-cut tombs. The best known is İntaş, with a main vaulted chamber and ten deep niches.

CYME

Just down the road from Myrina, by the Nemrut Limanı, west of Aliağa, is the site of ancient Cyme (*map B, 1*). Or at least, this is what the coins and the inscriptions found here suggest. Otherwise we are back to the sources. Strabo in Book 13 speaks of it as the best and largest of the Aeolian cities, but he was writing much later and Cyme's glory had by then faded. Little has been done about its archaeology. French, Czech, German and Italian archaeologists have all nibbled at the site, which is situated on two hills overlooking the harbour facing north towards Lesbos. Not much remains of the temple, the theatre or the fortifications, which were dismantled by the Turks in the 15th century. Ancient harbour installations have been traced underwater. Recently the site has been the object of renewed investigations; not the town, which is protected, but its surroundings prior to industrial development and road construction.

We now know that Cyme had three necropoleis spanning a period from the 8th century BC to Roman imperial times. In the one to the southeast along the old paved road to Smyrna, the fragment of a very large stele in high relief with traces of paint, presently exhibited in İzmir Museum in the entrance hall, was found. Further investigations have traced the remaining portion of the stele to a small museum in Ödemiş, a town 100km to the east. The new **museum at Ödemiş**, recently set up, had been filled with donations from the depots of other museums. The stele is now complete. Its large size, 136cm by 92cm, suggests that it belonged to a substantial funerary monument dedicated to a young man (on the right) who is shown being welcomed into the Underworld (symbolised by the snakes) by his ancestors, a man standing and a woman sitting on a very elegant chair. Four diminutive distraught servants complete the scene.

PHOCAEA

Going west, past Yeni Foça and the Haydar Aliyev Ormanı, a park dedicated to the memory of the late Azeri president, 'the saviour of modern Azerbaijan', the drive offers fine views but few beaches as the shoreline is all cliffs. When you arrive at **Eski Foça** (Phocaea), you can see why this harbour (actually two separated by a spit) was so successful. It is the only one that opens directly onto the Aegean while at the same time being well tucked away and almost invisible from the mainland. Not far from the shore, a number of little islands, the **Siren Kayalıkları**, are said to have a monk seal population, hence the name (Phocaea derives from the Greek word for seal).

According to tradition it was a group of Ionian Greeks who tricked Cyme into parting with this piece of land. Since then the people of Cyme have had to struggle with the reputation of not being too clever. Whatever the truth, ever since there have been people here, they have been noted as enterprising, daring sailors (again in contrast with the people of Cyme, who have a reputation as 'landlubbers', not too keen on the sea). Phocaea's list of colonies spans the length and breath of the Mediterranean: Tartessus (now Cadiz), Massalia (Marseilles at the mouth of the Rhône) and Alalia in Corsica, to name but a few. The colonising was accomplished in the 6th–5th century BC, when the Persians were becoming a threat. The town was not easily defensible by land, though it had a wall. When the Persians came, people moved out, with the statues of their gods, to nearby Chios and further afield. When the Romans arrived, in the 2nd century BC, the Phocaeans were unwelcoming, which was a bad calculation, but even so the town survived. It became a Byzantine episcopal see and later a busy port run by the Genoese, who had commercial interests in Anatolia and occupied nearby Chios for over 200 years. The Ottoman conquest in 1455 put an end to all that.

The archaeology of Phocaea remains to be undertaken (although it will probably never be undertaken fully, as the old town lies under the new urban development). Moreover, as fishing and agriculture have declined, tourism in Phocaea is given high priority, often at the expense of archaeology. Limited excavations have ascertained that the original settlement occupied an elongated peninsula looking over two harbours (Kücük Deniz to the north and Büyük Deniz to the south). On the summit of the peninsula an Ionian, 6th-century BC temple of Athena, built of tufa and preceded by a shrine dedicated to Cybele, has been located. The peninsula was walled off and had a gate on the isthmus. A stretch of the defence showed signs of destruction with burnt beams and ballista bolts. The Beş Kapılar Kalesi to the north is an over-restored portion of the defences. What is left of the theatre on the mainland, on the slopes of

Değirmenli Tepe to the east, has been excavated. According to Ekrem Akurgal, the Roman agora was on the peninsula. The land wall was 5km long. It incorporates various styles from Archaic and Roman to Genoese and Ottoman. Notable in town are also a number of old Greek stone houses with large windows and vast portals. Most have become cafés and arts venues. Others have metamorphosed into three-storey concrete apartment blocks.

Just to the south of Phocaea, along the coast at **Kaleburnu**, the archaeologist Ömer Özyığıt has been studying a structure projecting into the sea with a very loose date from Genoese to late Ottoman. Here the rock has been trimmed to vertical faces and massive walls and arches have been built on an area paved with material scavenged from Phocaea. It is thought that the openings were slipways like those observed on Mount Athos in Greece.

LARISA

On the way to Larisa, just north of Menemen (*map B, 3*), you will go past the road to the Devil's Bath on the edge of Can Dede Tepesi, near the new cemetery. No devil and no baths. It is a family tomb of uncertain date cut in the rock.

According to the archaeology, Larisa on the Hermos, north of the Gediz river, was an Aeolian settlement developed on top of an earlier one of Anatolian character. It is situated on a hill overlooking the village of Buruncuk. According to Homer, the town was allied to the Trojans and was inhabited by Pelasgians, but the archaeology points east. As a gateway to Anatolia, it was well placed to control traffic, which may well explain the rich architecture of its acropolis. The town was destroyed in the Persian wars and Cyrus made a present of what was left to the Egyptian ruler of the time, which explain why it was known in Hellenistic times, when it was but a village, as 'Egyptian Larisa'.

The acropolis of Larisa was investigated in the early 1900s. The residential area may have been on the slope below. The necropolis, with a number of tumuli, has been identified to the east at the foot of the hill. The acropolis was surrounded by a massive trapezium-shaped wall with two gates, a main one to the north and a postern to the east; it had nine square towers. Inside, the area was clearly divided between the secular district (the ruler's residence) and the sacred (the temple) to the east. The original residence of the ruler, a megaron, a large room with a porch and two columns at the entrance, was replaced in the mid-6th century BC by a larger palace, very Oriental in style and Mesopotamian in its conception. Wide rather than long, it was fronted by two towers on either side of a porch with six columns. The roof had terracotta acroteria. To the east, the Temple of Athena overlaid a pre-Greek cult place and looked away from the palace. When the temple was replaced with a larger one in 530 BC, the new one had terracotta reliefs in the pictorial tradition of Asia Minor, acroteria and an altar in front. Larisa is unusual also for the large number of Aeolian capitals, some of which are thought to have belonged to the palace and which may have been sheeted in bronze. The number of unapportioned capitals and columns have suggested to Philippe Bettancourt that some may not have been structural but free-standing.

PRACTICAL INFORMATION

In **Bergama** the Tourist Office is on Cumhuriyet Cd. (*open Mon–Fri; 8:30–12 & 1–5.30*). A small booth, run by the Bergama Chamber of Commerce (Bergama Ticaret Odası) is on Bankalar Cd (*open Thur–Tues 8.30–12 & 1–6*).

In **Eski Foça** the tourist information office is near the otogar on Değirmenlik Cd.

GETTING AROUND

By bus: In Bergama the new otogar is 7km west of town on the D240. You can try and get a dolmuş to town from there. If you come from Istanbul, the Metro bus company will take you to the city centre. Local services, including to the new otogar, run from the Soma Garajı near the Kızıl Avlu.

WHERE TO STAY

Pergamon is blessed with a wealth of smallish pansiyons. Those in the older part of town to the north, closer to the acropolis, will be more expensive. Try the Akropolis Guesthouse (*akropolisguesthouse.com*), with swimming pool, in Kayalık Sk. Other options include the Odyssey Guesthouse (*odysseyguesthouse.com*) on Abacihan Sk just north of the Red Basilica in an old Greek stone house, or the Gobi Pension (*gobipension. com*) not far from the Archaeological Museum on Atatürk Blv. For a budget alternative, the Böblingen Pension (*T: 232 633 21 53*) south of the D240 (and therefore a distance from the acropolis) will do well by you. If you just want to sleep, the fully modern Hotel Anıl (*anilhotelbergama.com*) is a good choice. Alternatively, if you have your own transport, try the Berksoy Hotel (*berksoyhotel.com*), on the D240 right out of town to the west.

At **Eski Foça**, an area fully dedicated to tourism, you will find a wide choice. It can vary from the luxurious, like the Menendiotel (*menendiotel.com*) on Reha Midilli Cd., with views of the sea, the harbour and the sunset, drinks on the terrace and designer rooms, or something more cosy like a small guesthouse in an old Greek stone house; there are a number of them in the area of the 'small sea' (Kücük Deniz) to the north. The Focantique Hotel (*focantiquehotel.com*) at the tip of the peninsula, has plenty of character and exposed stonework. Another choice is the İyon Pansiyon (*iyonpansiyon.com*), a little bit to the north and away from the sea, in the İsmet Paşa district on 198 Sk. Bear in mind that these are small outfits and the area quickly fills up in the summer. Moreover the Rock Tatili Foça Festivalı or Foça Rockfest, which takes place for five days in July or August at İngiliz Burnu, the cape north of town facing İncir Adası, attracts some 90,000 visitors.

WHERE TO EAT

It is the usual problem. This is a heavy tourist area and the proliferation of fast food outlets (Turkish style or Western style) continues unchecked, drowning out local specialities. If you want to find real Turkish food, you have to go where the locals go.

Bergama: In Bergama the Meydan Lokanta, on Mustafa Yazıcı Cd. near the archaeological museum, will serve you Turkish home cooking. Look out for *gözleme*, a sort of savoury pancake with various fillings cooked on a convex griddle. Watch while it is done and eat it right away, well puffed up: it is much better than the ubiquitous, often stodgy *pide*. The technique harks back to the distant days of nomadic life when the Yürüks on the move had no ovens but were able to secure a small supply of flour, either by obtaining it from the sedentary population or by staying put long enough to harvest a crop. While the very thin pastry (*yufka*) used for baklava and börek is now factory-produced, the dough for *gözleme* remains homemade. For finer dining, Les Pergamon (*lespergamon.com*), in a small alleyway off Taksim Cd., has a good reputation for Turkish cuisine and also offers a fine selection of Turkish wines. Occupying a converted Greek school, it also offers a few rooms. Try and book one of them for a perfect stay.

Pergamon's apparent lack of Western-style cafés has been filled with the recent opening of the ambitious Cultural Centre (or BerKM for short) in the centre of town, on the site of the old bus station. One can only hope that among the cappuccinos, frappuccinos and lattes there will still be room for a properly brewed Turkish coffee.

Eski Foça: There are a number of fish eateries in the harbour area. The standard Turkish lokantas are tucked away in the streets at the back. For a superb fish dinner, try the Liman Balık restaurant on the north side of the peninsula, towards the end of the harbour. If breakfast in your pansiyon is not all you hoped for, head for the *börekçi* opposite the Turkiye İş Bankası and feast on Turkish coffee, sweet or savoury delights and excellent ice cream.

WHAT TO DO

In antiquity there must have been plenty of seals in the sea around Eski Foça, since the settlement is named after them. These days you may not lucky enough to spot one. Despite this, a **boat trip around the volcanic islands of Siren Kayalıkları** is well worth it. You might be lucky and catch a glimpse of Badem, a monk seal rescued off Didim in 2006 and later released here.

The **Bergama Kermesi** is a whole week of music, poetry and dancing. It happens in May–June and celebrates the visit that Atatürk paid here 82 years ago. The opening procession starts near the museum at the Monument of Atatürk, in which he is shown in Western leisure attire, wearing a jacket, plus fours and a flat cap (which according to pictures, were all pale blue).

İZMİR & THE ÇEŞME PENINSULA

According to a document published recently by the City and Regional Planning Office in İzmir, the geography and topography of the area are unsuitable for further settlement. In the period between 496 BC and AD 1949, there have been at least 20 destructive earthquakes: the Gediz graben continues into the Gulf of İzmir and is criss-crossed by active faults. Deforestation and overbuilding have increased the risk of floods, landslides and rockfalls. And yet, almost 3,000 years on, İzmir is still there—and still growing; its population will soon top the three million mark as people keep moving in from all over Anatolia. Perhaps defiance is the main characteristic of this metropolis, which like a phoenix constantly regenerates itself from its ashes. Because of this, you should not expect to find visible, spectacular antiquities here. But there is history, and plenty of it.

THE GULF OF İZMİR AND ITS CHARACTERISTICS

İzmir (*map B, 3*) is situated at the east end of a long gulf that stretches for some 35km. This gulf is the town's main asset and İzmir developed as a harbour linking the Aegean to the Anatolian interior. But there are drawbacks. The waters are shallow, just ten metres deep, and silting has always been a problem. Indeed the river, the Gediz Çay, the ancient Hermus (the main culprit), had to be re-routed, well to the north of its original course, in 1886. At that time its delta was due south of Menemem and enough silt was discharged to threaten the viability of İzmir harbour. Even so the coastline has steadily moved west, in places by over 1km. The ancient city and its sheltered anchorage are now completely on dry land.

The other problem was the wind, the İmbat, which funnels into the gulf from the west during the daytime. This made life difficult for sailing ships before the advent of steam. At night, the wind direction changes and a gentle breeze blows from the land.

A SHORT HISTORY OF SMYRNA (LATER İZMİR)

Evidence of early Neolithic occupation has recently come to light in the district of Bornova, during the course of excavations at Yeşilova Hüyük—now well inland close to the E87 but originally not very far from the deeper eastern reaches of the gulf. Later a defensive settlement developed to the northwest, on a ridge at Bayraklı (also called Tepekule), with a natural harbour (*see below*). Here the pottery goes back to the 3rd millennium BC. It was this spot, in the 11th century BC, that saw the development of Aeolian Smyrna, a name harking back to its mythical founder, a queen of the Amazons. Investigations have shown ten layers of occupation and evidence of trade from the 7th century BC. From humble beginnings with mudbrick houses, the architecture moved to stone. Houses became larger and a temple to Athena went up in strict Aeolian style, with columns made of wood at first and then of tufa drums 90cm diameter, with curly Aeolic capitals (now in İzmir Museum). The settlement had a defensive wall in polygonal blocks topped by mudbrick architecture. The entrance was to the northeast just above the harbour. At the south end there was a fountain, quite a novelty for the time. Finds show that the site had contacts with the Levant, Cyprus, Ionia and Greece. If you feel inspired to visit the spot (though there is not much to see), you can get there by İZBAN train, alighting at Bayraklı Station and walking along Ekrem Akurgal Cd. Ask for 'İzmir Hüyüğü'.

After it was destroyed, first by the Lydian Alyattes in c. 600 BC and then again by the Persians in 546 BC, Smyrna reinvented itself and by the 4th century BC the population was expanding, with some of the inhabitants living in courtyard houses. On the whole, however, the settlement was in decline. By this time Smyrna is likely to have been a cosmopolitan town, maybe more Ionian than Aeolian, having absorbed or been subjugated by people from Colophon to the south (if we believe Herodotus; *1,16*). Things changed under Alexander the Great. Whether he really came here and dreamed his visionary dream on the slopes of Mt Pagos (now Kadife Kale), and whether he ever consulted the oracle at Claros (*see below*), we shall never know. But his lieutenant Lysimachus carried out his wishes, moved the settlement to the southwest and gave it a new name: Eurydikea, after his own daughter.

The new site comprised the area from Mt Pagos, where the acropolis was, down to the sea, where a bay formed a natural harbour. From then on Smyrna (the name Eurydikea was short-lived) grew considerably, establishing itself as the main anchorage on the coast and making adroit political moves. Strabo (*14,1,37*), writing about it in the 1st century AD, waxes lyrical about its library, its paved streets laid out on a grid, its porticoes and its temple to Homer—until he remembers the lack of sewers. Archaeology has proved his memory faulty on this score: three aqueducts are known and they are Republican in date. It is the other features, so vividly evoked by Strabo, that archaeology cannot reveal to us.

The reason is not because they have not been found. The surviving remains (of the theatre, the temples, the stadium where St Polycarp was burnt alive in the mid-2nd century, the bouleuterion, the colonnaded street, the circus, the amphitheatre, the aqueducts and the fine houses which—in the words of Aelius Aristides, a 2nd-century AD local orator—made Smyrna 'the ornament of Asia') have all been located but they lie under a thick blanket of modern concrete or, in the case of the stadium, as an outline within the street pattern. The agora is also known and can be visited (*see below*). Knowledge of the grid layout is scant: the main east–west street led from Le Pont des Caravanes (*see below*) to a city gate and directly on to the harbour, roughly along today's west end of Anafartlar Cd, where it makes a loop. West of the agora it met a southwest–northeast axis that has been traced along Eşrefpaşa Cd. The rebuilt fortifications on the acropolis are Ottoman, incorporating earlier Hellenistic, Roman and Byzantine structures. The 1966–9 excavations have not been enlightening and the mosaics and buried columns that Charles Fellows saw in 1837 were used as building material and grave stelae.

The layout of the city wall, beginning here and descending to the sea either side of the harbour and taking in a couple of kilometres of coastline, was mapped in the 1950s. Considering the ups and downs that followed the end of Roman rule and the demise of the Byzantines, it is unsurprising that so many structures have disappeared.

Travellers coming to Smyrna, the main port of entry for the eastern Grand Tour, report seeing a lot of Classical architecture still standing as late as the 19th century. But the ease of transport by water, and later with the development of the railways, meant that Classical Smyrna was used as a quarry for building material, both locally and for Istanbul, and stone was taken for ballast by any ship in need of it. At the same time the market for antiquities was developing in Europe, causing artefacts to depart from Anatolia in a steady stream, necessarily also depleting Smyrna. In 1680, for example, Louis XIV, the French Sun King, began his royal collection with statuary from Smyrna's stadium. He chose Anatolia because his relations with the pope at the time were less than cordial and the Italian market was closed to him. His enterprise did not turn out as felicitously as he had hoped: the ship bringing back the Smyrna statues was hijacked and held to ransom by pirates and, when it was about to reach France, it foundered within sight of the coast of Provence. The wreck is still there but the statues were fished out and are now in the Louvre for all to admire. In the 19th century, foreign consuls played an active role as intermediaries and facilitators in the antiquities trade. When Greece put a stop to the export of its antiquities, the pressure on Asia Minor via Smyrna redoubled. By 1860 Smyrna was importing marble.

Late antique Smyrna made a seamless transition to Byzantine rule, only facing decline after the Arab raids of the 7th century. It was in the hands of the Seljuks for a short while towards the end of the 11th century, returning to the Byzantines not long after. Between that time and the arrival of Tamerlane in 1402, Smyrna flourished as a trading centre, co-operating with the Venetians, the Genoese, the Crusaders and the local emirs. The harbour remained in use. On its northern spur in 1344, possibly on top of an earlier Byzantine structure, the Knights of Rhodes built St Peter's Castle, thereby temporarily checking the maritime ambitions of the emirate of Aydın. The structure had a triangular plan with a curtain wall and a keep to control the port. When Tamerlane took it, inflicting serious damage in the process, the Knights hastened to Bodrum to build another stronghold. Meanwhile the castle lingered on and was only fully demolished in 1872. It was located in the area of today's (appropriately named) Hisar Camii (Castle Mosque). Its only remains are two marble plaques with the coats of arms of Ferdinand de Heredia, Grand Master of the Order of the Knights of Rhodes, and of the Italian admiral Domenico d'Allemagna. Both are now in the garden of İzmir Museum, after spending some time on the walls of Smyrna prison. As for the harbour, at the time when Chandler visited in the 18th century, it was only visible after heavy rains. It was eventually completely filled in and the area was turned into Smyrna's bazaar. Today, Anafartalar Cd, from the Clock Tower round to the Şadırvan Cami, marks its location. The new harbour has been moved to the north.

Under Ottoman rule Smyrna regained its role as a leading import/export harbour, run by an increasingly cosmopolitan community that earned the town the nickname of Giaur İzmir (Infidel Smyrna), because so many non-Muslims lived there. The Armenians had flocked in from the late 14th century, when their Cilician kingdom had collapsed. The Greeks had always been present and more had migrated from Anatolia. Jewish, Maltese and European merchants added to the variety. Smyrna was Turkey's window on the west. Capitulations, ensuring privileged status, were granted to foreign investors, who could rely on the presence on the spot of their own consuls and the more distant protection of their motherland. By the turn of the 20th century, Smyrna's economy was internationally integrated, with Ottoman and foreign banks financing improvements in the harbour infrastructure and in transport (trams and trains) and providing capital for trade in any commodity they could find, from carpets from as far away as Niğde, to dried figs and raisins. The transport was by camel train (*see box below*). During WWI, İzmir suffered as it was severed from its hinterland, foreign ships patrolled the Aegean and agricultural output plummeted as labourers joined the army. Its only trading partners were the Central Powers and they had their own share of troubles. The events of 1922, with the Great Fire and the exodus of the Greeks, sealed the fate of Smyrna as a cosmopolitan city. The newly reborn İzmir is a completely Turkish metropolis, with little to show for its recent past, as churches and other buildings have been demolished or turned into depots, cinemas or fitness centres.

LE PONT DES CARAVANES

In İzmir, Yeşildere Cd. (the D300) follows the course of the ancient river Meles, now nowhere to be seen. After skirting the acropolis on its east side, the stream spent itself in the marshes of the Bornova Gulf to the north. At about the height of the ancient harbour it was spanned in the recent past by a stone bridge known as Le Pont des Caravanes (it does not appear to have had a Turkish name at that time). It serves as a reminder of the role of camel caravans in the transport network that supplied Smyrna. Camel caravans were a frequent sight in Turkey up to WWII; indeed, this writer remembers seeing one in the early 1970s in eastern Anatolia. In 1894 Anatolia still had a camel population of 160,000.

As a means of long-range transport, camels have been around for long time. They were domesticated around the 13th century BC, if not before, in the Arabian peninsula. By the time of the Arab conquest, camel transport had progressed thanks to the practice of selective breeding and the introduction of appropriate accessories such as saddles and loading equipment. As wheeled transport faded in the Middle East between the 3rd and the 7th centuries AD, with the degradation of a road system that was no longer maintained by the Roman army, the camel took its place. It was better equipped for the task than the mule or the horse, being more resilient and able to carry heavier loads. Its feet were adapted to both sandy terrain and stony ground. One driver could look after six camels.

In Anatolia at the time this development had relatively little effect. The area had been conquered by Turks, not by Arabs, and the climate was unsuited to the Arabian camel. It is thought that increasing contacts between nomadic Türkmen, Kurds and Arabs who were breeding camels in northern Syria, led to the successful hybridisation of an animal that could withstand the Anatolian climate. To start with, this form of transport remained expensive and camel caravans only transported highly profitable merchandise such as silk and other luxury goods, but in due course other goods were added to the list: madder, cotton, opium, mohair, hides and carpets. Camel trains, easily consisting of some 150 animals, each with a load of about 250kg, crossed the Anatolian plateau at a speed of 25 miles a day and arrived at Smyrna—then, with Istanbul and Alexandria, one of three main harbours for the region—via this little, single-arched stone bridge.

Successive Ottoman governments added a new twist to the story when they spotted an opportunity to move low-cost but vital merchandise, such as salt, and make huge gains in the process. They adopted a policy of 'encouraging' Türkmen and Arab camel drivers to settle in the Aegean area, where the government ran a monopoly on salt production. They then drove hard bargains with the drivers and forced each district to buy a yearly set quantity of salt. The profits were huge, and the rebellion that in due course ensued equally so. The practice of settling drivers in the area has left a trail in the ancient toponymy (a number of villages were formerly called Araplar, meaning 'Arabs'). It also explains why camel fighting (*deve güreşi*) is common on the coast of the Aegean but not in the homeland of the camel.

Visiting İzmir

Visiting İzmir can be relatively quickly done. You may wish to explore the 18th-century **Kemeraltı Bazaar** and the Kızlarağası Hanı on Anafartalar Cd. and stock up on Ödemis Silk, an old industry that is being revived, and on good luck charms (*see box opposite*) or alternatively sip a coffee on a terrace and watch the world go by in the shaded alleyways of the **Kültür Park** in the centre of town or by the seaside.

There are at least half a dozen museums in the town, three of which are well worth a visit. The first **archaeological museum** in İzmir dates from 1927 and was located in the disused church of Hagios Voukolos in the district of Basmane. The new museum (*open Tues–Sun 8.30–5.30; charge*) on Halil Rifat Paşa Cd., south of Metro Konak, is a grander affair. It houses material covering a long span of time from the 5th millennium BC to the end of the Roman period, both local and from the wider Aegean area (the museum was built in 1984, when local museums were rare and finds tended to gravitate towards the nearest metropolis, in this case İzmir). Finds labelled in Turkish and English, from Tepekule, Aeolian İzmir (*see above*), are displayed here as well as material from Ephesus and Pergamon. The **Ethnography Museum** (*open Tues–Sun 8.30–5.30; charge*), occupying an architecturally interesting converted hospital building, originally a shelter for poor Christian families set up by the French in 1845, is nearby. Here you can get a flavour of old Smyrna, although very much through Ottoman eyes (a visitor with no prior information would ever guess that Europeans had lived in this town for centuries). Both museums will be eventually overshadowed by the **İzmir Museum of Aegean Civilisations**, set to rival the grand institutions in Urfa and Gaziantep, although the completion date at the time of writing was no more than a vague 2023 (the 100th anniversary of the Republic).

The open air **Agora Museum** (*open 9–12 & 1–7; charge*) occupies the part of the agora locally known as *namazgâh* (open-air prayer place), just east of Eşrefpaşa Cd. It is thought that this was first used as a civic space in Hellenistic times, but excavations have found nothing earlier that the 2nd century BC. The visible remains are Roman and Ottoman. The area was used as a cemetery from the end of the Byzantine period onwards, which accounts for the large number of Muslim tombstones neatly stacked; there are some very fine stone turbans. On the whole the agora is best seen from the air; that way one can appreciate the plan and does not see the skyscrapers that surround it. It was laid out as a rectangle with two stoas running north–south and a basilica with interesting graffiti closing the northern edge. The bouleuterion to the west, with an opus sectile floor, was quarried for stone in Ottoman times; recent excavations have uncovered the remains of a large building (60m by 25m) with a mosaic floor facing it to the south. Beyond, after the removal of encroaching buildings, a huge Roman bath has come to light. In the agora, columns and stones have been re-erected. The cryptoporticus is no longer hidden in the foundations as it was meant to be, but is open to the skies. Columns do not support anything, arches lead nowhere. In its present state, visitors may find it difficult to be excited by this motley collection of architectural elements. The planned archaeological park, the result of long, painstaking, meticulous and extensive investigations by Turkish archaeologists, will undoubtedly make the visitor experience more satisfactory.

A number of 19th-century **Levantine houses** that survived the Great Fire of September 1922 and have been restored, can be seen in the districts of Bornova to the north of town and of Buca to the east.

NAZAR BONCUĞU

Given how widespread it is in Turkey, one could be forgiven for believing that the Evil Eye Charm is typically Turkish and comes from an ancient tradition. It is in fact not Turkish but it does come from an ancient tradition. A very early such charm was found in a neo-Assyrian excavation level (early 1st millennium BC) in Tarsus. It was apparently used by priests for incantations and had been popular around the Levant and the Aegean since the mid-Bronze Age. It would not necessarily have been made of glass; a banded agate or chalcedony would have served equally well. The beads that we find today in bazaars all over Turkey apparently began life as the *İzmir Boncuğu*, here in İzmir after WWII, when some Arabs from Palestine set up shop on Kadife Kale, the ancient acropolis, and started producing the now-familiar lovely blue beads with concentric circles of differing colours.

Nazar, meaning 'sight' is Arabic, refers to the Evil Eye that the bead will repel. It is the colour blue that works the charm (though sometime the bead is green). The concentric circles (white, yellow or black; rarely red) simply mimic the eye and have no particular power. Although nowadays mass-produced in any possible material from plastic to cloth, and applied to all sorts of supports (horse harnesses, cars, costume jewellery), the original *nazar boncuğu* was hand-made from recycled glass, champagne bottles providing the best raw material. The Palestinian Arabs on Kadife Kale manufactured each bead by hand in a horseshoe oven with a rounded cupola, working with thin rods to shape the beads and apply the coloured circles; it was a long process as each addition entailed time in the oven to settle. They used copper oxide for the blue; yellow was a mix of zinc and lead; and blue and yellow together made green. For white they used a sort of porcelain; black was iron oxide; and the red was obtained from recycled red glass (which is perhaps why red is rare). When the bead was finished it would be placed in a special place in the oven and allowed to cool slowly. Thus was born a fashion that took Turkey by storm.

THE ÇEŞME PENINSULA

The deeply indented Çeşme peninsula (Erythrae in antiquity; the present Turkish name refers to the abundance of springs while the old name refers to the flaming sunsets), which forms the south edge of the Gulf of İzmir, has been described by some as İzmir's playground since its livelihood is now based on tourism, with a substantial prevalence of Turkish holidaymakers. Historically it was a producer of oil and wine, with the recent addition of tobacco. However select and high-end the tourism aims to be, it is still mass tourism, as the fine beaches and the excellent conditions for windsurfing are a great pull. The six-lane motorway that crosses the peninsula all the way to the town of Çeşme on the western tip has been built to accommodate the large number of visitors. They are spread out mainly on the north coast. In 2008 a plan to develop the south coast further, with new hotels,14 golf courses and the consequent loss of vast stretches of forest and beach, was overturned by the İzmir administrative court, to the relief of environmentalists, especially as it had been approved by central government.

Geologically, the sea to the north of the peninsula has the same features as the town and the Gulf of İzmir. The peninsula itself is a hard schist horst rising in places to almost 1300m. When earthquakes have struck in the past they have occasionally created tsunamis. Such a precarious situation is somehow compensated by the abundance of hot water springs, especially in the area between Balcova to Şerifhisar, prompting the development of thermal tourism away from the beaches. In antiquity a few towns grew up on the peninsula but a lack of fertile land meant that they could never grow to any extent and none of them thrived for long. Remoteness provided protection but enforced isolation. The town of Çeşme at the peninsula's very west end is, in a way, the only success story, due to its close proximity to the island of Chios.

Coming from İzmir you can safely bypass the **Baths of Agamemnon**, 800m south of the motorway. It is now a modern spa with water gushing from the bowels of the earth at over 70°C. It has no proven connection with the Greek hero. It has been suggested that its current name is a corruption of *Ağa memnun* (the happy ağa).

KLAZOMENAI

Klazomenai (*map B, 3*) occupies a stretch of flat coast north of Urla, divided by an elongated island (Karantina Adası). Being by the sea, it was mercilessly plundered for stone for Istanbul. Very little remains *in situ*. According to the official version of history, Greek colonists arrived here in the 10th century BC, and found the place deserted. The archaeology, however, shows human activity from the Neolithic and Mycenaean contacts in the Bronze Age. Originally the settlement was on the mainland and the fortified island was used as a refuge (the inhabitants moved there during the Persian Wars, for example). At the time, Klazomenai was a renowned producer of pottery. Its clay sarcophagi with their characteristic iconography of griffins, sphinxes and the occasional gorgon, extolled the virtues of the dead and at the same time protected them on the difficult journey of transition to the Underworld. Workshops and pottery kilns have been found, together with olive presses and ironworks. Klazomenai traded with Miletus. More renowned still were the philosophers Scopelianus and Anaxagoras, both born here. They went on, especially the latter, to leave their mark on the history of thought (*see box*). Hellenistic Klazomenai gave itself two proper harbours by building a causeway linking the mainland to Karantina Adası, with its cave and sacred well on the west side. Today's causeway runs alongside the old submerged one. Klazomenai supported the Romans against the Seleucids but even so it eventually sank slowly into obscurity and by Ottoman times was no more than a village. Recently, Turkish archaeologists have been investigating the harbour and have identified submerged structures. On the mainland, the location of the theatre that Chandler saw in the 18th century has been identified.

BLUE SKY THINKING IN IONIA

Ionia is well known for its abundance of thinkers and philosophers. Every city seems to have at least one and the list is impressive: Anaxagoras and Scopelianus from Klazomenai, Thales from Miletus, Heraclitus from Ephesus and many more. What they had in common was a rational way of thinking, perhaps a reaction to the overburden of myths and legends in the ancient Greek world, and a willingness to pursue esoteric lines of enquiry—what we would now label 'blue sky thinking'—in the pursuit of a truth that did not involve deities or external, unaccounted-for influences. That meant moving from the enumeration of facts to looking for causal links.

Philosophy later became associated with Athens, with figures such as Plato and Aristotle. So why did this intellectual ferment start here and not on the Greek mainland? According to Ernst Heitsch, it was all due to contact with the cultures of the East, either by sea via the Levant or by land along the Meander Valley. In the East, writing and the transmission of knowledge had been current for a long time, and speculative and intellectual endeavours were more developed.

Unlike literature, where Eastern influences on the Greek writers can be traced, philosophy has not left much hard evidence, except for a few exceptional cases. One of them is Herodotus (*1,74*) where he describes a solar eclipse that so frightened the Lydians and the Medes that they laid down arms. He goes on to say that Thales from Miletus had shown as early as the mid-6th century BC that solar eclipses were natural phenomena that could be predicted. There was nothing to fear, no divine intervention. This shows that the application of rational thinking, i.e. philosophy, had moved a step forward in Miletus from the astronomical observations that the Sumerians and the Babylonians had conducted for millennia. Thales, relying on these observations, the work of many generations, had spotted the pattern that enabled him to postulate a prediction; he had worked out a rational cause of the event.

The desire to understand the natural world rationally also encouraged thinkers to look for a unifying principle, something that had existed ab origine. Some opted for water, others for air or fire, while Anaxagoras introduced the concept of a small element that could not be further reduced, in other words, an 'atom'. More than the actual result was the willingness to discuss, debate, explore, take an empirical approach and aim for rational conclusions. In this rests the glory of the Ionian philosophers.

ERYTHRAE

At the west tip of the Çeşme peninsula, in a fine bay facing Chios, Erythrae (*map B, 3*), near Ildır, is a fast-expanding tourist destination. It may not be yet 'paradise on earth', as some of the promotional literature would have it, but the sheltered bay closed by the little islands, the Hippoi (today going under the collective name of

Kara Ada), with the Ak Dağ towering to the north (the ancient Mt Mimas, 1200m), is enchanting. No wonder it was settled early. It was better-favoured than Smyrna, which had a long shallow gulf and troublesome winds.

Erythrae was, according to tradition, a Cretan foundation and an extension of Chios onto the mainland; if we believe Herodotus (1,18), in his day the two communities spoke the same dialect but did not get on very well. Historically Erythrae was an Ionian city, a member of the Ionian League with a thriving trade in wool, wine and stone. It came under Lydian domination in 560 BC and under the Persians shortly after that. As free city, minting its own coins, it later oscillated between Sparta and Athens. It never regained its former importance: the geopolitical situation had changed and not in its favour. Pirates infested the sea and the Galatian Gauls raided the city in the mid-3rd century BC. Later the Egyptians unsuccessfully besieged it twice; the Carian Mausolus, a benefactor according to an inscription, probably offered assistance at some point, but he was too far away. Erythrae had no territory to speak of and Smyrna, in due course, stole its trade. It dwindled with the establishment of the Roman province of Asia and the Ottomans largely ignored it. Freya Stark, in the early 1950s, found it deserted. On the ground remains are scarce. It was used as a quarry from the 19th century: the quays of İzmir are made from Erythrae's city walls.

The place has never been thoroughly investigated. The wall circuit (4km), with four gates, is known. It enclosed the town up to the acropolis, which was defended by its own circuit; there were no defences along the shore. The wall had towers that Hamilton, in the early 19th century, still saw standing but which are no more. Made of limestone and trachyte, the late 4th-century BC wall, 3–5m thick, made no provision for the use of heavy artillery, even though this was a time when such weaponry was in use. The wall must therefore have been built on the cheap by the local community. It was later repaired by the Byzantines.

The theatre sits in a hollow on the north side of the acropolis. Most of the seating has been stripped out and there is no trace of the skene. Erythrae was famous for its Sibyl (depicted by Michaelangelo on the ceiling the Sistine Chapel, shown studiously leafing through a book). She looks very young there, but she lived to be 900. She also appears in inlaid marble on the floor of the duomo in Siena. Greatly respected in antiquity for her prophetic gifts, the Sibyl of Erythrae, Herophile by name, is also part of the Christian tradition as an early announcer of the Redemption. Some of her prophetic verses, collected in the Sibylline Books, were in due course seized by the Romans for the Capitoline Temple of Jupiter, where they were destroyed by fire. Her workplace at Erythrae was a cave which has never been securely located. Equally elusive is the location of the Egyptianising Temple of Heracles, about which Pausanias writes enthusiastically (7,5,5–8).

ÇEŞME

Çeşme, at the very tip of the peninsula, catches all the wind you will need for wind- and kitesurfing. It is the 'wind capital of Europe'. The clear sea and the fine sands mean that are several good beaches. One even promises diamonds (Pırlanta Plajı), but the reference is to the glittering sand. The castle by the harbour may now fly the

Turkish flag, but it is originally Genoese. Genoa had a lot of commercial interests in Anatolia and much of its merchandise flowed through Çeşme harbour. Moreover Chios, just opposite, was in the hands of the Giustiniani family from Genoa until 1566, when they lost it to the Ottomans. Bayezıt took possession of Çeşme Castle sometime in the 15th century and it has now been more or less rebuilt by the municipality to house the Archaeological Museum (*open Tues–Sun 8.30–5; charge*); it houses material of various periods from the area and includes a couple of rooms magnanimously commemorating the great Ottoman naval defeat of July 1770 at the hands of the Russian fleet of Catherine the Great. The sultan's fleet was annihilated and 11,000 Ottoman sailors drowned.

TEOS

Teos (*map B, 3*), about 1km south of Sığacık, was Freya Stark's 'favourite place to live'. To capture the atmosphere that so enchanted her back in the 1950s, you should avoid the summer altogether. Teos has now been discovered and is not a very well-kept secret.

Teos began as one of the twelve Ionian cities, minting its own coins (its emblem was an iris). It appears to have had an undistinguished political career. It was dwindling in Hellenistic times—according to Thucydides (*8,16*) its defences had been dismantled by the Persian satrap Tissaphernes in the early 4th century BC—and it was not strong enough to oppose Lysimachus when he removed an unspecified number of its inhabitants to the newly-founded Ephesus. Manpower was one of the most valuable commodities in antiquity and was used to give weight and importance to a city and to carry out the required public works. With the rise of Smyrna, Teos eventually sank into complete inconsequence.

Geographically, Teos is well positioned, on an isthmus of a north–south peninsula (this neck of land was narrower in antiquity; the south end of it, where one of Teos' harbours was, has gradually silted up with alluviation). Harbour installations have now been identified on dry land. The north harbour is presently under the town of Sığacık. Teos has attracted interest over time but there has been no sustained investigation until recently; the work of the University of Ankara has produced an exhaustive tourist booklet in Turkish/English, which is available online, as well as a programme of excavation and restoration.

The Temple of Dionysus (*see below*) had become a focus of attention locally by the 18th century, since a marble business was set up inside it. At the same time inscriptions, friezes and building material were steadily being incorporated in Sığacık's castle, its mosque, houses and cemetery. As a result in 1924, all the French archaeologists could see were the foundations. Today the basic layout of the Hellenistic occupation on the isthmus is known; it overlays an earlier Archaic development.

THE RUINS
Starting from the acropolis, a 35m elevation (now Kocakır Tepe) affording a commanding view over both harbours, you are at the north end of the 4m-wide

Hellenistic wall circuit, partly in ashlar limestone blocks with small towers, gates and posterns, which extended to the south harbour. Like the one at Erythrae, it was cheaply built, without provision for heavy artillery. On the acropolis, a **temple to Zeus Capitolinus**, on an east–west axis and fronted by an altar, overlays an earlier Archaic temple of the Ionic Order. The **gymnasium** to the northeast, still largely unexcavated, was co-educational according to an inscription, with boys and girls learning reading, writing, literature, music and sports. The 2nd-century BC **theatre** on the south slope has remains of the cavea and of a scaena, a Roman addition (early 2nd century AD). Whereas the theatre has been extensively robbed, the **bouleuterion** has preserved most of its 16 rows of seats divided into four sections. Statue bases give the names of prominent members of the community and hint to a fundamental overhaul of the building in the 1st century AD. An inscription suggests that the building was also used for musical and literary performances. To the southwest, the **agora area**, with scant remains of a small temple, is as yet little understood.

The **Temple of Dionysus** to the west, a peripteros of the Ionic Order, the largest in Anatolia (35m by 18m), dedicated to the god of wine and song, was first excavated by the Società dei Dilettanti in the 19th century. With its deep pronaos, distyle in antis, and peripteral colonnade of 30 columns, it has been compared to the Temple of Athena at Priene and may be the work of the same architect, Hermogenes. It was surrounded by a temenos shaped like a trapezium with four stoas (Doric: north and south; Ionic: east and west). Originally Hellenistic, the temple was renovated in the Roman period. Here Dionysus was honoured under the epithet of Sitaneios, connected to his role in the fertility of the land.

The **cistern** along the city walls going south (*sarnıç* in Turkish) is Roman in date and is connected to the water supply system. With a barrel-vaulted ceiling and a stucco lining all around the interior, it is roughly rectangular in shape, 4m long and c. 6m wide, with blind arches on the outside.

TEOS AND ITS LEGACY

Teos's wealth came partly from its role as a trade hub, but lay partly also in its famous pots, woollen cloaks and Africano marble (apparently named after the workforce), which was quarried in the immediate hinterland, in the Karagöl area 3km to the northeast of the ancient city. Part of the quarry is now submerged in a shallow lake (hence the name, Karagöl, which means 'dark lake'). Here the multicoloured marble, for which Teos was famous in antiquity, was quarried. Most of this coveted stone was not used in Anatolia but was exported to Rome for prestigious public imperial buildings.

Teos had, besides, one additional claim to fame, namely Anacreon, who was born here in 485 BC. Critias, the late 5th-century BC Athenian politician, summed up Anacreon's contribution to world's happiness thus: 'Anacreon, stimulator of banquets, deceiver of women, lover of the lyre, remembered for ever; a gift from Teos'; indeed his role in introducing Lydian music and a love of the good life generally cannot be understated: it earned him a commemorative statue on the Athenian acropolis (where he is represented in his cups).

There remains to be explained the large Temple of Dionysus. This ambitious project may be connected to the bestowing of a great honour on this small city at the end of the 3rd century BC, when Teos was chosen as the seat of the Asiatic Branch of the Artists of Dionysus. These were professional itinerant actors and musicians who performed at various festivals. Being the seat of this body conferred a certain number of financial advantages on the city. It made its territory sacred and inviolable; there were tax privileges to be had. Unfortunately these artists were highly strung and temperamental and had a terrible reputation—apparently not entirely undeserved. They were moved to Ephesus, then to Myonnesus and then to Lebedus, all small places down the coast (*see below*), ending up in Priene at the time of the great romance between Anthony and Cleopatra. He wanted to please her. Eventually they made their way Rome, wherefrom the Asiatic Branch of the Artists of Dionysus is heard of no more.

SOUTH OF THE ÇEŞME PENINSULA

MYONNESUS

When Livy (*37, 27*) talks of Myonnesus (in the Doğanbey area, south of Teos; *map B, 3*), referring to the time when the Romans were about to engage the Seleucids in a naval battle in the area in September 190 BC, he described it as a rock in the shape of an obelisk connected by a causeway to the mainland. He also mentions the high cliffs undermined by the waves and pirates hiding at the top ready to strike. So it is difficult to believe that there was a city there in 500 BC, as the written sources maintain. It must have been on the mainland and it must have been there that the Asiatic Branch of the Artists of Dionysus (*see above*) decamped when they moved out of Teos. The mainland has not been investigated. On the rock itself the plastered cisterns are Ottoman, but there must have been some form of defence since the rebel emir Cineis took refuge here in 1424 when the Ottoman Sultan Murat conquered İzmir, the town of which he was governor. After his men mutinied, Cineis surrendered and was murdered in his tent.

LEBEDUS

Further east, by the coast at Cumhuriyet, is Lebedus (*map B, 3*). A small town, yet one of the Twelve Ionian cities, it was poorly situated without a good harbour and squeezed for territory by the proximity of Teos, Colophon, and Notium and Claros. Small wonder that it did not thrive. It is known only for having played host to the Artists of Dionysus (*see above*), at a time when it wanted to improve its image and perhaps make some money from their performances. This would have been sometime in the 2nd century BC, after it had been subjugated by the Egyptians in 266 BC, when it was known as Ptolemais and had lost some of its population to Lysimachus's new city of Ephesus. It is known that it was still minting coins in the 2nd century AD and that it had a bishop; his church has been identified.

Lebedus was sited partly on the headland, with an extension on the mainland. The headland section had a wall with four towers and three gates: the Byzantine church is within the walls to the east; to the southeast, a ramp cut into the rock led down to the sea. On the mainland, the acropolis, with defences all around and a theatre on the slope, has been identified, together with the foundations of a building, possibly a temple. Some geophysical investigation prior to excavation would be helpful. One should also consider the possibility that the abundance of hot water and mud baths in the area may have supported some thermal tourism in antiquity, which would have helped Lebedus to survive. The hot springs at Karakoç to the west, and the nearby old bath installations, may hold the key.

COLOPHON

Further east, near the village of Değirmendere, is the inland site of ancient Colophon (*map B, 3*), reputedly the oldest of the Twelve Cities of Ionia. The site, on an elevation (hence the name, connected to the Greek word for summit), was surrounded by good land, today's Cumaovası, where beautiful horses were reared. It is not surprising that evidence of earlier settlers has been found nearby, in a cemetery thought to be Mycenaean. Colophon prospered in the 6th century BC, in part also thanks to pilgrims to the temple of Claros. That did not save it from the Lydians and the Persians. It later resisted Lysimachus (unsuccessfully as it turned out) when he wanted to move its people to Ephesus (or Arsinoë, as it was then). It is said that those that fell were buried in the tumulus that can be seen in the area. Colophon was eventually refounded in Notium as New Colophon (a fact not accepted by all scholars).

The people of Colophon had a reputation for loving luxury, according to remarks in the ancient sources. They probably enjoyed high living standards because of their favourable economic situation, with the easy money from the horses and the pilgrims. But the idea of 'punishment for hubris', as in the case of Sybaris in southern Italy, was a recurrent theme often used to explain undignified exits from history. According to John Freely in his *Western Shores of Turkey*, the Colophonians had a special relationship with dogs, training them to fight alongside horses and to work as guard dogs. They saw it as a good investment, since the animals did not have to be paid. If we can believe Pausanias (*3.14.9*), they also sacrificed puppies to Hecate. Whether they ate the sacrificial meat afterwards is open to question.

The site, which has been poorly investigated, is spread over three hills. It was walled with a circuit of well-cut, large blocks of grey-blue limestone, some 4km long and dated to the 4th century BC. It had twelve towers in 1881. Survival has not been good and the gates are not identified. The acropolis is to the west. Stretches of paved roads and house foundation are known.

CLAROS AND NOTIUM

Claros (*map B, 3; open daylight hours; charge*) is the site of a temple and an oracle of Apollo. It was situated by the river Hales, the coldest river in Asia Minor, celebrated in ancient poetry. This trait guided Richard Chandler, who was the first to identify the location in the late 18th century. There is indeed plenty of water around: the river frequently overflows and as the watertable has risen, the ruins now emerge from the water in an idyllic setting.

According to tradition, there has been an oracle here since time immemorial, before the Trojan War (which it had predicted, stating that Helen was going to be the ruin of both Europe and Asia). The oracle's fame dipped a bit during Hellenistic times; pirates (who obviously escaped the oracle's radar) did some damage, but the temple flourished again under the Romans, spreading its fame over a wide catchment area from the Pontus to Corinth to Crete, rivalling Delphi and riding high on the fame achieved when it correctly warned Germanicus of his impending death in AD 18. The rise of Christianity, earthquakes, encroaching water and consequent silting led to abandonment and decline and inevitable pillaging. Recent archaeology has confirmed early human activity. Two caves have been identified below the temple, with a spring—possibly the one the priest drank from for inspiration from Apollo (which enabled him to answer the question before it was formulated). According to the excavators, the monumentalisation of Claros began in the 6th century BC. A temple to Apollo and a much smaller one to his sister Artemis were built. The complex was expanded on a grander scale, with a propylon entrance to the south and larger temples and altars, later in the Hellenistic to Roman periods. With the introduction of the Claria Games in the early 2nd century BC, Claros joined the international sacred games circuit, along with Olympia, to cite one example. In due course, to the east of the Temple of Apollo, Hellenistic structures were removed to create an area for a hecatomb, the sacrifice of 100 head of cattle. Four rows of reused marble blocks with rings to tether the animals have been identified. Statues of Roman grandees went up. A marble arm over 3m long is thought to belong to a lost outsize image of Apollo.

A recently investigated wreck, off the coast to the west at Kızılburnu, was found to have been carrying eight column drums and a capital (altogether making a single column of the right size for the temple) together with marble slabs and unfinished blocks. The size and the isotopic analysis of the marble, which came from the Sea of Marmara, matched perfectly the known remains of the Temple of Apollo at Claros. Up to the 1st century BC, Proconnesian marble, as the stone from Marmara Island was known, was only moved locally. This shipment was a new development and it is thought, from the analysis of its construction, that the vessel was a purpose-built marble carrier.

NOTIUM

By the 7th century BC a sacred way linked the sanctuary of Claros to Notium to the southwest (*map B, 3*). According to Herodotus (*1,149*), Notium was an Aeolian foundation, its southernmost (though some dispute its identification with the settlement in question here). Notium, perhaps just the port of Claros, was situated on a hill with two eminences and a saddle in between, facing the sea to the south. From high up one can see to Ephesus and beyond; on a clear day, you can catch a glimpse of Mt Mycale and Miletus. Notium benefited from the proximity of Claros and the pilgrim trade but was forever quarrelling over it, with Colophon also staking claims to Claros. Booming Ephesus had an adverse effect on the development of

Notium, draining it of business and resources. By Roman times, Notium was no more. On the hill, which has been only cursorily investigated, one can see some remains. The early 3rd-century BC wall with towers and gates was 3.2 km long and also controlled access from the sea (defence against pirates). A temple of Athena has been identified. The agora was in the saddle, not far from the theatre. A swim off the sandy beach nearby is a beautiful way to round off a visit.

PRACTICAL INFORMATION

TOURIST INFORMATION

There are several information centres in İzmir: at the Adnan Menderes Airport; by Clock Tower on the seafront; and by the Hilton and Büyük Efes hotels, both on Gazi Osman Paşa Blv. not far from the Atatürk monument.

GETTING AROUND

By air: İzmir's Adnan Menderes Airport, to the south of town, is an international hub with flights to and from a number of European destinations. However, most connections within Turkey are via Istanbul or Ankara. The airport is served by the metro and by a bus service directly to the İzmir Yeni Otogar.

By train: İzmir has two railway stations: the Basmane Garı on Fevzipaşa Blv for regional trains, and the İzban Alsancak İstasyonu on Şehitler Cd. to the north, which is the main terminus for intercity trains with fast connections to Afyon and Istanbul; both have a metro stop. The station was built in 1858 (it was then known as 'La station de la pointe' because here the coastline makes a kink, closing the harbour to the north) and it still maintains some of its Ottoman charm, especially inside. Basmane Garı is

slightly later and was designed by a young Gustave Eiffel, well before he built his famous tower.

By bus: You can get to İzmir from anywhere in Turkey, arriving at the İzmir Yeni Otogar/Büyük Otogar, which is some way away from the town centre to the east. The İlçe Peronları (platforms serving local destinations) are on the upper floor.

To get into town, use local buses (54 and 191). Bus 204 serves the airport. These buses leave from the ground floor, from platforms (*peron*) 2 and 3. Alternatively you can take the metro to Halkpınar.

By metro: İZBAN, as İzmir's metro is locally known, is a suburban railway line that runs from the north at Aliağa beyond Menemem, with possible extensions at some point in the future to Bergama, Cumaovası and Selçuk/Ephesus. At present you can get as far as Selçuk from the airport with the local train. A shorter east–west light railway line crosses the İZBAN at Basmane.

Public transport in İzmir is fully integrated (city buses, local trains, İZBAN and ferries). You can buy an İzmirimkart valid for three rides or a card that you can load with as much credit you think you will need.

WHERE TO STAY

İzmir: If you decide to stay in İzmir, bear in mind that at the beginning of September the İzmir International Fair and Festival will fill the town. You can splash out on the Key Otel (*keyhotel.com*) on Mimar Kemalettin Cd., right on the edge of the sea next to the Halkbank, or on the Büyük Efes (*swissotel.com/hotels/izmir*) on Gazi Osman Paşa Blv., which has spacious rooms, sea views, indoor and outdoor pools and a fine garden. (The chef here in the 1960s was İlyas Ertü, who in January 1966 became the darling of the nation after winning First Prize at the International Hotel and Catering Exhibition at London's Olympia. For his success in bringing to the attention of the whole world the delights of Turkish-Ottoman cuisine, a pleasure both to the palate and to the eye, he was presented by the Minister of Tourism with a Hittite copper pitcher.) The Kilim Otel (*kilimotel. com.tr*), on Atatürk Blv. just south of the eponymous statue, has a fine view of the sea. For cheaper alternatives, forsake the sea and look around Basmane Station, bearing in mind that if you are sensitive to noise, a side street is a better bet. The Zeybek Hotel (*hotelzeybek.com*) on Fevzipaşa Blv. is quite reasonable.

Çeşme: Gone are the days when the peninsula was one single uninterrupted olive grove. A multiple-lane motorway now crosses it from east to west and it is all very built up, especially on the north side. Çeşme has an abundance of accommodation but is also a very popular destination. The Melisa Hotel (*melisa-hotel.cesme.hotels-tr.net*) on Hürriyet Cd. not far from the sea and the Tekke Beach, is comparatively quiet, as is the Pasifik Otel (*pasifikotel. com*) nearby at the top end of the same street. If you want to be in the thick of things, the Tanı Pansiyon at Çarşı Sk 5 (T: 232 712 62 38), just south of the castle, or the Yalçın Hotel (*yalcinhoel. com*) on 1002 Sk will do well.

To the east of Çeşme, **Ilıca** has been fast expanding as a tourist destination with the help of its thermal springs (the meaning of *ılıca*). The Çeşmeplus Hotel (*ceshmeplushotel.com*), on Şifne Yolu at the east end of town, is a good choice. **Alaçatı** used to be a separate village to the south but is now a suburb of Ilıca, a windsurfing paradise off the south coast. It offers a choice of accommodation, for example the Asmahan Otel (*asmahanotel.com*) in a quaint old-fashioned stone house just off Atatürk Blv. to the south, or the Viento Hotel (*vientoalacati.com*) on 11039 Sk, similar to the above but in a different colour scheme: the woodwork is painted green. Alaçatı, thanks to the lure of its windmills, organic food, wine, herbs and general atmosphere, has become a known destination among the *cognoscenti* and as a result is not cheap. The ingredients are all there to a certain extent, but you need to visit outside the peak season.

WHERE TO EAT

İzmir: There is plenty of choice here. If you want a fine view and a coffee, stroll along the Kordon in Alsancak, which is where everyone seems to go in the evening. Alternatively try İzmir Asansör, at the top end of an elevator built in 1906 to negotiate the steep rise in the land; the food is of a variable quality. To find it, look out for a tall brick tower on Dario Moreno Sk. Dario Moreno was a native of Smyrna. He went on to make an amazing career as a singer in France, where he partnered Brigitte Bardot on screen when she was at the height of her fame. The Altınkapı Restaurant, not far from the Atatürk Museum, has now been going for almost 40 years. It has a well deserved reputation for its kebabs and has recently opened a fish section. You will find a number of smaller eateries in the Kemeraltı Bazaar and the area around it, starting with Ömür Balık Lokantası for fish near the Hisar Cami. Should you happen upon a döner kebab fired with coal instead of gas, that is a must; this is how it should be done, using lamb meat and abundant onion juice and spices, not the inferior chicken. If you feel nostalgic for Western food, you can relax at the Café La Cigale on Cumhuriyet Blv., which offers a choice of French and Italian fare.

Çeşme: There is abundant choice around the harbour and near the castle but this being said, the offering is not particularly inspired. The Meydan Restaurant on Cumhuriyet Meydanı has a well-deserved reputation for mezes, meaning you do not get a serving all to yourself but help yourself from the choice of dishes spread out on the table. If you are prepared to go a way out towards the top of the peninsula, the Cevatin Yeri at Dalyanköy will reward you with amazing delicacies ranging from deep fried stuffed zucchini flowers to salt bonito and fish böreks. For something sweet, go to MADO in the Çeşme marina. This franchise can be found all over Turkey,

even deep in the east, as well as in many locations abroad. It specialises in desserts and ice creams.

Alaçatı (a suburb of Ilıca) should be approached with caution and a well-stocked wallet. There is a lot of hype. Restaurateurs here do not have a vegetable garden, they have a *potager* (and it goes on in that vein).

If you are keen to explore the **local wines** (it is said that one fifth of Turkey's wineries are on the Çeşme peninsula), make a trip to Urla Şarapçı (*urlasarapcilik.com.tr*) at Kuşcular Köyü, south of Urla beyond the motorway.

As you travel around, you will see signs for *çöp kebab* and *kokoreç*. Try them both: the first one comes on characteristically short wooden skewers, the second is a traditional dish of the Balkans, the west coast of Turkey and Azerbaijan (and also parts of northern Greece). It is made of sheep and goat offal wrapped up in intestines and grilled on a spit. It tastes like delicious bits of meat. Ask to see it in the kitchen.

WHAT TO DO

The **Çeşme Music Festival**, which takes place towards the end of June, offers a week of Turkish music, fashion shows, classic cuisine and more.

The **Ot Festivalı** in Alaçatı (early June) is all about herbs. You will be taught how to plant a mastic tree and how to recognise different herbs. Food will be on sale: look out for cookies (*kurabiye*) and for böreks filled with spinach and other greenery, and for jams to take home.

EAST OF İZMİR, THE GEDİZ VALLEY: MANİSA, SARDES & KULA

East of İzmir, the long valley of the Gediz (the ancient Hermus) was traditionally the border of Aeolia and Ionia with Smyrna, fluctuating between the two. Its destiny in antiquity, however, was not to divide but to provide access to the interior, at least as far as Sardes, and to Ephesus via the Karabel Pass, a mere 500m in altitude; further south, mountain passes connected the area with the Büyük Menderes, whose valley cuts deep into the east, giving access to the Anatolian Plateau.

The early development of the area is still little understood; however, the very recently discovered large late Bronze Age settlement near Gölmarmara at Kaymakçı Tepe, north of Sardes, may have hosted ancestors of the Lydians after the demise of the Hittite Empire in the late 2nd millennium BC. The destiny of the two main cities of the Gediz Valley (leaving out Menemen, a relative newcomer) has been shaped by geography: inland, Manisa was surrounded by productive agricultural land while Sardes, now a mere village but with a powerful past, prospered as a traffic hub.

As for the valley itself, it is one of the four grabens that cut the Anatolian peninsula between Bergama and Kuşadası. This means a wide, flat valley, with sides steeper to the south than to the north, abundant, fertile alluvium from the valley sides and from upstream, and a delta that grows and grows. Indeed the delta of the Gediz, thought to be threatening İzmir's harbour, was relocated further west in 1886.

Not far from the sea, the volcanic Yamanlar Dağı mountains exceed the 1200m mark and immediately south of Manisa, the Sipil (or Spil) Dağı, the ancient Sipylus, a limestone formation now a national park, has benefited from a programme of reforestation. With a maximum height of 1500m, it can have abundant snow in the winter while in the summer it is a favourite for picnics, family outings, camping and mountaineering. In the spring it is covered in blooms, among them the famous red Manisa tulip (*Manisa lalesi*), which sometimes deceptively looks like a red anemone. It is possibly best not to pick any flowers: tales abound of heavy fines meted out to transgressors.

MANİSA

There was a city somewhere in the environs of Manisa (*map B, 3*) in antiquity. Precisely where is not sure, but it left enough spolia incorporated in later building developments to show that it was no mean settlement. Richard Chandler placed it on the north side of the Gediz; Archibald Sayce thought it was at the bottom of a lake drained in the 1850s, where he later saw classical columns reused to embank an irrigation channel.

HISTORY OF MANİSA

Traditionally Manisa was founded by Thessalian veterans of the Trojan War; it certainly had a history later on, as a Lydian city, morphing into a Persian one and eventually coming under Hellenistic and Roman influence. Its life-changing experience came in AD 17, when it was hit by a massive earthquake that damaged twelve cities of the Roman province of Asia. The city was then Roman and Emperor Tiberius stepped in to provide financial assistance for a wide-ranging restoration programme of public buildings. After that comes another blank until Manisa resurfaces as a Byzantine city of some importance in the early 13th century. This is the time when the Crusaders were in Constantinople and the Byzantine Empire was split into four (Latin Empire, Nicaean Empire, Trabzon Empire and Despotate of Epirus). John III Dukas Vatatzes, the Nicaean emperor, endowed Manisa (where he had his treasury and mint) with a citadel, whose battered and yet-to-be-investigated remains are lost among the olive groves of Sandık Tepesi, 3km south of town at the foot of the Spil Dağı; he was buried there. It is thought that his palace was lower down, closer to the modern town. The emperor spent his winters further south, in the town of Nif (anciently Nymphaeum, now Kemalpaşa) where he had another palace, ruins of which are still standing in the town's outskirts (ask for Kız Kalesi). Later, when the Latins were ousted from Constantinople, the Byzantines held Manisa until 1313, losing it to Sarukhan, a Turkish emir who attacked it from sea.

The beautification of Islamic Manisa started then. It was mainly financed by agricultural wealth and the revenues of the port of Phocaea, which at the time was run by the Genoese, who paid the emir handsomely for the privilege. The Ottomans turned the city into a training ground for future rulers (*şehzade*, meaning crown princes). That entailed the building of palaces for the young men and their mothers in town and up the Sipylus for the hot season and for hunting, as well as the construction of imposing public works witnessing their Islamic piety. When the Ottoman Empire extended east, that function was taken over by Amasya and Trabzon, though the practice did not last beyond the 16th century. Crown princes preferred to stay in İstanbul, close to the action. Manisa settled down as an agricultural centre (cotton, tobacco, sundried tomatoes) with an early railway link. Trade and industrial production boomed. The events of 1922 left a deep scar, as the town lost a significant proportion of its buildings in the hostilities, but it soon recovered. It is now a very pleasant place to visit, with green spaces and a cablecar that takes you high up the Sipylus in 15mins.

Visiting Manisa

Start with the **Archaeological Museum** on Murat Sk (*open Tues–Sun 9–12 & 1–5, longer hours in summer; charge*), housed in the madrasa and in the imaret of the Muradiye Cami, a late 16th-century Ottoman construction. There you can admire an unusual piece of Ottoman armour dated to the 15th century and intended to protect the lower arm. The iron contraption is richly ornamented with gilded inlay, which makes one think it was rather a matter of prestige than practicality. Other finds include material from the synagogue at Sardes (fountain and mosaics) and Hellenistic and Roman remains testifying to a beautiful city whose precise whereabouts are still uncertain.

Leaving the museum, go east and then take 1818 Sk north and, after Esnaf Parkı, you will see the **Hatunyie Camii** at the corner of Atatürk Blv. and Borsa Cd. The complex, a külliye, includes a mosque, a han, a bath, a primary school (*sıbyan mektebi*), as well as a soup kitchen that is now no more. It was willed by the mother of Sultan Suleiman II and was built at a time when the future 'Magnificent' was learning the ropes as Crown Prince in Manisa. A document of 1497 shows that the complex was endowed with the revenues from the market. The mosque is surrounded by greenery; the original park was larger. The outer walls are made in brick and cut stone (andesite and marble); note the elaborate minaret. Originally the porch was open to the elements. Capitals and columns are Byzantine. To enter the prayer hall you pass an inscription stating that the mosque was completed in 1491. Inside, the area is dominated by a huge dome. Note the beautifully carved mimber (1495). West of the mosque is the mektep mentioned above. The market (Kurşunlu Han) is on the other side of the road to the south. It owes its name to its lead-clad roof. It is arranged on two floors and originally had 21 shops. Today it is used as a student residence. All the buildings have been heavily restored.

To the south of Murat Cd., on the edge of Mt Sipylus along Ulutepe Cd., is the **Ulu Cami**, an older monument built by the Emir Muzafereddin Işak Çelebi in the second half of the 14th century. Mosque and medrese are a single building, an arrangement not dissimilar to the İsa Bey Mosque in Selçuk. Both were built with reused Byzantine blocks of various sizes. The entrance is to the north. There are two additional doors, one to the east and one to the west leading to the school. Inside, a diminutive courtyard is surrounded by a wide portico with fine Byzantine capitals and columns. It leads to the prayer hall, with a large cupola supported by eight pillars. The mimber (1366) is by the very same woodworker from Antep to whom we owe the mimber of the Ulu Cami in Bursa. The minaret is a later addition. The medrese to the west of the mosque had to accommodate changes in the level of the ground. The result is a unique plan set on two storeys, with no portico and only one iwan to the south. Students had the choice between standing in the yard or retiring to their rooms to study. The türbe of the founder is between medrese and mosque; its entrance is flanked by two fine Byzantine columns and leads to a room with four sarcophagi, one of which presumably belongs to the founder.

The ruins of the **hamam** are to the northeast of the Ulu Cami. Here in 1410, the Emirate of Sarukhan that succeeded the Lascarids came to an end with the execution of its last official by the Ottoman Sultan Mehmet I.

OUTSKIRTS OF MANİSA

There are a couple of popular destinations for a day out in the country on the outskirts of town. On the very edge of the built-up area to the south, the **Niobe Rock** has been the object of particular veneration since time immemorial. Pausanias himself made a note of it in his travels. He does point out that if you want to see the weeping Niobe, grieving for the loss of all her twelve children killed by a vengeful god, you have to look at the rock from the right angle and in the right light. Under such conditions, you will see a prostrated woman in tears. These tears, according to the legend, created the lake mentioned earlier and now drained. At the time of writing the municipality had built an open-air theatre next to the rock. Works have damaged it and the increased number of visitors has resulted in a lot of litter strewn around, adding to Niobe's desperation.

Further east, on the way to Sardes around Akpınar, high up on the rockface of the Sipylus to the south and above an amusement park, is a 6m tall relief variously called **Taş Suret** (stone figure) or **Sipylos Heykeli** (the Sipylus monument). Said to be Hittite, it has been known to travellers and antiquaries for a long time and represents a seated figure said to be a mother goddess or a mountain god. Over time the limestone has eroded and so have the Luwian hieroglyphs, which can no longer be read. Opinions will remain divided.

AIGAI

Aigai (*map B, 1; open Mon–Sun 8.30–5*) can be reached from Yenişakran on the busy E87, the İzmir–Bergama road. Coming from the south, look out for a right turn marked 'Anadolu Lisesi' and drive on through two villages. At the third, Yuntdağı Köseler, a sign will direct you to the entrance of the site across the village. If you are lost, ask for '*Aigai antik kent*'.

Aigai is a site for the truly adventurous. It is located inland, high up in the mountains on a volcanic spur north of Manisa at the east end of the Güzelhisar Dam. It is the only large settlement on this mountain chain known as the Yund, the ancient Aspordenon. The site is also called Nemrutkale, an appellation that betrays the presence of unexplained massive buildings, the work of the god Nemrut in popular lore.

HISTORY OF AIGAI

Little is known of this mountain city. One of the twelve mainland cities of the Aeolians, but never a member of the Delian Confederacy, it appears to have flourished when it was in the hands of Pergamon; later, as part of the Roman province of Asia, it received financial help from Emperor Tiberius after an earthquake; most surviving monuments date from that period, the beginning of the 1st century AD. Coinage from Aigai is known from the 3rd century BC to the 3rd century AD. The *polis* faded after late Antiquity; a small chapel in the northeast corner of the acropolis suggest a muted Byzantine presence.

A plan shows an elongated settlement on a spur between two streams, the Sellik Dere to the west and the Koca Çay, the ancient Pythicos, to the east. The topography is quite similar to Pergamon's, except that Pergamon is in a plain, while Aigai is surrounded by yet more mountains. The city was certainly well defended but quite isolated; what did these people live on? Wool production and weaving are a possibility, but are not the complete explanation. The architecture reflects the nature of the terrain, which required the building of sturdy terraces. It has been suggested that Attalus I generously paid for the buildings but also sent along his architects and masons. Being so isolated, Aigai was allowed to crumble, there are no lime kilns in view and scavenging for building material has been minimal. On the other hand, the necropolis to the south and east has been thoroughly scoured for 'treasure', leaving behind a cemetery of broken cist graves and sarcophagi.

Visiting Aigai

Exploring the site requires good shoes, a stick and some warm clothing just in case. At 360m, Aigai catches lot of wind and can be overcast and cold. On a good day it is an excellent spot for a picnic. Visitors are rare and you will quite possibly have the whole site to yourself. The trail is well marked with a number of excellent explanatory panels. Three wall circuits separating the acropolis from the rest of the town and then marking the expansion of the civilian settlement can still be made out.

After the car park and a short walk, you will be entering the town from the north. After passing the remains of the North Bath and a couple of city gates now known as Yeni Kapı and Demir Kapı, you head straight for the **bouleuterion**. The building has been recently investigated. Measuring 24m by 14m and sitting on an east–west slope, it consisted of three parts. An entrance to the west was marked by a portico with six Ionic columns and led to a semicircular feature with twelve stairs and a seating capacity of approximately 180 (too small for a theatre). On the east side, fronting the main street, was the façade with a dedicatory inscription on the architrave block to Zeus Bollaios, Hestia Bollaia and the Demos (the people) set up by a local benefactor, one Antiphanes son of Apollonidas. At the foot of the seating, beyond the semicircular orchestra, an important number of statues and statue bases representing deities and local worthies and their families, have been identified. A couple of libation pits (bothroi) have also been investigated. One of them contained material earlier than the proposed date for the building (c. 2nd century BC), suggesting that the present building is on top of an earlier one.

After the bouleuterion, the **market building** is along the old path paved with huge slabs. When the German archaeologists recorded and photographed it in 1889, it stood to roof height; at 11m the gable was still visible. Now some of the andesite blocks have come tumbling down but it is still impressive. Built on three storeys on a platform 80m by 40m, it much resembles the market in Alinda. The ground floor had a row of shops and back rooms with beautiful doorways and window frames. The second storey was a single hall, divided lengthwise by arches and massive piers with narrow slits for air and light, while on the third level the open space was punctuated by a row of columns supporting the wooden truss of the ceiling. An additional colonnade to the west marked the access to the agora. The structure has offered a precious insight into Hellenistic construction techniques, with headers and stretchers and rubble filling. Now, however, as the site is being showcased for visitors, this beautiful building has become a true conservator's nightmare. It has survived amazingly well thus far but that was when the place was deserted. It did not matter if a stone was brought down by the wind or by the not-infrequent earth tremors. Andesite tends to weather and crumble and the structure is very exposed on the edge of a ravine.

To the east of the market on the edge of the ravine, a small circular paved structure with four steps going down towards the centre has been interpreted as a **macellum** (meat market), though the fact that it is a sunken feature means that it would have been impossible to keep clean if it really sold meat and fish (there is no trace of a drain anywhere). Other features worth exploring are the **theatre** to the west, and the remains of a **temple** possibly dedicated to Athena set in its temenos. Beyond the remains of a cistern is the area of the **gymnasium** with its baths. Just follow the bright red arrows and mind where you put your feet.

If you have been gripped by Aigai, bear in mind that excavations resume in the summer and some tour operators offer a day's digging as well as sightseeing.

SARDES

The only archaeological site with a symphonic poem to its name (*Sardis* by Kamran İnce), Sardes, also Sardis or Sardeis (*map B, 4; open daily 8–7, shorter hours in winter; charge*), has been a reference point since antiquity for power, riches, luxury and the frailty of human endeavour. However, when you get here (a short journey east of Manisa on the E96 to the village of Sart), you may be disappointed. There is a lot and at the same time very little to see, considering that the site boasts a history of urbanisation spanning 1,300 years. The landscape, beautifully green in the spring to early summer, with glorious fruit trees, the imposing Tmolus mountain (the modern Bozdağ) to the south, a field of outsize tumuli beyond the Gediz to the north, not to mention the reconstructed ruins themselves: all these speak of greatness. But the city as a network of streets, houses, palaces and public buildings remains elusive.

The Pactolus, which brought down gold dust from the mountains and riches to the Lydians is now a plain, ordinary stream, the Sart Çayı, all its glitter a thing of the past. The communication network has changed: in antiquity the Royal Road, now Kenan Evren Cd. south of Sart village, an ancient highway linking the Aegean to Susa, the Persian capital, three months away on foot, ran across Sardes bringing

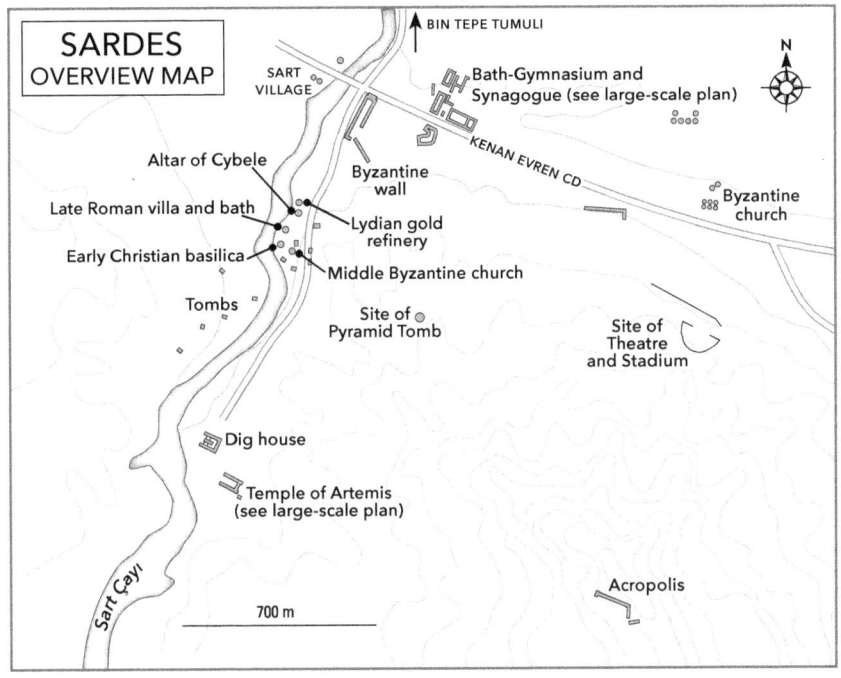

SARDES OVERVIEW MAP

BIN TEPE TUMULI

SART VILLAGE

Bath-Gymnasium and Synagogue (see large-scale plan)

KENAN EVREN CD

N

Altar of Cybele

Byzantine wall

Byzantine church

Late Roman villa and bath

Lydian gold refinery

Early Christian basilica

Middle Byzantine church

Tombs

Site of Pyramid Tomb

Site of Theatre and Stadium

Dig house

Temple of Artemis (see large-scale plan)

Acropolis

Sart Çayı

700 m

armies, trade and ideas. Now the six-lane motorway linking İzmir to the east has been shifted north to spare the archaeology presently under the fields.

To get an idea of the shape and extent of the Lydian city, use Google Earth. With the white blobs of the bath-gymnasium and synagogue (wrongly labelled Temple of Artemis) to the left of the screen, look at the disrupted field pattern immediately north of Kenan Evren Cd. edged by an unnamed minor road, follow the course east almost to the modern motorway then south to Çaltılı Köyü, up the slope to the acropolis and down again close to the starting point; this corresponds roughly to the ancient fortifications, both Lydian and Roman (these were in due course enlarged to take in developments to the west of the town). The plan shows the magnitude of the task awaiting the archaeologists (mainly American, Sardes has always been in their hands) and explains why, after over a hundred years of research, only three percent of Sardes has been excavated. Moreover, work has concentrated on visible features (the Artemis Temple, of which two tall columns are standing to this day, and the area to the north of it, for instance), some of which are *extra muros*. The city proper, terraced on the slope of the acropolis and continuing down the plain to the north, has suffered heavily over the centuries, while in the plain, remains have been deeply buried under the crumbling conglomerate washed down from Mt Tmolus. Add to this that the area is short of good building stone, which has led to a lot of scavenging and to the use of mud brick, in antiquity as well as in the recent past, which leaves scant traces in the archaeological record.

SARDES FROM EARLIEST TIMES TO TODAY

The earliest evidence of occupation for Sardes as a village dates to the late Bronze Age and has been found by the ford of the Pactolus, together with evidence of Anatolian and Mycenaean contacts. Here may have lived those Maeonians mentioned by Homer in the *Iliad* (2:865), early Lydians according to some, but more likely victims of the Lydians who subjugated them. About the latter one knows little. Their language was Indo-European and written in a modified form of the Greek alphabet. Unfortunately the corpus of inscriptions, limited and formulaic, provides little insight. One can see the Lydians emerging in the 12th century BC from the implosion of the Hittite Empire and the ensuing confusion.

Lydia had a number of capable rulers who eventually extended their power to control vast swathes of western Anatolia to the Aegean coast. Sardes was the capital, a city dominated by the acropolis high on the slopes of Mt Tmolus and with prestige buildings on terraces rippling down to the plain below. The wall circuit mentioned above was its defence. It cut off the original settlement to the west by the Pactolus, now turned partly into an industrial area and a necropolis. Some of its kings were buried in the huge tumuli of Bin Tepe 1km to the north, beyond the Gediz river.

The last and best known Lydian king was Croesus, the epitome of the extravagant wealth that could not fail to attract the interest of the Persians (both the rulers and the armies), showing that the Royal Road was no one-way street. Croesus was duly beaten and chastised for his hubris and his naivety (he trusted oracles, especially when they said what he wanted to hear, and failed to interpret *double entendres*). Fate was kind to him: Cyrus wanted him burned alive but Apollo intervened with a timely shower and the Persian ruler relented. Croesus ended his days in gilded exile in Persia, courtesy of his captor. From 546 BC to the time of Alexander the Great just over 200 years later, Lydia was a Persian satrapy; Sardes was known as Sparda.

Archaeologically, Achaemenid Sardes is more or less invisible apart from an impressive destruction layer. There are some improvements to the fortifications (the mud-brick rampart had been breached by the Persians with the aid of the siege mound in its northeast corner). The rebuilding was in stone, and a separate fort with a triple defensive wall was created on the acropolis. Hardly any architecture (domestic, ritual or prestigious) is typically Achaemenid, though some elements have been found reused in later buildings. Some changes of habit can be seen in grave markers, where the dead, shown at funerary banquets, recline in true Oriental fashion; the pyramid tomb on the west slopes of the acropolis hill is also attributed to this period. It could be that the Lydians carried on with their business (mainly trade, textiles and metalwork). They borrowed money from the Temple of Artemis (now in its earliest phase). Temples served both spiritual and material needs; in the case of the latter, financial transactions were policed by the gods and the power of a divine curse. Taxes and tributes, military obligations and forced labour were part of the deal made with the

Persians when Lydia became a satrapy; one does wonder under what terms and conditions Lydian masons toiled at Pasargadae (a long way east: not far from Shiraz in Iran) on Cyrus's royal tomb, which is built in the pure Lydian tradition of neatly squared blocks with drafted margins and rustication. Some locals did well for themselves and took an interest in music, carefully preserving the image of the pleasure-loving Lydians; when they died, they were buried in true Lydian-style tumuli. Satraps enjoyed the lush countryside, perhaps building hunting parks (*paradeisoi*), which leave little trace in the archaeological record

After the death of Alexander the Great, Lydia fell into the morass of the wars of succession, eventually coming under the influence of Pergamon and in 133 BC being incorporated into the Roman Empire. The Romans smartened it up, even more so after the terrible earthquake of AD 17, when the town suffered huge damage described by Tacitus in his *Annals* (2:47). A fund was created by Emperor Tiberius for restoration and rebuilding. First, buildings were dismantled and huge dumps of spolia created (some have been excavated) and emergency housing was supplied; then rebuilding took place on a grand scale and the water supply was improved. The city walls were repaired to fend off a Gothic incursion of the late 3rd century. Later, Diocletian placed one of his imperial weapons factories here. The Sardes of the 4th and 5th centuries prospered as a civil and ecclesiastical capital, with a trading and manufacturing community in which Christians lived and worked side by side with Jews, whose synagogue dwarfed any of the known churches of the period.

Decline set in in the 7th century, when the Persian Sassanids left a huge destruction layer behind them. Parts of the town were abandoned, others were repaired with spolia from fallen buildings. Lime kilns started appearing in among the ruins, a sure sign of bad times. By the end of the 7th century, the acropolis had been enlarged and could house the reduced settlement. Sardes had broken up, with various clusters huddling around crumbling antique structures. Later in the 13th century, a church was built on the west bank of the Pactolus. A small, multi-dome building inside an earlier, larger ruined ecclesiastical structure, it was the work of the Lascarid Byzantines ruling from Nicaea. They also had a strong presence at Manisa and at Nymphaeum (*see above*), from where they could keep an eye on the marauding Turks. Their interest in Sardes was part of that plan. When they left to go back to Byzantium, as courtiers in the restored empire after the demise of the Latins, Sardes was left completely undefended. Its fate was sealed by Tamerlane, who razed it to ground in 1401. Sardes was no more. When things picked up with the caravan trade from İzmir to the east and travellers and antiquaries paid a visit, they witnessed the destruction of the remains as they were turned into lime, a practice still ongoing as late as the end of the 19th century. The establishment of a railway station at Sart might have helped to resurrect ancient glories but the main local centre had already moved to Salihli to the east, where the market was. What one sees today mainly belongs to the Roman period, with minor Byzantine additions.

Visiting Sardes

The point of reference is the stretch of Kenan Evren Cd. running south and parallel to the motorway, cutting across the village of Sart (*marked on the plan on p. 73*). You cannot miss, after some tourist facilities, the partially reconstructed Bath-Gymnasium.

The Bath-Gymnasium
The complex is huge, totalling 23,000 square metres. It is in the tradition of the imperial-style baths, where young people would cleanse their bodies while exercising their minds in congenial company. Similar set-ups are known from other cities in Asia Minor such as Ephesus or Aphrodisias. Here, because it has been partly reconstructed you can see and experience it in 3D. Starting from the east, you will be in the palaestra, an exercise yard with a portico all around housing storage facilities and changing rooms. It is followed by a marble court, whose main function was to impress the beholder with the might of the Roman emperor, and a number of ceremonial rooms that might have been devoted to the imperial cult (though not all agree). The bathing pools, with the usual facilities, are further to the west. The complex was completed c. 2nd century, with later alterations. When it came tumbling down in the 7th century, after an earthquake, it fell out of use, though it was already in poor shape by then. Stones and architectural elements were left where they fell, a lime kiln was installed and squatters moved in.

The reconstruction that took place between 1964 and 1973 concentrated on the 18m high marble court, by far the most extravagant feature, very much reminiscent of the skene or scaena of a theatre, truly Baroque in style with its staggered columns, the expensive use of coloured marbles sourced for *giallo antico* from distant Numidia in north Africa. Fragments of stucco and mosaics have been found, which would have given colour to the brick vaults. Floors were in opus sectile, statues probably everywhere, though only some bases and fragments have survived. It has also been suggested that the marble court had a velarium or awning, just as theatres did. The quality of work is quite variable, however, with widespread use of mortared rubble cores. It is a far cry from the precise Lydian ashlar technique. Some of the walls, in stone with levelling brick courses, look almost Byzantine. Here is an early use of the technique. The pioneering reconstruction work has opted for solidity rather than authenticity. As far as possible, original material has been used, while concrete replicas have filled the gaps. A reinforced concrete frame is embedded in the wall. The beautiful inscription in red-painted letters on the first floor of the façade, stating that the building was dedicated by the citizens of Sardes to the emperors Geta and Caracalla and their mother Julia Domna, is original.

It is thought that the early Christians of Sardis had their first quarters to the west of the town outside the walls, where two small churches have been identified. Large ecclesiastical buildings have so far proved elusive; they were probably within the city walls by the 5th–6th century. On the north side of the wall circuit, a couple of ruins in brick with abundant mortared spolia and massive piers in a building style similar to the Basilica of St John at Ephesus, can be seen. One of them could be the cathedral.

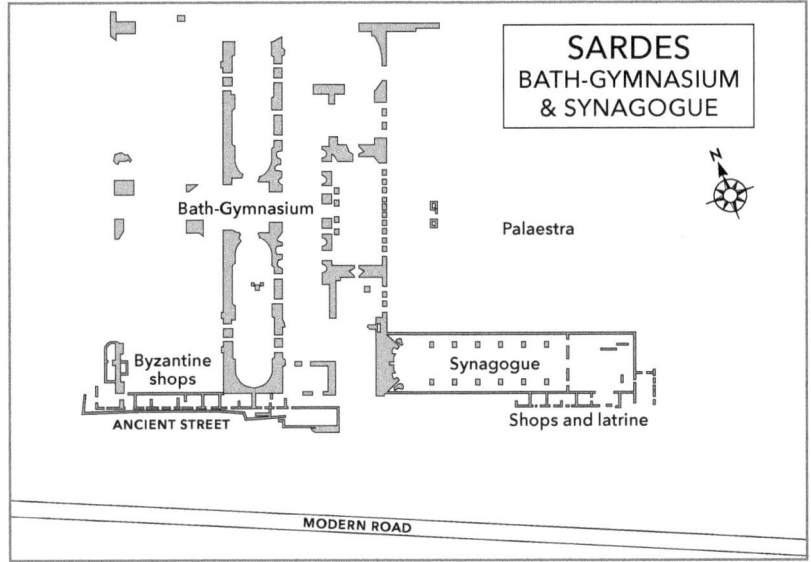

The Synagogue

At some point in the late Antique period, the south portico of the palaestra was given over to the Jewish community, who converted the space into a large synagogue, which has been excavated and partially restored. Future plans include more extensive reconstruction. The space can house up to 1,000 people, suggesting a sizeable Jewish settlement and a community with considerable influence since it could command the use of a public space in such a prominent position. Where the dwellings of this community were is not known.

The synagogue, discovered in 1962, was entered from the east via a forecourt surrounded by a portico with Ionic columns. The vessel in the middle, functioning as an ablution fountain, is a copy (the original is in Manisa Museum). The hall itself was some 50m long with two rows of six piers. The roof was of wood covered in tiles with a possible clerestory. At the far end, the apse, with tiered stone seating, marked the space for the elders and distinguished guests. On the marble paved space in front of it and beyond the semicircular donor mosaic, a marble table was possibly a lectern. Two pairs of life-size stone lions of Persian manufacture were seated on either side. The building was richly decorated with mosaics, mainly geometric, covering the floor, while the decoration was continued on the walls with inlaid panels and a wealth of inscriptions. At the exit on either side two small shrines housed the Torah and other important scrolls.

Locally-sourced spolia were liberally used, showing that the community could command access to disused ancient monuments; it seems that elements of the Temple of Cybele, mentioned in the written sources, ended up here. The dating of the building is debated. A coin hoard under the floor suggests the mid-4th century but there may have been an earlier phase. It could be that the space was given over to the Jewish community as early as the 3rd century AD; by then there had been a Jewish presence in the area some 400 years if, as some say, the Seleucid ruler Antiochus III brought 2,000 Jews, veterans and families, here from Mesopotamia about 215 BC. The synagogue went out of use after 616 when the community dispersed.

The Colonnaded Street

Immediately to the south of the synagogue, an important discovery was made in 1961. A stretch of a colonnaded street with a 5th-century date was discovered. Only the north side survived; the south side was buried under a later road. The idea of a colonnaded street was popular in late antiquity, as can be seen in Ephesus and Corinth for example. It was seen as a way to revitalise an urban space; financially it was a sort of public (imperial) and private partnership. The marble paved street, some 15m wide and flanked by 5m deep porticoes with mosaic floors on either side, was laid on top of an earlier Roman monumental thoroughfare, part of the reconstruction after the earthquake of AD 17. The shops, with an upper storey accessed by a ladder, doubled as living quarters and storage space.

Various businesses have been identified: dyers, potters, taverns. The space was mainly given over to retail as certain types of production could have entailed a fire risk. Here Christians and Jews worked, lived and died side by side, leaving tell-tale graffiti on the walls. Stylistically it was all very disparate with abundant use of spolia. Around 660, when Sardes was more or less deserted, the Byzantines built a road on top of the pre-existing one, sealing the shops that had been abandoned after the Persian incursion of 616. Later the Ottomans laid a road linking İzmir to Ankara exactly on the same spot. It remained in use until 1952. At the far west corner of the row of shops was a latrine, a necessary component of any shopping avenue. It had two rooms, suggesting that it was segregated, each accommodating some twelve people. A continuous stream of water flowed in front of the marble seats and a deeper channel connected to the baths ensured a regular, thorough flushing.

The Gold Refinery

On the way to the Temple of Artemis, 1km south along the banks of the Sart river, the ancient Pactolus, one crosses a beautiful stretch of countryside that in earlier times was given over to the industrial production of the gold that made Lydia and Croesus so famous (just think of his extravagant contributions to Ephesus and Didyma), and financed the military expansion of Lydia. So famous indeed was the term 'Pactolus' that in at least one language the ancient name of the river is still synonymous with wealth and profit. That is what 'pactole' means in French, its first recorded use dating from 1698, in one of Boileau's satires.

In 1968 Andrew Ramage, then a young graduate student, was given the task of recording and clearing what looked like a Persian destruction layer below later domestic occupation. The area, showing evidence of burning, was strewn with broken pottery and overfired bricks. Perceptions changed when small gold globules, bits of gold foil and lumps of lead oxide started to appear. Conservators were alerted and the true nature of the site was exposed. This was a Lydian gold refinery employing processes that can be traced to documented medieval practices for separating gold from silver; the layer was dated by the pottery. Ancient written sources are unanimous about the abundance of gold in the area, either in mines on Mt Tmolus or washed down as placer deposits in the streams originating from it. By Strabo's time, in the 1st century AD, the supply was exhausted. Lydians have been credited with the invention of coinage, which is not quite correct. Lumps of silver of a set weight, to settle accounts and pay mercenaries, go back longer. What the Lydians achieved was the creation of a true bimetallic system, with gold and silver coins of consistent purity and therefore of a stable value. The Sardes refinery employed different processes in order to achieve that goal: two have been identified in the archaeology: cementation and cupellation. Cementation was the process whereby gold was separated from silver and other base metals. The process required layering gold ore, scraps and electrum with salt and heating the load for a long time in small mud brick furnaces. During the process, the silver was absorbed by the bricks and pure gold was produced in a cloud of noxious fumes. Cupellation required small, bowl-shaped hearths made of pottery sherds set in a clay-lined dip in the gravelly earth. The heat came from above. The temperature of c. 1100 degrees required for the process entailed the use of tuyères, which have also been found. The end result was pure metallic silver extracted from the bricks and sherds of the cementation and cakes of litharge (lead oxide) as waste. It remains to be ascertained what raw material was fed into these processes. It has long been believed that the deposits in the Pactolus and related streams were contaminated with silver, therefore producing electrum when smelted. Recent research, however, has shown that these local deposits are remarkably pure. It has therefore been suggested that rather than a large-scale state-controlled operation, the refinery was a small business recycling jewellery scraps and obsolete electrum coins rather than processing natural ore.

The altar in the area, a box-like structure in rough stones and mortar, is believed to belong to the cult of Cybele because of the two crouching lions and a graffito. It may have later been turned into a Persian fire altar.

The Temple of Artemis

Further on past the ancient necropolis, the Temple of Artemis sits in an evocative rural location flanked by a diminutive early Christian church. The standing remains (six monumental columns with an architrave in the 18th century, now reduced to two) were a point of reference for early travellers. Excavations started early in the late 19th century. The crane of English manufacture, which is still there, was brought in by the American team to shift heavy loads in 1911. The remains had originally been identified with the temple of Cybele mentioned by Herodotus (*5:102*), torched by the Greeks in 499 BC when they made a surprise attack, coming not along the main road but from the back of the acropolis over the pass, the Üçler Geçidi (1200m). The excavated remains told a different story, however, and the temple of Cybele remains to be located.

Around 400 BC there was some form of cult here, but no temple, only an open-air altar. The stepped structure made of clamped tufa blocks, possibly clad in marble, was later incorporated into a second structure of the same sort but larger. The unusual orientation of the temple that followed c. 300 BC (facing west rather

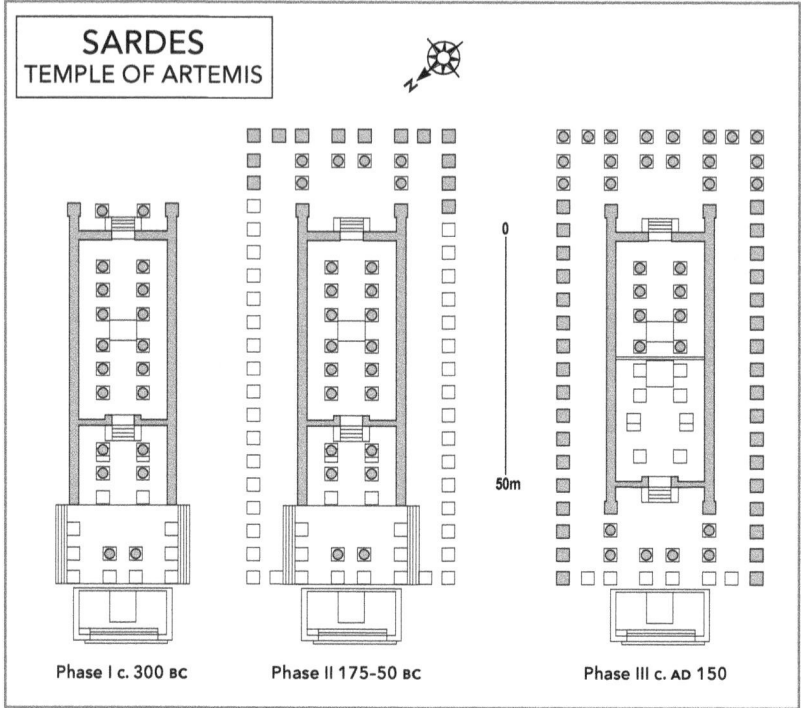

SARDES
TEMPLE OF ARTEMIS

Phase I c. 300 BC   Phase II 175–50 BC   Phase III c. AD 150

than east) is probably due to the presence of this structure that was not removed but incorporated into the entrance. The cult of Artemis Sardiane is attested in an inscription from Ephesus and it is fitting that the goddess should have a temple with her acrolithic statue here since Croesus had financed the rebuilding of the Artemision in Ephesus. The original temple, 67m by 23m on a high platform, was later improved and enlarged with the addition of columns inside and outside, turning it into a pseudo dipteros. After its destruction in the earthquake of AD 17, reconstruction—which was never completed as the unfluted limestone columns show—turned it into a shrine of the imperial cult. The cella was divided in two; gigantic portraits of members of the Antonine dynasty have been found both inside it and out. The structure, still unfinished in the 4th century, was gradually abandoned. With the advent of Christianity it was quarried for building stone and exorcised by having crosses carved on it. What was not looted was buried under successive landslides.

Near the southeast corner of the temple, a chapel (Church M) made of bricks, field stones and spolia set in mortar and covered in painted plaster, was used by the growing Christian community between the 4th and the 7th centuries. The three-arched windows in the apse belong to a second building phase, when an additional room was built to the east. The structure was buried under repeated landslides.

The Theatre and Acropolis

The rest of Sardes is yet to be uncovered. Going east, on the lower slopes of the acropolis, remains of a stadium and a theatre (*see plan on p. 73*) have been located. Platforms have been identified, suggesting monumental buildings like the palace of Croesus praised by both Pliny the Elder and Vitruvius. Well-to-do citizens probably lived here on the slopes, in mud brick structures on stone foundations that have left little trace.

The acropolis (*also marked on p. 73*), the strategic high point, can be reached after a scramble from the west or the southwest. There the early Byzantine fortifications with towers, gates, cisterns and vaulted corridors are but one development of a highly disputed area—so disputed, in fact, that the fortifications came of use in 1919 in the Turkish War of Independence, as attested by the graffiti in a corridor. From the acropolis you have a fine view over the late Roman ruins north of the road: to the east possibly a bath, immediately north of it the monumental remains still deeply buried may belong to a cathedral and to a basilica.

THE BİN TEPE TUMULI

Well in the distance north of the Gediz are the Bin Tepe tumuli, not numbering exactly one thousand, as the name seems to imply: there are in fact 116 of them. In the 1940s there were as many as 149; the loss is due to agricultural work. Nevertheless, this still remains the largest tumulus cemetery in the world—and one of the most beautiful, with a haunting, eerie atmosphere.

Here well-to-do Lydians were buried in style, beginning with **King Alyattes, Croesus' father** (619–550 BC). His was by far the largest tumulus, over 350m across. Sitting on top of a limestone ridge to the very east, it attracted the attention of the German consul in Smyrna, Ludwig Peter Spiegelthal, who in the 19th century tunnelled though it from the south side. When he reached the mortuary chamber, it was to find that it had already been plundered. The identification of the tumulus is based on information on its size and location in Herodotus (1:93). The chamber, in beautifully carved blocks in true Lydian tradition, has a roof of limestone beams. The stonework at the edge of the tumulus has disappeared. According to Teoman Yalçınkaya, a labour force of 2,400 men and women (according to Herodotus, prostitutes toiled there too) could have built the structure in two and a half years with the assistance of 600 pack animals.

Karnıyarık Tepe to the west is on a similarly grand scale. It has more recently been investigated by excavation and remote sensing. It turned out to be a double tumulus, one inside the other; as a result, the crepis wall of the earlier structure has been preserved, as well as the robbers' tunnels of Roman date. The chamber has not yet been uncovered. The name refers to the gash on the side (the result of a collapsed tunnel) that gives the mound the appearance of a halved and stuffed aubergine (*karnıyarık*), a delicacy of Turkish cuisine.

The other tumuli have not yet been investigated by archaeologists.

KULA

Some 40km east of Sardes is the town of Kula (*map B, 4*), at the centre of an area known in antiquity as Katakekaumene, the 'burnt country', which produced a famous wine and was also a source of pozzolana, a necessary ingredient for concrete. Such gifts are the result of millennia of volcanism that only ceased some 12,000 years ago. It has left wonderful sights in the landscape, with 'fairy chimneys', columnar basalt, extensive lava fields and volcanic cones. You can see examples in the Kula Volcanic Geopark along a specially-constructed walkway. The various features are scattered over a large area approximately 300km square. To arrange a visit, talk to Ali Karataş (*T: 0543 217 7581*), who is in charge of guided tours. In Kula itself, do not miss the Ottoman Quarter, where a number of houses have been restored and are open to the public.

PRACTICAL INFORMATION

TOURIST INFORMATION

Information about Sardes and guided tours are easily available from any of the coastal hotels from where day trips are organised.

GETTING AROUND

By bus: Both Sardes and Manisa are on main routes and bus connections are good. Manisa has a new otogar in the periphery of town; in order to get to and from it, use bus line 2, which stops in front of the Hükümet Konağı (government offices).

By train: Manisa is on a railway line connecting Afyon to İzmir. The station is to the north of town. Bear in mind that generally train connections are slower and less reliable than bus links.

WHERE TO STAY

Sardes: Accommodation in the immediate Sardes area is for tourists,

whether they want to see the ruins or luxuriate in the thermal waters. It tends to be rather expensive, so if you are on a budget it may pay to visit Sardes in a single day or, if you have your own transport, to stop out of town at Turgutlu at the Bulutpark Otel (*bulutparkhotel.com*) just off Route 300, the İzmir–Uşak road. Alternatively try Salihli, east of Sardes. The Ozcelik Hotel (*T: 236 715 35 35*) on Orhaniye Cd. near the Belediye (Town Hall) is quite a reasonable choice.

Manisa: Manisa is a bigger place. Try Hotel Anemon (*T: 326 233 41 41*) out of the city centre to the south of town. Part of a chain, it is not a particularly inspiring choice but it is quiet. More central are Hotel Arma (*hotelarma.com. tr*) or the Oreko Hotel (*oreko.com.tr*).

The Boz Dağ: If you feel adventurous and have your own transport, you can explore the Boz Dağ to the south of Sardes (*map B, 4*), where there is some hospitality infrastructure because of kayaking and skiing. There are a couple of outfits in Birgi, such as the Cinaraltı Pansiyon (*birgicinaralti. com*) and the Derviş Ağa Konak (*dervisagakonakpansiyon.com*), a nice old stone house with interesting fittings. While you are there have a look at the Çakırağa Konağı (*open Tue–Sun 9–12 & 1–5; charge*), an Ottoman period mansion recently restored.

For the truly adventurous there is the Gölcük Göl Pansiyon (*golcukgolpansiyon.com*), by the lake of the same name on the way to Ödemiş at 1000m altitude.

Kula: In Kula you can spend the night in Ottoman comfort at the Anemon Otel (*T: 236 816 25 55*).

WHERE TO EAT

Eating in **Manisa and in Sart** means trying the local lokantas. In Manisa there are a number of them in the centre of town. Try the Ulupark Cafe Restoran or the Gediz Kebap Salonu, where you can have your kebab in a green setting. The restored Yeni Han on Sadık Ahmet Cd., not far from the Belediye (Town Hall), has various coffee houses with music and sisha, and shops with local carpets and metalwork.

If you go to the **Boz Dağ** (*see Where to Stay, above*) you will have a rare chance to sample a *kuyu kebabı*, normally lamb meat in chunks or on a spit, cooked in a one-metre-deep pit lined with bricks. A special metal contraption holds the chunks of meat and the spits.

WHAT TO DO

In Manisa, after Midday Prayers on the Sunday following the Spring Equinox, towards the end of March, thousands of colourfully wrapped sweets are tossed from the domes of the Hatuniye Camii at the south end of Atatürk Blv. to huge expectant crowds. The event is preceded by a parade. The sweets are known as *Mesir Macunu* (Mesir Paste) and are said to cure all sort of diseases. They are made of a concoction of some 41 ingredients, which of late has been nicknamed the 'Sultan's Viagra'. Traditionally it was invented by Merkez Efendi, a mosque official in the 15th century, to cure the mother of the sultan. His statue can be seen on a roundabout in town.

EPHESUS

Because of the distances, the heat and the crowds, Ephesus (*map B, 3*) and surrounding sites are not for the faint-hearted. Ephesus, a UNESCO World Heritage site, conveniently located within reasonable distance of a seaside holiday, attracts tourists in vast numbers. Do join them, but read up on the site before you go. A little advance preparation will help you to get the most out of your visit.

UNDERSTANDING EPHESUS

Understanding Ephesus is particularly challenging because of its environmental development. Nothing has stood still here in the last ten thousand or so years. This is a land of continuous change and it is fitting that one of the city's main philosophers, Heraclitus, made relentless change the basis of his theories ('*Panta rhei*', as he famously said; Everything is in flux). Just as you cannot dip your foot twice into the same river, so you cannot look at the landscape here and assume that it is set in stone and is immutable. Change has been ongoing here from the beginning of time, accelerating with man-made interventions, shaping human development, favouring it, hindering it until it came all crashing down. Ephesus today is a dead city, peopled at night with the ghosts of over 2,500 years of history and an indefinite, little known, period of prehistory.

Of late, archaeologists, geographers, geologists and geomorphologists have joined forces to understand how land and sea have interacted over the millennia, how rivers have contributed to the natural accretion of land, how land has been reclaimed by human action. The study of past environments is all-important in explaining why a monument or a feature is where it is, why settlement developed the way it did and why settlement eventually collapsed. This chapter deals first with the site as a whole from an environmental point of view; it is then followed by sections covering the individual sites (the Artemision, Ephesus, Ayasoluk, Selçuk and Belevi), their history and archaeology and what there is to see.

ENVIRONMENT AND PREHISTORY OF THE SITE

It is clear to anyone arriving by air or by road that Ephesus is not on the sea. Indeed, from the town, the sea is some 8km away. Presently the area is dominated by one river, the Küçük Menderes ('Little Meander'), the ancient Cayster, coming in from the northeast and meandering in its wide graben, edged on the south side by a rugged and rocky horst. The reason why you cannot follow the river all the way to the sea is the drainage and irrigation canal (the Yeni Menderes, 'New Meander') built in the last century. It takes the water

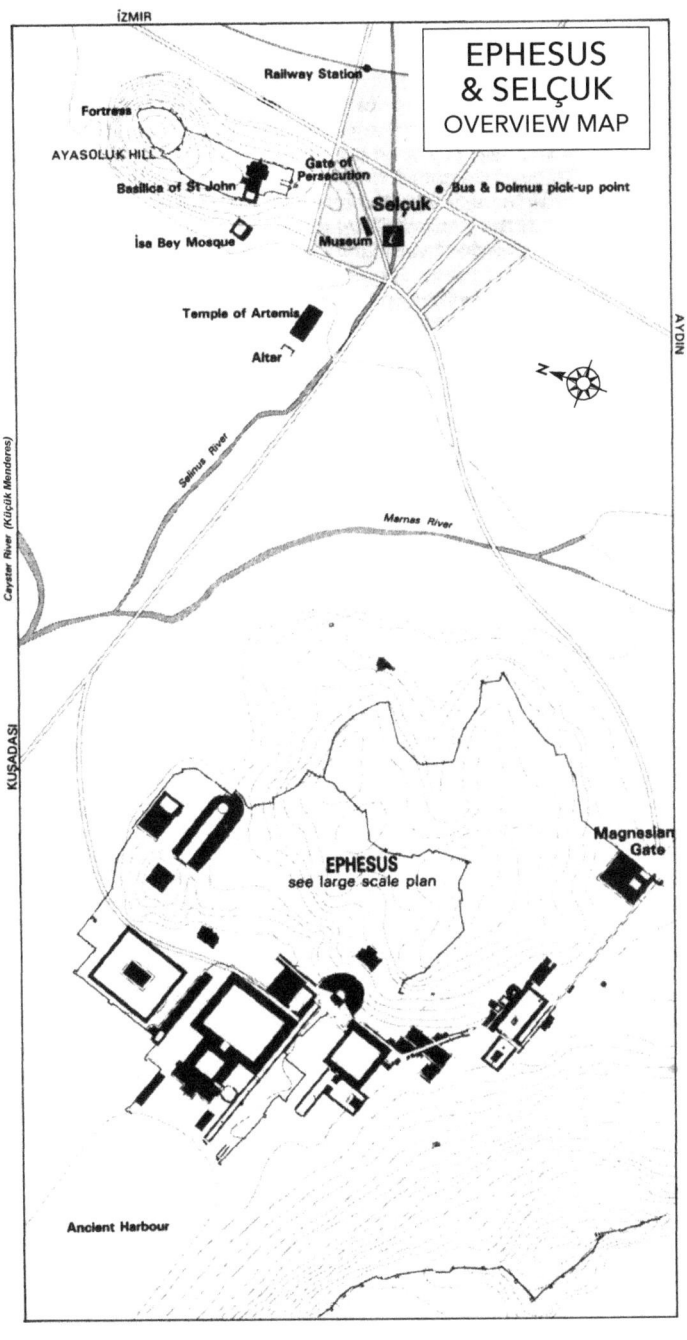

from the river in a straight line to the sea north of the original delta. Cores have established that c. 10,000 years ago this entire area was a marine embayment, with the sea reaching well inland and turning the hill of Ayasoluk into an island. To the southwest stood an elevation (Mt Pion), the site of the future Ephesus. Between the two the sea occupied a bay, filled over time with lime by two streams, the Marnas and the Selinus. The Temple of Artemis (Artemision) is in this shallow valley.

You can get a picture of the situation looking up the site on Google Earth. With the sea to the west, the east end of the airport runway to the north of the ruins of Ephesus and the Temple of Artemis beyond Dr Sabrı Yayla Blv., the location of the first settlement is to the east on Ayasoluk, marked by the later feature of Ayasoluk Kale. Note on your screen the cultivated fields penetrating south and east into the rugged mountains. They represent the extent of the marine transgression and subsequent alluviation that filled the depressions, providing good agricultural land. This state of affairs lasted more or less to the time when archaeology starts to yield finds, c. 1000 BC; the deep indentation into the coast provided a sheltered anchorage and access to the interior through the river valleys. From the very beginning, Ephesus was a place where East met West. And so it lasted for over two thousand years until everything silted up and sea access became difficult. Now the coastline is quite a way to the west and runs in a straight line due north of Kuşadası.

The prehistory of the area is little known. It was easily buried under the tons of sediment and until recently has not been a research priority. Work at Çukuriçi Hüyük c. 1km east of town overlooking the floodplain, has found evidence of a settled community with connections to the Aegean (harvesting marine resources and importing obsidian from Melos) as well as with the immediate interior (hunting leopard, possibly with a ritual angle); evidence for this community spans the Neolithic Period from the 7th to the 3rd millennia BC. Later Bronze Age finds of Mycenaean material (now displayed in the archaeological museum in Selçuk) testify to movements in the opposite direction. Contacts with the Hittites, who never ruled the Aegean coast but certainly had some sort of presence there before 1200 BC (when both Mycenaeans and Hittites met their doom) are a possibility. Indeed, in the archives at Boğazköy there are tablets mentioning the kingdom of Arzawa to the west, a client kingdom of the Akkiyawa identified as Mycenaean. Here was the city of Apasa, a name that does truly sound like Ephesus (alternatively it might have been the old name of Artemis herself). We know no more: these finds however must be put in context with the Mycenaean remains in Miletus, in Iasos, around Kuşadası and up the valley, east of Belevi.

According to tradition, Ephesus was a very early Ionian colony (c. 8th century BC), under the leadership of one Androclos, a tradition that rules out foundation by the ubiquitous Amazons. That said, it is not quite clear where the settlement was. The area was certainly not empty; there is talk of an earlier, small Carian settlement. The Greek presence may have been on the north slope of Mt Pion (thought to have been the site of the acropolis and a temple of Athena) and to the east where the Cave of the Seven Sleepers now is, with as a focus around a temple to Cybele. This location overlooks the site of the Artemision, where the oldest certain archaeology is. It is fitting to start from there.

AUSTRIAN ARCHAEOLOGY IN EPHESUS

Like any other ruling European dynasty, the Habsburg monarchs were avid collectors of antiquities (their passion had begun in the 16th century). Things changed in the 18th century under Empress Maria Theresa, who showed a distinct preference for home finds, things that were related to the recent development of the empire. The artefacts from distant lands that filled the cabinets of curiosities of her peers failed to impress her. So much so that she financed no excavations—and all this at a time when the British, the Germans and the French considered the acquisition of antiquities as part and parcel of their imperial ambitions. Later, Chancellor Metternich would not even allow Austrian archaeologists to work with the German Archaeological Institute newly founded in Rome in 1829.

Over the years, and not from a lack of talented individuals, the Austrians continued to lag behind in the field of archaeological exploration. Meanwhile, the Germans forged ahead, taking on sites like Pergamon, Troy and Olympia. The fact is that with the Ottoman Empire (some of the most promising ground for exploration; whole temples were there for the taking while in Italy it was too late), the Habsburgs still had a difficult relationship, tainted by not-so-distant memories of invading armies; moreover, the Balkans were still a constant cause of friction between the two empires, Ottoman and Habsburg.

The turning point was the visit of the Sultan Abdülaziz to Vienna in 1867. He came as a valued guest, not as a conqueror. Relations mellowed and there was a successful return visit to Istanbul. Official funding became available. The first permit was for the island of Samothrace. Unfortunately the stunning *Winged Victory* had already taken flight to the Louvre but there were still treasures to discover for the museums of the capital. Then, in 1881, Felix von Luschan dipped his toes into Caria and Lycia. The great breakthrough came in 1893, when a firman for the exploration of Ephesus was granted. The British, who had been working there, were probably overextended and may have found financing problematic. At the time, the British excavations at Ephesus were still privately funded by wealthy patrons. The Austrian excavations yielded shiploads of statues for Vienna and the Austrian Archaeological Institute was set up in 1898. Ephesus is still firmly in their hands.

THE ARTEMISION (TEMPLE OF ARTEMIS)

Once one of the Seven Wonders of the World, the Temple of Artemis at Ephesus (*admission free; for location, see map on p. 85*) was a sure reference for European antiquaries and travellers alike: ancient written sources referred to it from the mid-6th century BC, when Croesus built it, to the 4th century AD, when it was quarried for spolia. This is what spurred John Turtle Wood, a British engineer engaged in building railways in the Ottoman Empire, to look for it when he was given the concession for the stretch from Smyrna to Aydın. The track he laid ran very close to the site of the temple and was useful when he needed to deliver material to the British Museum, who had covered part of his expenses.

With the help of a providential inscription and some shrewd digging, Wood found the sought-after temple, lying under seven metres of alluvium. A medieval lime kiln stood on its entrance steps. It did not look like a world wonder: it was in a truly sorry state. Between them, however, Wood himself, and afterwards David Hogarth and from the early 20th century the Austrians (*see box above*), were able to piece together the site's history. There is not much for visitors to see, apart from a hole in the ground more often than not filled with water. Even the one still-standing column has been re-erected. And yet people worshipped here for almost two millennia.

The first people were the Mycenaeans, who left evidence of their presence here, although no building. Later, c. 800 BC, two structures went up: an altar to the west (*see below*) and the temple. This has suggested to some that there were two communities worshipping separately. The temple was a peripteros, open to the west towards the altar; it had a floor of hard-packed clay and no roof. Inside, a six-column structure may have supported a baldachin for the xoanon of the deity. This first temple was rebuilt twice. Floods and Cimmerians were responsible for the damage. The second temple, built on exactly the same spot, was willed by Croesus at a time when Lydia was rising power in western Asia Minor. He had the financial means for an extravagant display thanks to the gold of the Pactolus. At the intersection of the building's two main axes, a rich foundation deposit was laid in a purpose-built structure made of green schist known as the central basis. The treasure, a single deposit of some 200 objects, contained 93 electrum coins, amulets, ex-votos, ivory and bronze furniture fittings, rock crystal lenses, scarabs and various ornaments, all in good condition. Additional precious material, not contained within the central basis, was also found and was described by David Hogarth, who excavated the deposit, as 'holy rubbish', i.e. temple objects that could not be thrown away but which did not belong to the foundation deposit. The central basis in which the objects were packed, layered with sand for stability, was used as a base for the statue of the goddess.

Built c. 560 BC, Croesus's temple was an Ionic dipteros some 46m by 115m; it was the first edifice in the Greek world to be entirely in marble, unlike the contemporary Heraion on Samos, which is comparable in size but lower and built of stone. Some of its columns were truly exceptional, being ornamented with reliefs on the lower portion of the shaft. Some of these *columnae caelatae* (the Latin name for such columns) can be admired in the British Museum. Some bear inscriptions in Greek and Lydian.

The general configuration of the temple was very Oriental, beginning with the name of the chief priest: Megabyzos, certainly not a Greek word; it appears more Persian. The temple may have been dedicated to Artemis, but the manifestation of the goddess here was very different from the lithe sister of Apollo, ferociously chaste, shooting her arrows with merciless precision and running barefoot in the woods (*see Images of Artemis, overleaf*). The temple was a major tourist attraction in its own day. Its size, its richness, its prime location, right by the sea and close to an international harbour, made it world famous. It even had its own anchorage.

As the story goes, it was exactly this that caused its undoing. In 356 BC a madman burned the temple down so that his name (Erostratos) would be forever remembered. One should treat the tale with caution, however. It is not the easiest of tasks single-handedly to burn down a structure of that size, supported by 13-metre marble columns and with a full complement of attendant priests. The only wooden elements were in the coffered ceiling. It is true that Artemis was busy elsewhere, at Pella in Macedonia, where the future Alexander the Great was born that very night. Perhaps the priests had used this as an excuse for their lack of vigilance. It is more likely, though, that the priests themselves were the arsonists. They had a serious problem on their hands that even the divine power of Artemis was unable to solve: their temple was sinking. It had been built on marine deposits and mud and moreover it was threatened by the relentless alluviation of the Selinus River.

A fresh start was needed. Apparently changing the temple's location was not an option. To this day the deep attachment to this specific place has not been fully explained. The visit of Alexander the Great in 323 BC, when the Persians had been driven from Asia Minor, proved a suitable time to start talks about the rebuilding. Alexander offered financial aid (with conditions attached), which was politely refused. The ladies of Ephesus valiantly stepped in with their jewellery; Ephesus maintained its independence.

The new Ionic temple was even larger than its predecessor, reaching some 32m in height. The foundations, of stone slabs set in clay, supported a massive platform (64m by 128m) accessed by 13 steps, tall enough to lift the construction away from the encroaching sea and the alluvium. Some of the earlier decorated columns were reused, new ones were added. The temple suffered greatly from the Goths in 263 and was gradually abandoned as Christianity spread. It was plundered for the construction of the Hagios Theologos basilica (*see p. 102*) and some of its 18m tall columns were transported to Byzantium for the Church of Hagia Sophia. The lonely column now standing was reconstructed in the 1970s, to the delight of nesting storks. Investigations, with the assistance of pumps to counteract water seepage, are ongoing.

The altar

The separate altar, west of the temple, was apparently built by Croesus before the temple, on top of an earlier cult structure and remodelled in Classical times. The colonnaded court, in a horseshoe shape with relief panels, is reminiscent of the Pergamon altar but smaller. Inside, a statue base and a burnt area for animal sacrifices have been identified. Its relationship with the temple is not clear. The proceedings within the altar could not be seen from the temple, which has suggested secret ceremonies; alternatively, it may be that each structure catered for a different community.

IMAGES OF ARTEMIS

The well-known representation of the Ephesian Artemis, with legs like a tree trunk, a columnar torso, a body dotted with mysterious signs and accretions (for want of a better description), arms stretched forward, a tower-like construction on the head, is known from the 2nd century BC when it was reproduced in stone or in terracotta. It harks back to the original image Artemis, made in wood from a real tree trunk.

Xoana, as wooden three-dimensional images are called, are the precursor of marble statues. They were intended to be clothed and ornamented with jewellery; they could have ex-votos pinned on them. They are the forerunners of the divine images in churches today that are sometimes dressed up for specific ceremonies. The later evolution of the Ephesian Artemis has maintained the characteristics of a xoanon in that the greater plastic freedom afforded by the use of clay or stone has not been used to create a more lively figure: she still stands stiff as a poker.

The accretions have been interpreted in different ways. Some believe they are breasts, others opt for bull's testicles. In both cases the meaning is clear. Artemis is the giver of life. She brings forth the next generation, not in the literal sense because she is a virgin, but by feeding, nurturing and protecting it. She is the goddess of fertility (hence the identification with bull's testicles) as well as the guarantor of the continuity of the family and of the city. There is yet a third view on the accretions. It was a Hittite practice to hang bags (kursas) on statues as tokens of good luck and fertility. The bags could contain anything, depending on what the goddess was prepared to bestow on mere mortals. They never occur in the archaeological record since they were made of perishable material, but they are known from Hittite reliefs. The earlier image of Zeus from Labranda, a bronze statue with arms stretched forward and three 'breasts', suggests this was an Anatolian trait. It seems that in the case of the Ephesian Artemis it was taken to extremes: eventually the entire surface was covered with bags (or breasts) and even signs of the Zodiac (a sign of Egyptian influence, with a reference to the afterlife). Thus arrayed, the statue of the goddess was carried in procession, in a way recapitulating, by visiting its various monuments, the history of the town under her protection.

EPHESUS

Ephesus, as the city whose ruins can be seen now, came into being in 290 BC in the Hellenistic period when Lysimachus, a contender for Alexander the Great's inheritance, founded it, so to speak *ex novo*. A Lydian settlement may have already been present to the east of the Artemision, at the foot of the slope of Ayasoluk. Otherwise settlement was probably scattered: one does have to wonder where those ladies lived, who are purported to have paid for the rebuilding of the Temple of Artemis with their jewellery (*see p. 89*).

A SHORT HISTORY OF EPHESUS

The arrival of Lysimachus in 290 BC was a life-changing event for the people of the area. The heart of the city was to be on the west slope of Mt Pion, now Panayır Dağ and along the corridor between this elevation and the one immediately to the south (the Bülbül Dağı, the ancient Mt Preon), extending further towards the plain to the southeast, giving a total size of roughly 2km by 4km. This corresponds to the layout of the city walls, 10m high and of stone, which Lysimachus built, hugging the heights for strategic reasons. Much of the land inside the circuit was unused. The harbour was to the west, where some facilities probably already existed. The Persian Royal Road to Susa had started here. The harbour was protected from silting-up by the Marnas and the Selinus but threatened over time by the progression of the Cayster delta to the north. As an elevation with sea access, the area was probably already occupied. The first Greeks had settled nearby.

The processional way connecting the Artemision to Ortygia to the west (the mythical location of the birth of Artemis and her twin brother Apollo) skirted the east slopes of Mt Pion. However, there were insufficient Ephesians for this ambitious undertaking and Lysimachus forcibly moved people in from the surrounding villages and from further afield (from Lebedus, for example). The new settlement was laid out on an orthogonal grid as far as was compatible with the topography. Some of it has been identified.

Lysimachus called his city Arsinoë, in honour of his Egyptian wife, but he did not live long enough to see it thriving: he was killed in the battle of Curopedion in 281 BC and his wife had to flee disguised as her maid. The city reverted to its old name, Ephesus. The town meandered its way through the complicated allegiances that preceded the imposition of Roman rule. The last of the Attalids, who bequeathed the kingdom of Pergamon to the Romans in 133 BC (*see Pergamon*), included Ephesus, which he owned at the time, in the bequest. For Ephesus this was a great coup. Pergamon had no immediate sea access; Ephesus did, as well as ready access to the interior.

The Romans made Ephesus the capital of the newly-founded Province of Asia and the seat of its governor, the proconsul. The 'metropolis of Asia' was extensively beautified as a showcase of Roman power, with emperors and notables outdoing each other in their extravagant contributions. All this required land, which was indeed in short supply. By the 2nd century AD the coastline had already developed its near-straight stretch to the southwest from the northern tip of Ayasoluk. Any urban development in that area would be below the floodplain. The city was extended to the northwest by deliberate infilling and some contribution from the advancing Cayster delta. This reclaimed platform housed many civic buildings facing the port area. The Roman town was planned with insulae larger than the previous Hellenistic one. While many civic and a limited number of high-status residences have been excavated, it is not known where the ordinary people lived. It is strongly possible that their dwellings were outside the Hellenistic walls, since up until the arrival of the Goths in the mid-3rd century AD, defence was not a priority: the *Pax Romana* was sufficient.

Port facilities, i.e. the great harbour of Ephesus, were a serious cause of concern, also because the various measures taken by well-intentioned rulers tended to exacerbate the problem. In around 190 BC, according to Livy's description (*37, 14–15*), access had already narrowed to a slim channel. Regular dredging and the extension of the moles to the west, giving the harbour a polygonal shape that has been compared to the Port of Trajan at the mouth of the Tiber, proved no solution. The emperor Hadrian (r. 117–38) considered diverting the course of the main culprit, the Cayster, by constructing a dam. His was not the first. According to an inscription, Caesar had had an 18m high dam built earlier on. Whatever Hadrian did—and we have minimal details—it proved to be no solution, partly also because the Ephesians themselves were contributing to their woes by using the harbour as an industrial dump and sewer outlet. By the 5th century AD, sea-going vessels docked outside the harbour canal and transferred their cargo using shallow draft boats.

Christianity came early to Ephesus. St Paul visited it several times, although he was not entirely welcomed. He had a public spat with a silversmith who made a living by making silver images of Artemis and saw his livelihood threatened. The clash sparked a riot—not the first one in Ephesus; the Ephesians were well-known in antiquity for their hot tempers. Paul retreated to Macedonia. Other Christian figures are associated with Ephesus though not on very firm ground (*see below*). Nevertheless, by the 5th century the Artemision had been abandoned and two of the most important ecumenical councils of the Early Church were held in Ephesus, in 431 and in 499. This may be a reflection of a vigorous Christian community or it may simply have been a matter of logistical convenience (easy access and availability of accommodation) and wealth. Certainly there were many who had not adopted the new faith: as late as the mid-6th century the local bishop was still converting and persecuting pagans. Late antique Ephesus enjoyed a reputation as a centre of magic and miracle working, not an unusual phenomenon in a cosmopolitan harbour city.

The decline of Ephesus came about from a combination of the waning of Roman ruling power, the relative weakness of the Byzantines that succeeded it, external threats (first the Goths, then the Arabs, by sea; twice in 655 on their way back from Byzantium, and again in 696) and finally the Turks, coming down from Anatolia along that very route (the Royal Road) that had made

Ephesus's fortune. Environmental degradation and the rise of Ayasoluk (*see below*) and, farther away, of Smyrna, were also contributing factors.

By the 8th–9th century, the city had shrunk considerably and had broken down into separate clusters. The new, reduced defences of the 7th–8th century protected the harbour area and the immediate hinterland on Mt Pion. By the 9th century, however, the Byzantines were sailing from Phygela, later the Scala Nova of the Genoese and now Kuşadası.

By the beginning of the 14th century, an important settlement had grown up to the east, on the slopes of Ayasoluk (*see p. 102*); yet the harbour was still functioning. In Ephesus itself, part of the population was deported in 1304; those who stayed had a difficult time and were forced to part with precious relics (a piece of the True Cross, a shirt woven by the Virgin and the manuscript of the Apocalypse) in order to buy food. According to the Austrian archaeologists, in the period between the 14th and 15th centuries, a new harbour had been built 3km to the west, in the Cayster delta. It was used by Italian traders, including a group of outlaws expelled from Lombardy, so there is a sense of piracy in the air, with Ephesus an entrepôt between Anatolia and the island of Chios. It would have been particularly useful to Venice, chronically short of grain, with the Black Sea closed and Egypt difficult of access for political reasons. Apart from the graffiti, excavations have revealed a hoard of some 2,000 coins from Rhodes and Naples, hidden in the Artemision. Money was clearly being made by some.

The town is known to have suffered at the hands of Tamerlane, who besieged and conquered it in 1402, wresting it from short-lived Ottoman control. Later it was contended by various emirates, by the occasional adventurer and by Venice and Genoa.

After the 15th century the evidence becomes thin on the ground; Italian documentation ceases. Early 17th-century travellers found the ruins deserted (Evliya Çelebi provides the background sound-effects with his mention of howling jackals). Malaria set in too, because of the breakdown of the water supply. According to Jordan Pickett, the city's waterworks were maintained until well into mid-Byzantine times (8th century), for domestic, ornamental and industrial purposes. Five aqueducts converged on Ephesus. You can see the remains of one of them if you arrive from the east by road or rail.

Visiting Ephesus

The site of the city of Ephesus (*open summer 8.30–7; shorter hours in winter; charge*) has been welcoming tourists since the beginning of time. They came first as pilgrims to worship at the Artemision; later, they were on a quest for early Christian landmarks; today they arrive as holidaying visitors. The suggested time that a visitor should devote to the town itself is given as a minimal 45mins, which is unrealistic and will involve having to see things in a rush. However, since at the time of writing there were no visitors' toilets inside the site, it is difficult to linger too long. In addition to this consideration, there are also Ayasoluk, Selçuk and the Artemision to consider, as well as the landscape as a whole; you need to give yourself enough time to take it all in. Bear in mind that this is a very popular destination and book your tickets in advance (*muze.gov.tr*). There have been complaints about the high price of tickets (it is worth examining the various combinations; you may be able to save some money).

There are two entrances for visitors (*marked on the map overleaf*). One to the south by the Magnesian Gate (it can be reached along Meryem Ana Yolu, south of Selçuk) and another to the north (on Efes Yolu, on the way to the airport). Both have the usual complement of cafés, souvenir shops and toilets. The description below begins from the south entrance.

For early visitors to Ephesus, until the mid-1950s, faded glories were a leitmotif. 'Standing solemn and dignified in death' is the kind of description one encounters, in an attempt to express the weird, haunted feeling that not even the solitary goatherd could dispel. In those days the stone edifices had toppled, had been plundered and what was left was buried underground. Reconstruction, excavation, conservation and promotion have been at the forefront of the research led by Austrian teams engaged here since the late 1890s.

Visiting Ephesus today is marketed as an experience akin to seeing Pompeii— which is a fair comparison since most of the reconstructed monuments belong to the Roman Imperial period, when Ephesus was at its height, with c. 250,000 inhabitants. However, there is another Ephesus to be unpacked, namely the Hellenistic town.

Starting at the Magnesian Gate means tackling the very heart of Hellenistic Ephesus, going straight into its main civic space, the upper agora.

The Upper Agora

The area, c. 56m by 160m, was considerably altered in Roman times with rebuildings and additions; however, its size and shape were maintained. Past the Magnesian Gate (of which not much remains) and the ruins of the East Gymnasium, look north. Beyond the elongated **basilica (1)**, a colonnaded hall in Ionic style dating from the time of Augustus, with colossal statues of the emperor and his wife Livia, you can see the **odeion (2)** built around the mid-2nd century AD by Publius Vedius Antoninus; it was used both for assemblies and performances. The **prytaneion (3)** to the west, originally Hellenistic and rebuilt by Augustus, housed the sacred flame of the city that was never allowed to go out, thereby ensuring the protection of Hestia/Vesta, the goddess of domesticity and of the family. Here civil and religious dignitaries were welcomed. Two statues of Artemis, of Roman date and in the traditional hieratic form (now in the museum in Selçuk), were unearthed here. One had been carefully buried. In the 3rd century AD the prytaneion was robbed and material reused in the Baths of Scholastikia (10). The **Temple of Divus Julius and of the Dea Roma (4)**, between the odeion and the prytaneion, was the work of Augustus, Caesar's adopted son. The small **Temple of Isis (5)**, on a platform on the west side of the agora, has been attributed by some to Mark Antony (who certainly had a connection with Egypt); remains of a colossal statue of him were found nearby. Elements of the temple were reused in the Domitian Fountain (*see below*).

The scant remains of the **Temple of Domitian** close the agora to the west. This building marks the beginning of official imperial worship in Ephesus towards the end of the 1st century AD. Set on a high terrace some 50m by 100m, the temple was a rather small prostyle with four columns in front. The cella contained a huge statue of the emperor. According to one tradition, the Ephesians themselves started dismantling the temple when they heard that the hated emperor had been murdered. However, according to a different source, as they did not want to lose the coveted neokorate, the right of imperial worship, they rededicated the temple to Domitian's father, Vespasian, a less controversial figure.

The agora is also a place of water as at least two of the five aqueducts of Ephesus arrived here: they fed baths such as the Baths of Varius, dated to the 2nd century AD to the northeast outside the agora, and also supplied fountains. Three of these were clustered in the northwest corner of the agora, one next to the monument to Caius Sextilius Pollio, the architect of Marnas aqueduct. Also known as the **Domitian Fountain (6)**, it is an apsidal structure verging on the monumental, with recumbent statues of personifications of rivers and of various deities. Remains of two more fountains can be seen beyond the south side of the agora. Water provision in the agora was still functioning in the 5th century when it was used to operate a mill. The whole area was under restoration at the time of writing.

The Street of the Curetes

Exiting the agora from the northwest, visitors pass the **Gate of Hercules (7)**, so called because of the characteristic image of the demigod wrapped in a lion skin. The two-storey structure with a large, central, arched opening is dated to the mid-4th century. Here starts the Street of the Curetes (so named by the Austrian archaeologists because of the columns reused from the prytaneion, which bore yearly lists of priests, the *curetes*). The whole colonnaded street, leading to the Library of Celsus, is Late Antique in date, made at a time when such development were all the rage, with repairs, refurbishments and the reuse of earlier material, mainly from the Upper Agora. The Byzantines called it 'Embolos' (the wedge, the insertion). Connected to another public space (the Tetragonos Agora or Lower Agora; *see below*), it was the main artery of town, planned as an 11m wide thoroughfare, and was constantly being remodelled as new monuments went up and refurbishments and repairs were carried out. On the slopes on both sides, the erection of monuments and statues, prestigious houses, fountains, baths and temples offered the elite an opportunity to show off their wealth and patronage. The latrines and the brothel testify to their human frailties. The ever-present traders had their shops behind the ill-assorted colonnades.

The **Fountain of Trajan (8)**, up the hillside to the east, was a memento of the devotion to the early 2nd-century emperor willed by Tiberius Claudius Aristion; one of his many benefactions to the town, which earned him an accolade from Pliny the Younger in one of his letters. The monument has been partially re-erected but the statues (the emperor and family, Aphrodite and Dionysus among others) are in the Selçuk Museum. They stood around a rectangular pool in niches in between columns.

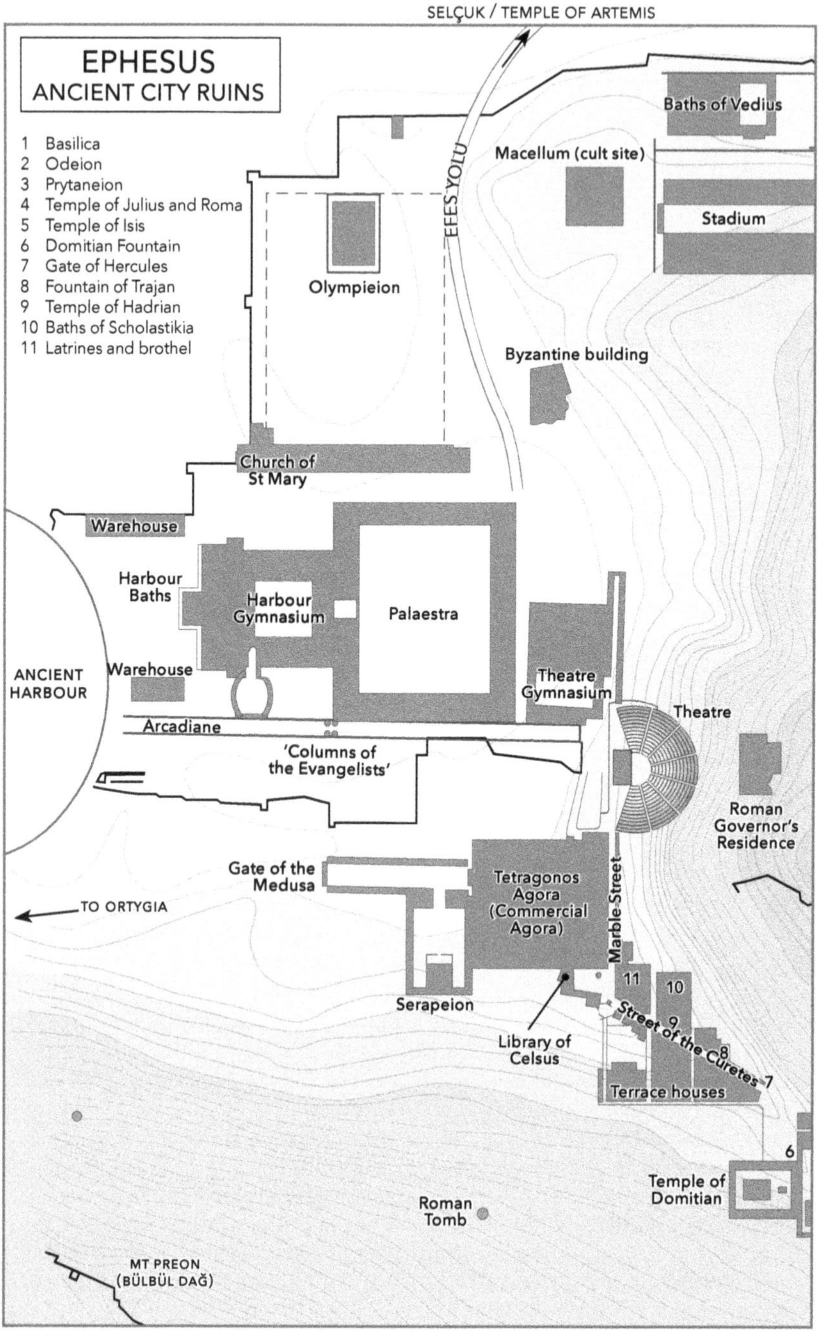

SELÇUK / TEMPLE OF ARTEMIS

EPHESUS
ANCIENT CITY RUINS

1 Basilica
2 Odeion
3 Prytaneion
4 Temple of Julius and Roma
5 Temple of Isis
6 Domitian Fountain
7 Gate of Hercules
8 Fountain of Trajan
9 Temple of Hadrian
10 Baths of Scholastikia
11 Latrines and brothel

EFES YOLU

Baths of Vedius

Macellum (cult site)

Stadium

Olympieion

Byzantine building

Church of St Mary

Warehouse

Harbour Baths

Harbour Gymnasium

Palaestra

ANCIENT HARBOUR

Warehouse

Theatre Gymnasium

Theatre

Arcadiane

'Columns of the Evangelists'

Roman Governor's Residence

Gate of the Medusa

TO ORTYGIA

Tetragonos Agora (Commercial Agora)

Marble Street

Serapeion

Library of Celsus

11 10
9
8
7
Street of the Curetes

Terrace houses

Roman Tomb

6

Temple of Domitian

MT PREON (BÜLBÜL DAĞ)

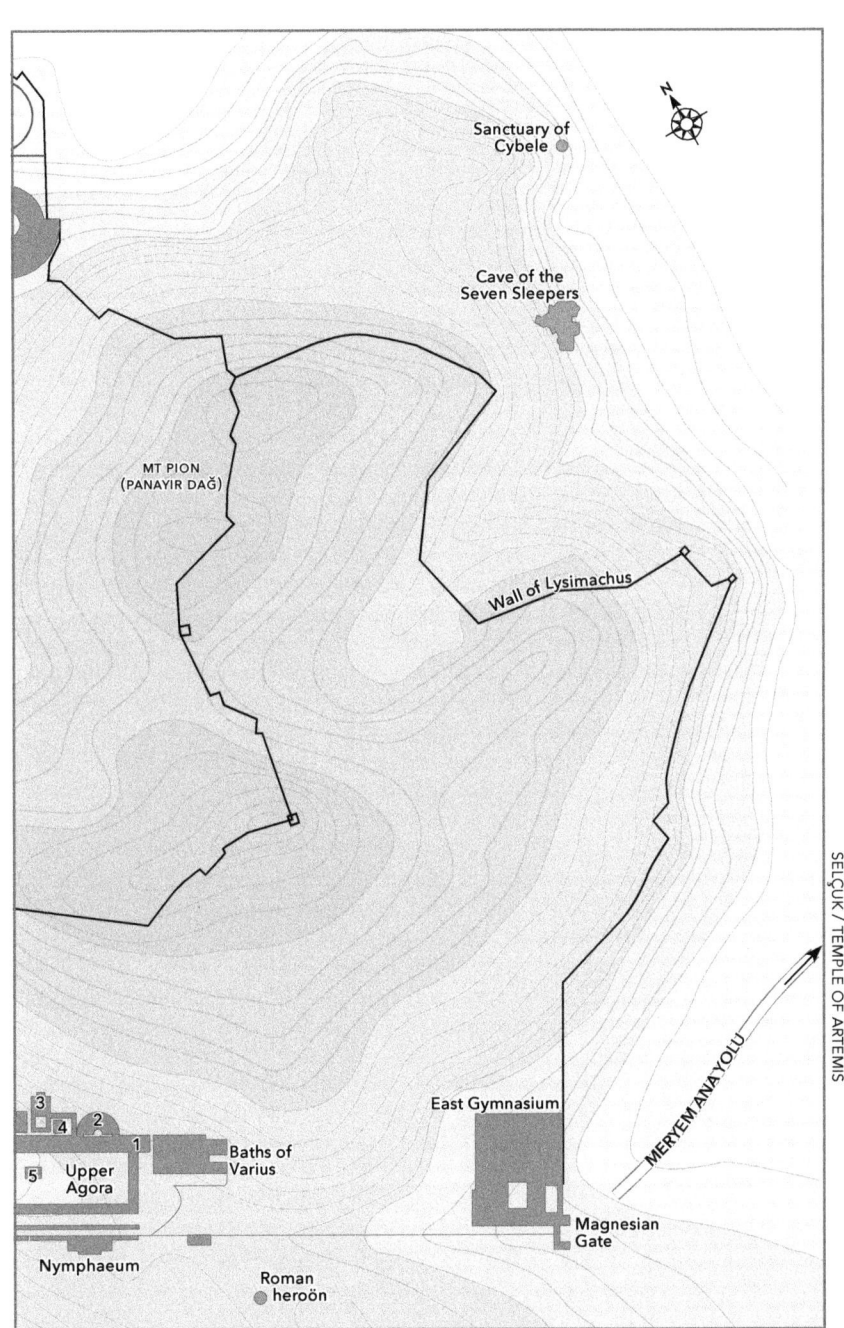

Sanctuary of
Cybele

Cave of the
Seven Sleepers

MT PION
(PANAYIR DAĞ)

Wall of Lysimachus

SELÇUK / TEMPLE OF ARTEMIS

MERYEM ANA YOLU

East Gymnasium

Baths of
Varius

Upper
Agora

Magnesian
Gate

Nymphaeum

Roman
heroön

Further on on the same side is the so-called **Temple of Hadrian (9)**, as much an icon of Ephesus as the Library of Celsus is; it was re-erected in 1959. Recently doubts have been cast on its attribution to the builder-emperor. In fact, it may not even be Hadrianic. It has been suggested that it may originally have been the monumental entrance to the Olympieion (*see p. 102*), reused from there. That would explain the inscription on the architrave: the Olympieion was indeed Hadrian's project. The present arrangement of the structure dates from the very early 5th century, after repairs due to earthquake damage. At that time it acquired new relief panels (now in Selçuk Museum), clearly scavenged from elsewhere; one of them shows scenes of the legendary founding of Ephesus, with Amazons and Androclus chasing the boar, just as the Delphic oracle had predicted. The four inscribed bases in front bore statues of the Tetrarchs at the time of Diocletian, when he found the empire unwieldy and divided it up, replacing the single ruler with four, two senior (the Augusti) and two junior (the Caesars).

The **Baths of Scholastikia (10)** were a benefaction of a wealthy Ephesian lady. She enlarged and repaired them in the 4th century AD using material from the prytaneion in the upper agora. In the process she unwittingly preserved the original mosaic floor, by covering it with marble slabs. Immediately adjacent to the baths are the **latrines (11)**, which would have been regularly flushed with waste water from the baths. The room, which has a floor mosaic, was only roofed around the edges, where the marble seating was positioned. The rest was open to the sky. The **brothel** is not far off; it is accessible from the Embolos and from the Marble Street that follows it to the north. It owes its reputation to the statue of Priapus excavated there. Otherwise it is an ordinary atrium house with small rooms on the ground floor. The marble slab with the carved foot may be a reference to pilgrims; the heart and the picture of the woman on the same slab may be more meaningful. The tunnel connecting it to the Library of Celsus (allowing scholars a little diversion from their books) remains to be located; it may just be a malicious rumour.

On the slopes on either side, seven high-status **Terrace Houses** (*closing time earlier than that of the main site; charge*) have been excavated, restored and opened to the public. A visit is well worth the cost of the extra ticket and is recommended. You can even watch the archaeologists and conservators at work. Bear in mind that numbers are limited, so plan your visit carefully. The houses have beautiful mosaics and wall paintings; the proconsul of Asia may easily have lived in one of them. They span a period from the 1st to the 7th centuries and compare well with some of the villas in Pompeii and Herculaneum. The reconstruction has been sensitively carried out, with re-erected columns to give a sense of height, view points with unimpeded vistas and a well-designed walkway, occasionally with transparent floors, allowing maximum access. Some of the walls stand to full height as the houses, after abandonment, were buried by landslides.

The Library of Celsus

The famous Library of Celsus is the high point of a visit to Ephesus and a compulsory stop-off on your tour of the site. Contrary to the above-mentioned Temple of Hadrian, we are here left in do doubt about the nature of this monument: everything is set forth in the inscriptions on the façade. Neither Celsus nor his son were of a modest disposition (*see box*). The building was excavated in 1903–4 and reconstructed in 1969. In the interim, since it was not at first clear what the jumble of columns, statues and reliefs was, some items were allowed to leave the site. Some statues went to Vienna while other pieces may have ended up in the agora in Smyrna, without an identification. What you see now is the reconstructed façade of the monumental tomb of Celsus, to which he attached a library in order to be granted burial in town, in the most prestigious, central location.

READING WITH CELSUS

Who was Celsus and how could he command the use of such a prominent spot, the nodal point of the procession from the Artemision to Ortygia? The answer is very simple: he was a self-made man from Sardes who rose through the ranks in a stellar career in the Roman imperial army and administration, eventually being appointed proconsul of Asia in 105–7. The emperor would have been happy to publicise this ascent to power of a humble provincial, an epitome of the social mobility offered to those who cast in their lot with the Roman Empire.

The library was a clever idea as it allowed Celsus to remain visibly promoting the Roman cause even after his death. Ordinary mortals were laid to rest outside town in the necropolis. The *cursus honorum* of Tiberius Julius Celsus Polemaeanus was there for all to read in the inscription on the (now re-erected) façade, both in Latin (north side) and in Greek (south side). It does not appear to have been very well designed (either that or the stone cutter was second rate). For the not-so-literate, the virtues of Celsus were exemplified by four statues (originals lost, copies *in situ*) in the recessed façade evoking his knowledge, expertise, courage and judgement. The fasces and the axe symbolised his position as consul and the eagle stood for eternity. The display was completed with two equestrian statues of the dead man on either side of the entrance steps. An inscription stipulated that on his feast day (presumably Celsus's birthday), his statues should be garlanded; it has been suggested that there may have been other likeness of Celsus around the town. Financial provisions were also made for upkeep of the building, care of the scrolls and acquisition of new ones, and for the payment of annual salary to the staff.

The whole structure was preceded by a flight of steps which raised it above level of the square by almost two metres (note the menorah graffito on one of the steps). The arrangement of the aedicular façade over two storeys was inspired by a theatre skene. It showed off not only the statues but also the monolithic columns in Phrygian pavonazzetto, from the Dokimion quarries some 400km away. The construction technique, using big, perfectly-shaped blocks held together only by metal clamps, is an example of opus revinctum. If any restraining measure was needed, it would have been placed at the back where marble cladding hid the library's core construction of brick, articulated over three floors. In the basement Celsus was laid to rest in his sarcophagus—he is still there. The other two storeys housed the library, with manuscripts in Greek and Latin and an estimated capacity of 3,000 to 17,000 volumes. Draining facilities dealt with the possible accumulation of damp, so deleterious to scrolls.

Public libraries began to appear in Rome in the late Republican period. There is no reason to believe that they were on anything like such a grand scale. Even that in Pergamon—the very cradle of book collecting—was not housed in a particularly impressive building (though its identification is uncertain; *see p. 36*). The only comparandum is the Library of Trajan in Rome, which is roughly contemporary. Celsus's vertical architecture finds a natural comparison in Trajan's Column, which held the ashes of the emperor and stood in the forum between two libraries, Greek and Latin. The complex opened in 112 while Celsus's tomb was completed by his son in 120.

In 262 the structure burnt down following an earthquake. The Goths completed the destruction in the same year. About a century later the façade was reconstructed as a backdrop to a nymphaeum, whose basin was made with the slabs of the Parthian Monument which according to sources had been set up somewhere in Ephesus (whereabouts unknown) by the emperor Lucius Verus in the middle of the 2nd century. What was left of the library was backfilled. A quake in the 10th century sealed its doom until the beginning of the 20th century.

The Tetragonos Agora

The Tetragonos Agora (also referred to as Commercial Agora) was a square measuring 111m on each side with a stoa all around and commercial rooms behind it. Originally Hellenistic, it was rebuilt for the last time in the 5th century. It had three monumental entrances, of which the south gate connecting it with the library is the best known. The inscription states that the structure with three arched openings was erected by Mazaeus and Mithridates at the very end of the 1st century BC and was dedicated to Augustus and named members of his family. The spelling of the inscription leaves something to be desired suggesting that Mazaeus and Mithridates, two freedmen who had clearly done well for themselves, had received only scanty education. Remains suggest an abundance of statuary in the agora but none have been found; only the bases remain. The round structure in the centre, originally interpreted as a Hellenistic building, turned out to be the remains of the **horologium**, known from an inscription. The structure was like a small round temple with a pointed covering and no cella; it worked as a water clock and as a sundial. It is dated to the mid 1st century BC, when such devices were fashionable. It has affinities with the Tower of the Winds in Athens, though smaller.

Beyond the west gate of the agora, a colonnaded street with porticoes and shops extends to the **Gate of the Medusa**, a structure with three passageways. The capitals of the entrance pillars have Medusa heads on them. They are dated to roughly AD

400, showing that Christianity had not completely extinguished paganism at this stage. From the south portion of the colonnaded street, a flight of steps leads to the **Serapeion** and its massive, monolithic columns. It was identified by the numerous fragments of statues of Egyptian deities. Moreover, the profusion of water pipes suggests that there was a re-creation of the Nile here, a well-known feature of Egyptian temples. When in late antiquity the cella was turned into a church, the water supply was diverted to the agora to glass and metal workshops and to cisterns in the vaulted substractions. From this location you can catch a glimpse of the **Wall of Lysimachus** which enclosed Hellenistic Ephesus, a 9km circuit bristling with towers complete with gates and posterns. It has been calculated that for the wall alone, 200,000 cubic metres of limestone had to be cut and shifted, all by forced labour. No wonder Ephesians old and new (those that had been deported here to provide manpower) did not take to their new ruler. These were the walls of a true tyrant.

The Theatre, Old Harbour and Arcadiane

There follows an area that was extensively developed in Roman and Byzantine times by reclaiming large swathes of land to the north and west. Indeed, it became the nucleus of the shrunken Byzantine town of the 6th–7th centuries, running from the theatre to the stadium and down to the harbour. Unfortunately, the upper layers of this area, containing much evidence of the last rebuilding programme by Theodosius I at the very end of the 4th century, were cleared away by the first excavators.

The **Theatre**, on the hill slope, is a Roman extension of the earlier Hellenistic structure. It had a capacity of 24,000. Beyond the skene, of which little survives, spectators looked across to the harbour and the sea. In its final days it was no longer used as a theatre but was turned into a bastion affording much needed protection.

At the end of the 1st century of the current era, the swampy land to the west was reclaimed and the Harbour consequently moved. The social fabric of the city was altered by this. Big families backed by imperial favour moved in to reap the benefits of the booming international trade. The **Arcadiane** or Arcadian Way, the street running from the Theatre to the new harbour, started as a connecting passage to the sea and was gradually monumentalised. In its present form it belongs to the 5th century, when the emperor Arcadius turned it into a 600m long, 11m wide marble colonnaded street with wide porticoes on either side and lit at night. The four-column monument halfway along it may have been intended for images of the four Evangelists or four of the Apostles. As the statues are no longer there, it is difficult to tell. On the north side of the street a monumental bath to the west and a gymnasium framed a wide open space 200m by 250m for a huge palaestra. By 614, when the Persians caused much damage and the two agoras and the Embolos lay in ruins, the baths and gymnasium were no more. The street level had risen and the whole area was covered in a thick maze of unplanned housing development.

The Church of St Mary and the Olympieion

Beyond, to the north, the **Church of St Mary**, with a well preserved baptistery, is signposted. Excavations have shown that this small structure was is the successor to a larger one, long and narrow. Considering the two great Councils of Ephesus (in 431 and 449), the conclusion that the earlier church was the cathedral that is mentioned in the written sources, was tempting but the dates do not coincide. The building occupied and adapted the south end of a market and basilica complex, known as the **Olympieion**, willed by Emperor Hadrian in the early 2nd century when the city obtained its second neokorate (the right to build a temple for imperial worship). Hadrian's temple, in which he was worshipped as Zeus, stood in the precinct to the north. The complex, a 23m tall marble structure with Corinthian columns, was not long-lived. It was pulled down at the beginning of the 5th century and largely turned into lime. In Byzantine times the area was residential and there was a lot of plundering and re-employment of material. The church, with an episcopeion with private baths at the east end, was a domed structure built in brick on limestone foundations. It dates to c. 500 and was destroyed around the 7th century, possibly by the Arabs, to be replaced by a smaller building made partly of wood, when the focus of Christian Ephesus had shifted (*see below*).

The north part of the site

The tour ends to the north, past the location of the Stadium; the so-called '**Macellum**', a cult site marking the location of the acropolis of the first Ionian settlement in the 8th century BC; and finally of the ruins of the **Baths of Vedius**, built to a standard Roman layout of the 2nd century. From the exit, a well-paved road leads to the **Cave of the Seven Sleepers**, claimed since antiquity as a sacred site by pagans, Christians and Muslims alike. It is thought that there was an ancient Temple of Cybele here and that it was for this that the processional way from the Artemision to Ortygia ran past here. For the faithful, this is the site where seven Christian youths fell asleep for over a century, waking at the time of Theodosius II and therefore avoiding persecution. They are thought to be buried here; in fact, there is a rock-cut church with burial chambers in the cave. According to Muslims, the cave is the burial place of Mary Magdalene.

SELÇUK & AYASOLUK

Across the floodplains of the Marnas and the Selinus is the continuation of Ephesus, where the relief topography picks up again. The hill of Ayasoluk, an island in antiquity, 87m high, the Helibaton of the Byzantines, lacks fresh water and until late antiquity was only ever very sparsely settled. The fortification wall that circles its top, with 20 towers and three gates, now impeccably rebuilt, was more a refuge than a defence; the structure, originally largely built with spolia, went through several phases and was abandoned in 1764.

Over time a settlement gradually developed to the south, around the **Basilica of St John, Hagios Theologos** (*open Mon–Sun 9–5; charge*), which eventually gave the place its name, of which Ayasoluk is a corruption (for the Italians, it was Altoluogo, another corruption of the same). Which St John was buried here is not certain. Scholarship and Christian tradition are not agreed about the identities of John the

Apostle, John the Evangelist and John the Divine, the author of the Apocalypse. We may possibly be dealing with three different people (it is unlikely that the apostle, a fisherman, was literate). The truth is likely to remain murky.

The basilica, being excavated, restored and rebuilt at the time of writing, was financed by Justinian, which places it in the middle of the 6th century. It marks the spot where the eponymous St John was buried and where a small mortuary church was built. When Justinian decided to erect his new church, Ephesus was certainly not in decline. It had a circuit of walls while Ayasoluk was not defended. What then prompted his decision to build here, in the latter spot? Ephesus was already densely populated; within the wall circuit and there was not much level land available for a large building project; other extramural locations by the old Hellenistic city may have been unsuitable. The planned church was on a monumental scale: it needed space and a good line of sight to be fully appreciated. It was to provide a new focus for Ephesus. Moreover, the nearby Artemision, by that time abandoned, could be turned into a valuable supply of building blocks—as indeed came to pass. The inspiration for the new structure came from the churches of the Holy Apostles and Hagia Sophia in Byzantium, though there were significant differences. The basilica, measuring 110m by 60m, was designed in the form of a Latin cross with six domes and elegant pillars, now re-erected. The roof was of lead. The wide colonnaded atrium at the west end measured 34m by 47m. Later, the Ottomans built a cistern in it. Capitals in the nave bore the monograms of Justinian and of his wife Theodora. The walls were clad in marble and opus sectile and there was a synthronon at the east end. The tomb of the saint was located under the central dome, which was adorned with glass mosaics; dust from the tomb was thought to be miraculous. A baptistery, belonging to an earlier phase of the building, was located on the north side of the nave. Structures to the south and east of the basilica are believed to have belonged to the bishop's palace.

The site was already in decline in the 12th century, when Odo de Deuil, a historian and participant in the Second Crusade, reported that the tomb of the saint had a protective wall around it. In due course Ayasoluk turned into a nest of pirates (nominally under the Seljuks, whose base was several hundred kilometres away in Konya) and along the coast, the banner of Ayasoluk (a black wheel on a red field) came to be feared. In 1333 Ibn Battuta found a Greek virgin for sale here and bought her for 40 dinars; he also visited the basilica, part of which housed the horse market and stores; the remainder had been turned into a mosque. Later, when Seljuk power waned and the political scene fragmented, the area came under the control the emir of Aydın, Isa Bey. He built himself a mosque nearby, employing an architect from Damascus. The Isa Bey Mosque, 51m by 57m, consisted of a closed prayer hall with a flat roof and two domes, adjoining an arcaded courtyard. Spolia from the nearby basilica and elsewhere were liberally used for the elaborate decoration of windows and portals. This was the first monumental construction in the area since the time of Justinian and also the last. It was still functioning in the 17th century. At a later date, despite the two minarets, Richard Chandler mistook it for the Church of St John.

On the south side of the basilica, along a paved marble road, is the **Gate of Persecution**. Flanked by two towers, it represents the last surviving element of the wall circuit built in 7th–8th century to protect the settlement and the basilica, probably against the Arabs; the gate was constructed so as to trap invaders into a narrow courtyard where they could be quickly dispatched. The wall contained abundant spolia including entire sarcophagi. At least one of them, in the early days of archaeological exploration, was moved to Woburn Abbey in the United Kingdom, together with a fragment of the prominent relief that gave its name to the gate. It represented Achilles in combat and came originally from the theatre. The connection to early Christian martyrdom was inevitable.

The **Ephesus Archaeological Museum** (*open daily 8–7; shorter in winter; charge*) is also in Selçuk, due south of the Basilica. Recently renovated, it houses statuary and sculpture from the excavations (including the iconic Artemis).

MERYEMANA

Ephesus, from early on a centre of Christian pilgrimage, has several Christian connections, some fanciful such as the so-called 'prison of St Paul' (in reality a barrack room in the defensive walls) or the 'tomb of St Luke' (a Roman heroön).

While the assumed connection with a number of Christian saints fostered a lively trade in relics, Ephesus suffered from the 'Byzantium effect' as relics were requested for the capital (as occurred in the case of the bones of St Timothy). The whereabouts of Mary Magdalene's mortal remains, on the other hand, are disputed: she could be in Byzantium; conversely she is at rest in the Cave of the Seven Sleepers (*see p. 102*).

A later twist in the tale is Meryemana or Panaya Kapulu (*open daily 8–5; until 6 in summer; charge; 3km south of Ephesus, signposted*). According to tradition, the Mother of God died here after she came here with St John. The cult of Mary was actively fostered by the Church from 400, when the Virgin was given the title of Theotokos (God-bearer) and much thought was given to her true nature. As her cult grew, there were many contenders for a part in it. Byzantium, among them, was quite successful in taking the lead, with the help of imperial patronage. The imperial family acquired the bones of the Virgin from Jerusalem, where she was alleged to have died, and had a church built at Blachernae to house them. Ephesus, though it entered the fray much later, received help from an unexpected quarter, from a German nun by the name of Katherine Emmerich (1775–1824). Although Katherine was an invalid, had never visited Ephesus and was totally ignorant of the tradition of its connection with the Virgin, she was able to give a detailed description of the building that had been Mary's home in her last years, having seen it in a vision. On the basis of her description, a Lazarist father from Smyrna identified the structure at Meryemana. According to archaeologists, the T-shaped building in question can be dated to the 6th–7th century but it sits on an earlier structure, thus far undated and unexplored. Holy houses of Mary, taking into account that at the end of her earthly life her body was taken into heaven (the Assumption), became a potent replacement for her missing bones. The town of Loreto in the Marche region of central Italy houses one such, in a purpose-built basilica. According to tradition it was transported there by angels. In reality it appears to have been the work of the Crusaders. When they lost Palestine in 1294, they left with the holy relic from Nazareth. On arrival in Epirus on the Adriatic coast, they organised its transport to Loreto with the aid of the local ruling family, the Angeloi ('Angels').

BELEVİ MAUSOLEUM

For all its impressive appearance and commanding position on a high terrace, the monument (*signposted, by a brown sign, to the east from the centre of town at Belevi, after leaving Route 550 to Aydın*) remains to be fully excavated. It was left unfinished, judging by the incomplete frieze decoration, which makes it difficult to reconstruct its original appearance. Over time, elements of mausoleum, such as the sarcophagus, have found their way to Selçuk Museum, other remains were fed to a nearby lime kiln.

The mausoleum, built around an outcrop of rock, was cube-shaped, 25m by 25m, covered in marble blocks and surrounded on the upper part by a Corinthian colonnade. According to some, the pyramidal roof was topped by griffins, winged lions and charioteers, elements which suggest a Persian appearance, thus prompting a date c. 6th–4th centuries BC. Another school of thought, however, maintains that it was built by Lysimachus for himself, though he never used it. Alternatively it may house the remains of another Hellenistic king, Antiochus Theos, who was poisoned by his wife in 246 BC. The most interesting thing about the monument is its sheer size, second only to the mausoleum of Halicarnassus. It seems that this extraordinary construction was not a one-off but part of a trend.

The nearby tumulus, to the west, was also a grand affair with an 18m long dromos. Around the base, five courses of ashlar construction have been identified. The structure contains two grave chambers which were cut from above and covered with a corbelled stone roof. The scattered blocks on top may be the remains of a commemorative monument.

PRACTICAL INFORMATION

TOURIST INFORMATION

Information about Ephesus is available everywhere in Turkey. In Selçuk itself, the Tourist Information Office (*open 8.30–12 & 1–5.30; weekends 9–12 & 1–5*) is close to the archaeological museum; it offers free maps and plans as well as advice on getting around the various sites. Public transport (dolmuş) and taxis are a possibility (for Meryemana for example); otherwise you can hire a bike.

GETTING AROUND

By air: The airport north of Ephesus is only used for private flights. The nearest commercial airport is at İzmir.

By bus: The otogar in Selçuk is close
to the Belediye (Town Hall), just off
Route 550. The area is well served by
coaches and dolmuş in addition to the
numerous organised tours.

By train: The station is in the centre
of Selçuk, with connections to the east
(Aydın) and west (İzmir, with a stop at
Adnan Menderes Airport).

WHERE TO STAY

Ephesus is one of the most visited
sites in Turkey. While most people
will be here on a day trip, if you
want to stay you should make sure to
book in advance in the high season.
There are a number of reasonably
priced guesthouses in the centre of
Selçuk, such as the Anz Guesthouse
(*anzephesusguesthouse.com*) and the
Barim Pansiyon (*barimpension.com*). If
you are looking for something more
upmarket, Villa Dreams (there are two
of them; *ephesusvilladreams.com*), on the
edge of town (pick up arrangements
from the bus station offered), with a
view and a swimming pool, is a good
option.

WHERE TO EAT

Selçuk has many eateries to choose
from. On the whole, though, do not
expect to find genuine traditional
cuisine here. There is none. Ephesus
has been on the tourist trail for a long
time and the 'traditional' fare here is
the same as what you find anywhere
in Turkey. Having said this, the Ejder
Restaurant on Cengiz Topel Cd. has a
well-deserved reputation for its grilled

meat. For a cool drink and a bite to eat
in green surroundings, in the company
of locals who come here *en famille*,
head for the Carpouza Café just west of
the train station. The building, which
is old by local standards, used to be a
hospital in the 1940s.

WHAT TO DO

Take a stroll round the **Saturday
Market**, east of the Selçuk otogar, for
fruits, cheese and olives.

See the camels in their best finery
processing and performing in the
Camel Wrestling Festival (Deve
Güreşleri Festivali) on the 3rd Sunday
in Jan (the semi-finals; the concluding
event takes place in Aydın in March).
The festival is a family occasion for
Turks near and far who can appreciate
the finer points of the sport. As a
foreign visitor you will be greatly
outnumbered. It is highly likely that
you will be invited to share in one
of the many barbecues that sprout
up all around the Pamucak Arena (a
temporary structure set up by the local
municipality), where the spectacle is
held.

THE MEANDER VALLEY

Seen from the air on a physical map (centred on Denizli), the Meander Valley looks like a green ribbon extending from the Aegean deep into the east until it disappears into the valley of the Kufu Çay between the Çatma Dağ and the Ak Dağ through a narrow, 2km pass marking the crossing of an ecological boundary and giving access to the Anatolian Plateau with its treeless steppes. For centuries Isıklı has been the nodal point controlling access. Now that role belongs to nearby Çivril (*map C, 3*), which has better communications by rail and road. Archaeological exploration of the Meander Valley (550km long and measuring some 10km in width in the last 130km of its westernmost section) has been patchy and mainly confined to the western part, where the best-known sites are. Deep in the east, the site of Beycesultan, outside Çivril, shows occupation since the Bronze Age; Hellenistic and Roman presence with dwellings and public buildings, has been also identified at the foot and on the slopes of Sarıbaba Tepesi, guarding the entrance to the valley of the Kufu Çay. A Roman cohort had its fort in the vicinity in the 1st/2nd century. Before that, in 400 BC, Xenophon's mercenaries would have taken this pass to reach Mesopotamia along a true bottleneck of the Persian Royal Road, the main caravan route; communications have indeed been eased by the east–west alignment of the geology.

The Roman presence waned as the empire disintegrated but their place was soon filled by the Byzantines, who recommissioned the fortress of Eumenea on the slopes of the Sarıbaba and repaired the aqueduct fed by a water wheel, the remains of which are still standing. It was not a case of keeping the Royal Road open but of stemming the flow of nomadic Türkmen enticed by the green pastures of the lower land to the west, the coveted kışlas. By the 11th–12th century the Byzantines had abandoned the high reaches of the valley and the population had retreated to the cities. According to Peter Thonemann, the battle of Myriokephalon in 1176—in which the Byzantine army was successfully ambushed by the Turks—took place here in the narrow gorge of the Kufu Çay.

A further look at the physical map highlights the difference between the north and the south sides of the Meander Valley. Both are rugged and seemingly inhospitable. Settlement on the north bank developed ribbon-fashion on the alluvial fans and at the foot of the steep eroding slopes, on spurs, hillocks and terraces. On the south side the Carian granite massif is bisected by streams; erosion is less prominent, the valley sides are steeper and there are fewer pockets suitable for settlement, which is sparse, away from the river and higher up. Moreover, the valley is tilted to the south, where it is more prone to flooding. Traditionally, water has played a major role in the social order. Those living in the wide floodplain of this collapsed valley floor and tilling the fine alluvium have been the poorest. The better off occupied the mid-range, using the river as a source of water for fruit trees, olives and vines. The sparsely populated higher zone was the land of shepherds. While occupation

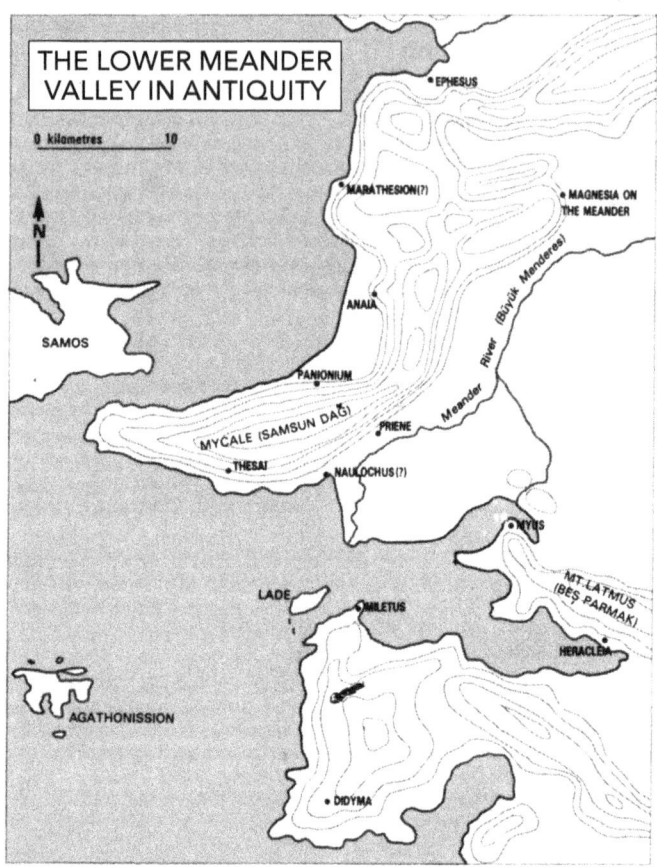

THE LOWER MEANDER VALLEY IN ANTIQUITY

is ancient, urbanisation away from the coastal influence is more recent, dating from the Hellenistic period, when Macedonian veterans had to be settled somewhere and the idea grew up of cities as showpieces of civilised values. Hierapolis and Laodiceia are just two examples.

Historically, the lower Meander Valley has been ecologically unstable. Back in time, the sea reached as far as Aydın, leaving to the north the Dilek Dağı (one of two Turkish names for the ancient Mycale), an island of gneiss with marble intrusions, and to the south the future site of Miletus, also an island but made of limestone; the Bafa Gölü was open sea surrounded by precipitous rocks. Today the valley is completely filled with alluvium and Miletus is landlocked. Various factors have contributed to this transformation: the width of the valley and the low gradient of the river have encouraged it to twist and turn and to deposit its load, while human intervention upstream has opened up areas for agriculture and encouraged erosion.

These days the Meander Valley is a fairly stable environment (bearing in mind the ever-present risk of earthquakes here, where two tectonic plates meet) with a

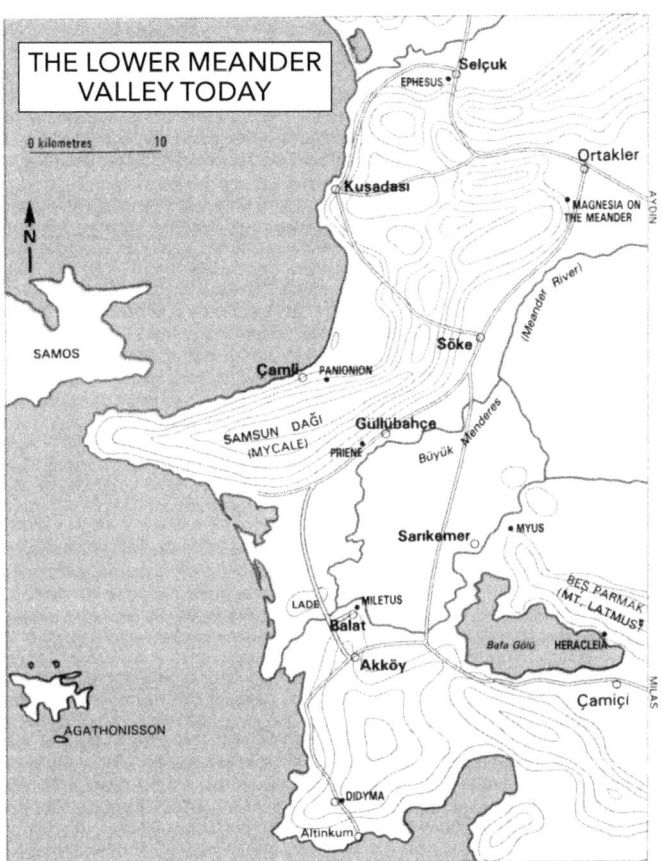

developed transport network. The delta is no longer a barrier to north–south traffic as it used to be, nor is it, as it was in Ottoman times and more recently, malaria infested. Agriculture from cotton to liquorice is thriving. The days of vast agricultural estates owned by absentee landlords and tilled by slaves, the *pedieis*, who dominated the scene from Hellenistic times to the Ottoman era, are over. And crossing the river is no longer an adventure, as it was in Freya Stark's day.

MILETUS

Of the four sites in the area of the mouth of the Meander (Priene, Didyma, Heracleia and Miletus), the last is by far the most important and also the most likely to disappoint—especially if you have just come from the reconstructed ruins of Ephesus. While Priene and Heracleia have been frozen in time, dead cities in the wrong location; and Didyma, a temple site rather than a settlement, has been buried under later occupation, Miletus (*map B, 5; open daily 8–7; charge*) has only recently been fully abandoned, having constantly reinvented itself throughout its long history. By the time of its abandonment (1955), after one earthquake too many, it was a squalid village called Balat (from Palatia), retaining in its name the memory of its former grandiose buildings.

When the sea reached 50km inland, the future Miletus consisted of small islands which with some imagination you can just make out from the top of the theatre facing roughly south (*see map on p. 114*). To the back is Kaletepe; further northeast is Humeitepe (a Turkish name with connotations of typhoid and malaria, showing environmental degradation). These stand out well on a physical map because they still have some elevation and are not under culture. Immediately opposite the theatre, roughly where the museum is, was another island, the nucleus of the prehistoric settlement beneath the site of the much later Temple of Athena. The mainland began 1.3km southwest, somewhere beyond the main road to Didyma. It was here, on the twin peaks of Kalabak and Zeytin Tepe, that the Archaic city eventually developed.

The maritime vocation of Miletus was clear from the very beginning. Excavations under the Temple of Athena have revealed occupation from the second half of the 4th millennium BC showing later Aegean and Cretan connections. Remains of buildings dated from the 18th–15th centuries BC suggest a strong Minoan link. The frescoes are in a style reminiscent of Thera. Linear A writing and seals, Minoan weights and distinctive Kamares pottery lend support to the theory that this was a bridgehead for overseas trade, with Anatolia's metal resources the main attraction. Moreover, Milesian pottery has been identified in palatial deposits in Crete. The settlement shows signs of violent destruction that has been attributed to the eruption of the volcano on Santorini, unless it was the work of the Mycenaeans. They were certainly here on the same quest a short time later, after a brief hiatus, as one can see in the architecture, cult practices and the pottery. They were ousted around the 12th century BC and this time the Hittites were blamed, though they themselves came to a sticky end round about that time. This then ushers in a lull, as trade dwindled.

By the time the Greek colonists arrived, in about the 10th century BC, people— very probably Carians—had moved in from the south. According to legend, the new arrivals quickly despatched the male members of the population and subjugated the women. As a result, Milesian women would never sit with their husbands nor call them by their name, in memory of the distant outrage. The colonists settled on the mainland, where the high point (the limestone hill of Kalabak Tepe, whose surface was artificially flattened) had been fortified with sturdy defence works in the 13th century BC. Bone remains suggest a consistent interest in animal husbandry. Over time, as the Meander 'worked', as Herodotus put it, creating land, the Archaic city spread from Kalabak Tepe (which became its acropolis) to the northeast. Miletus reconnected with its maritime vocation and set out to found daughter colonies, some 90 of them, around the Black Sea, in the Propontis, the east Aegean and in Egypt at Naukratis on the Nile delta. With this impressive network and direct access to the core of Anatolia, Miletus boomed, an economic power to reckon with, shifting merchandise but also actively manufacturing 'orientalising' bronzes; it sought its inspiration from its contacts and beyond, from deep into Anatolia as far as the Kingdom of Urartu by Lake Van.

Miletus expanded its maritime base by controlling the islands of Patmos, Leri and Lepsia, which offered welcome shelter to the population when danger threatened. Eventually its territory extended from Mount Grion (İlbir Dağı) in the south to mount Mykale (Samsun Dağı) in the north, up the Meander Valley on its north bank, as well as outward to the islands. Socially, it was a crucible, a hotbed of ideas where anything and everything could be discussed from the unifying principle of the universe to the process of town planning (*see box overleaf*). One can but wonder if some of this rubbed off on Aspasia, the local woman who became Pericles' partner and bore him a son. Was it her scintillating conversation that attracted the attention of the great man?

Trouble came from the Lydians and later from the Persians. The Greek colonists rebelled and were duly beaten at the battle of Lade in 494 BC. This was a naval battle, though today Lade (now Batmaz Tepeleri) is a hillock on dry land. The defeat proved quite a setback; the population was deported as far as Susa and Miletus was sacked. Although the city's fortunes rallied after Athens dealt decisively with the Persian peril, the new Miletus was diminished by Athens' triumph, its role reduced to that of a regional power. A marked change in the layout of the city was the building of a new defensive wall that cut off the acropolis on Kalabak Tepe and encircled the peninsula. The defence towards the mainland in a low and vulnerable setting, built in ashlar limestone with frequent towers and sally ports, was particularly heavy-handed. Miletus became like an island again, blessed with four deep water harbours, one by the theatre (the Theatre Harbour) and another immediately to the northeast (the Lion Harbour, so called because of the two massive marble lions guarding it; according to some, they held a chain strung across the opening). Two additional harbours are yet to be located on the other side of the peninsula. Most of the monuments we know come from this period and its continuation, when Miletus became an important free city in the Roman province of Asia.

The Roman period was a time of increased siltation as the Meander delta drew near. By AD 100, pavements had to be raised and the harbours needed frequent dredging. The incursions of the Goths prompted the construction of improved defences. Later emperors from Diocletian to Justinian lavished attention on Miletus, mending structures and building anew. The last major project was the building of the Church of St Michael in the 6th century, on top of a temple dedicated to Dionysus. Elsewhere Hesichius, a local worthy, had a column erected with the statue of the emperor on top. Miletus, though not yet dead, was nevertheless only just surviving. The scant information on that period shows poor building practices, the collapse of the grid, and the incorporation of buildings into the defences. The 2–3m thick 7th-century wall, with spolia from the Baths of Faustina, incorporated the theatre; the market gate was turned into a tower. The theatre itself became a castle with the addition of heavy walls and towers to its already sturdy structure. Houses and cisterns were built inside. The whole village fitted inside it. It was a self-sufficient unit, a defence truly worthy of the dark ages. The city's fortunes deteriorate from this time on. By the 12th century the only nucleus left was the theatre/citadel; the rest was dispersed settlement. When Richard Chandler visited in the 18th century he found the place 'mean'. Even the mosque was ruinous. The theatre was full of squatters and bats—but the local ağa was out hawking, suggesting that there was still some life in landlocked Miletus.

TOWN PLANNING IN MILETUS

Miletus was the hometown of Hippodamus, who lived in the 5th century BC and is credited by Aristotle (*Politics 2,8*) with the development of town planning on an orthogonal grid, dividing land into regular equal blocks with civic buildings in the centre, sometimes occupying more than one block but always respecting the grid. In antiquity the idea was particularly suited to newly-founded settlements for colonial settlers and veterans for instance; in more modern times it has inspired the layout of a number of cities in the Americas, from Manhattan to Buenos Aires. The idea of urban gridding has naturally been always present in the mind of the excavators at Miletus: did Hippodamus apply his principles in his home town? The expansion of the Archaic city to the north from Kalabak Tepe to the Theatre Harbour was the test. It had originally been thought that the development had been unplanned and organic, but recent investigations have shown that there was a grid, albeit in places with smaller insulae than the ones in the later plan of Miletus, which shows the Roman layout with larger blocks. And gridding had its effect: when the Temple of Athena was rebuilt in the Late Archaic Period it was realigned to fit it. With modern techniques such as remote sensing, archaeologists have been able to plot the gridded pattern of the city almost in its entirety, from the Hellenistic crosswall in the south, to the very tip at the north on Humeitepe. Public buildings, which constitute the bulk of excavated Miletus, conform on the whole to the grid, sometimes taking up several blocks (the south and the north markets, for example). There are exceptions though, like the Baths of Faustina east of the Theatre Harbour. They were built on a difficult, low area, recently reclaimed. Practical considerations prevailed.

According to Peter Thonemann, the silting up of the Meander delta was not an unmitigated disaster for the area, though the town declined markedly. Unlike the people of Myus, who watched their harbour silt up and moved away, the Milesians, as the silting shifted south and the coastline moved west, set about exploiting the new prime agricultural land, using the salt pans and the marshes for fishing and fowling and horse rearing. The sea bass and the grey mullet were famous. Murex shells suggest the production of dyes. In Byzantine times this was a land of vast estates, imperial and ecclesiastical, provided with sufficient capital to build drains and ditches and regulate water. Later, with the emirs, Miletus (now Palatia) was still a functioning port, accessible by light boats along a branch of the river; it was the emirs' main harbour. Here Venetian and Cretan traders would come to load up wheat and buy horses. They had a consul and a church dedicated to St Nicholas. There was sufficient trade inland to warrant the building of two caravansarays. The İlias Bey Mosque and two hamams with stucco decorations suggest some opulence. Fourteenth-century Palatia was also a pottery production centre. The local clay was excellent and the inspiration came from far afield: it was an imitation of the dark blue and white Chinese porcelain.

A walk through Miletus

It is best to start with the **theatre** because it is a clearly recognisable and prominent feature, north of the museum (*open 8.30–6.30, shorter hours in winter; charge*). The theatre was originally Hellenistic with a capacity of 5,000. It was reconstructed in the Roman period for three times as many spectators and adapted to gladiatorial fights. The remains of the skene suggest a set-up similar to that at Ephesus. The four standing pillars used to support a canopy for the imperial loggia. Substructures, vaulted passages and stairways are particularly well-preserved because of the subsequent history of the building, when it was filled in and built over. Note a couple of inscriptions. On the third row, one marks the place of 'the goldsmith of the Blues' (clearly Byzantium's horse-racing factions had spread beyond the capital). On top of the stairway to the west end, part of an inscription deals with a labour dispute which shows that the workers involved were free agents, not slaves. The dispute was referred to the oracle in Didyma. The answer shows a diplomat at work: 'make a sacrifice, do the job economically, consult an expert'. It must have worked, since the theatre was finished.

Behind the theatre is a section of the defensive wall and of the Byzantine castle, and further on are the remains of a Hellenistic heroön. The location of the **Lion Harbour** is downhill. It was surrounded on three sides by a Roman marble quay. The ruins further east belong to a 2nd-century AD bath. From there you can go south to the round feature of the **Delphinion**, more often than not with its feet in the water; it was surrounded by a large temenos The oldest known temple dedicated to Apollo, it has inscriptions dating to the 6th century BC, suggesting that the cult was brought by the early colonists. The visible remains are Hellenistic with Roman repairs. The association of Apollo and dolphins is very ancient: the god apparently used to travel on their backs.

At this point you are getting close to the heart of the city, where the public monuments were. From the Delphinion and facing south, to your right is the Harbour Stoa leading to the **North Agora**, the administrative and civic centre from the 3rd century BC, when it had a prytaneion and a bouleuterion. When it was monumentalised in the 2nd century BC, the bouleuterion was left untouched. The **Church of St Michael** is not far to the west; the episcopal palace may have been next to it. The **Baths of Capito**, next to the Delphinion, were donated by a Roman high official in the mid 1st century AD. The Hellenistic gymnasium with its ephebeum is followed by the **Ionic Stoa**, late 1st century AD, marking the beginning of the processional way to Didyma.

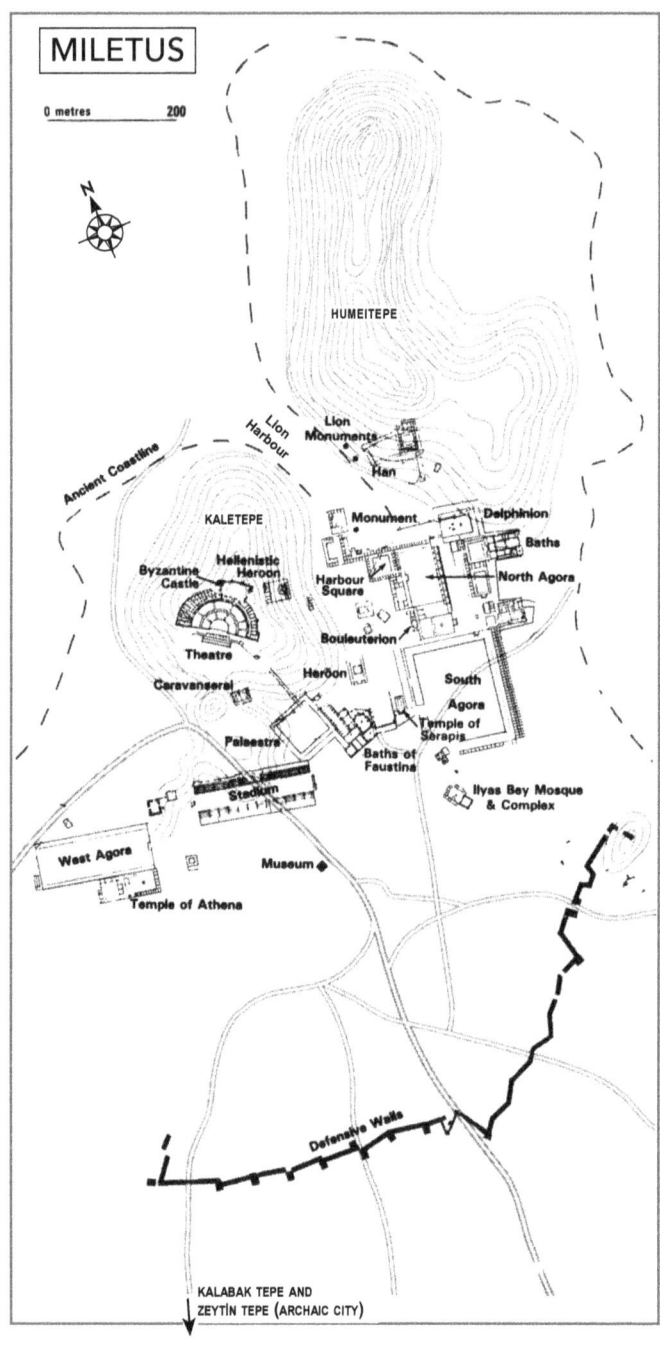

MILETUS

0 metres 200

HUMEITEPE

Lion Harbour

Lion Monuments

Han

Ancient Coastline

KALETEPE

Monument

Delphinion

Baths

Byzantine Castle

Hellenistic Heroon

Harbour Square

North Agora

Theatre

Bouleuterion

Caravanserai

Heröon

South Agora

Palaestra

Temple of Serapis

Baths of Faustina

Ilyas Bey Mosque & Complex

Stadium

West Agora

Museum

Temple of Athena

Defensive Walls

KALABAK TEPE AND
ZEYTİN TEPE (ARCHAIC CITY)

South of the market place, the well-preserved **bouleuterion** is one of the oldest buildings in Miletus, dating to the 2nd century BC; it sits on top of an earlier structure. It had a wooden roof. In the forecourt, the altar to the cult of the Roman emperor faced the entrance to the assembly room, a powerful reminder to the citizens of the real state of the balance of power.

The **nymphaeum** to the east dates from some four centuries later; it was supplied by aqueducts coming in from the southeast. Some of its statues of deities and nymphs are in the Istanbul Archaeological Museum, others are in Berlin in the Pergamon Museum; they graced the front, which is designed like a theatre skene. In the large 6th-century church to the south, a propylon with four columns was reused to provide a grandiose entrance.

The access to the **South Agora** was through the 2nd-century monumental entrance now re-erected in the Pergamon Museum in Berlin. The market was truly on a grand scale (164m by 195m), with shops and storerooms behind a Doric stoa. To the west, on the outside, a granary has been excavated and next to it a Temple of Serapis. Milesian connections with Egypt date to the time before the establishment of a daughter colony in the Nile delta. In 660 BC, the pharaoh Psammetichus I (Psamtik) had settled soldiers in the Meander delta in order to establish his rule, but nothing more is heard of them; however, Samos, Ephesus, Miletus and Erythrae all mark a surge in Egyptian imports.

The 2nd-century **Baths of Faustina** (wife of Marcus Aurelius) to the west, are of the standard design, built in brick and dressed stone. The statues and the ornament have all been removed. The local museum houses a reclining image of the River Meander. Other images of gods and muses are dispersed further afield. The stadium nearby, originally Hellenistic and enlarged in the 3rd century AD, could accommodate 15,000 people. Built on level ground, it attained the desired slope through the use of substructures. Note, at the east end, the Hellenistic gateway with an elaborate propylon with seven arched entrances flanked by pairs of Corinthian columns.

To the west, on the south edge of the **West Agora**, is an insignificant stone podium. It marks the location of the 5th-century BC Temple of Athena. Investigations of the area have revealed evidence of early occupation.

So far, archaeology in Miletus has been mainly about public buildings and yet it is said that the people built in stone available from the hinterland (limestone and gneiss) and in marble from Mt Mycale. Altogether we know very little of the lifestyle of the local people. Fine mosaics, now on display in the Pergamon Museum in Berlin, are evidence of luxurious residences.

The **İlyas Bey Külliye**, dated to the early 1400s, included, besides a mosque, a medrese (now missing), two hamams and a şadırvan (a recycled sarcophagus); the minaret, presently missing as well, was in brick, in the west corner. It has been suggested that the local petty rulers were using Miletus as a base for raids and, more sedately, for the trade of alum, wool and pekmez. The building with an elaborate façade made use of a lot of ancient construction material; the interior was colourfully decorated in impressed stucco with floral and geometric patterns. The külliye itself is not grand but makes an impressive statement given the time and the place.

End your visit at the newly refurbished **Museum**, with well-labelled artefacts from Miletus and the surrounding region and some fine reconstruction drawings. Then look for the imposing ruin of the **Sacred Gate**, some 400m from the museum exit going south. It marked the point where the processional way to Didyma, starting further north, exited the town and headed south. The structure, originally dated to the 5th century BC, was restored in the early 2nd century AD.

DIDYMA

Linked with Miletus for at least part of its history, the site of Didyma (*map B, 5; open 8–7, shorter hours in winter; charge*), with the grandiose Temple of Apollo housing an oracle well-known in antiquity, lies a few kilometres to the south. Its memory was never lost; in 1446 Ciriaco de' Pizzicolli, better known as Cyriacus of Ancona, saw the temple still standing; when Richard Chandler visited in 1764, a quake had felled all but three columns. The Società dei Dilettanti began some excavations which were later continued by the Germans. At that point, the east end of the cella had been filled with rubble and a windmill was standing on it, at a higher level than the original roof.

ORIGINS AND HISTORY OF DIDYMA

Didyma is not a Greek name, so one must assume a local development to start with, later taken over by Apollo, in one of his many manifestations. Cult centres developing around springs are quite common; more so in this area, which is normally dry, brown and barren. Legend has it that the water came all the way from Mount Mycale, to the north beyond the delta, having travelled below the sea bed. The scientific explanation is more prosaic. Here the limestone to the north meets less permeable marl and the water comes to the surface. Over the centuries the spring proved troublesome, at times drying up, which was interpreted as a very bad omen, although the cleaning of the pipes proved sufficient to placate the divinity. As there is currently no water anywhere in the temple cella, we must assume that the spring has again ceased to function and that no one has cleaned the pipes; alternatively, it has been dislocated by one of the frequent earthquakes.

The earliest remains predate the first temple, which is Archaic in date. There is Mycenaean pottery but no architecture to go with it. Later, around the 8th century BC, a mud-brick structure measuring 10m by 9m on a rocky ridge, marking out the spring, harks back to practices known from distant Mesopotamia and Anatolia, suggesting a local Carian cult. The simple structure was surrounded in the late 7th century BC by a colonnaded portico.

In the second half of the 6th century BC, a proper temple (in the sense that the Greeks would have recognised) took the place of the mud-brick structure.

This denotes the arrival of a cult of Apollo, claiming the place for the worship of Apollo Didymeion. With it came the myth of Branchos, a youth beloved of Apollo and the ancestor of the Branchidae, a Milesian clan who administered the temple, which by now was an oracular site, until the Persians burnt it down in 493 BC. From the scant remains, archaeologists have reconstructed an 85m by 38m Archaic temple, a Ionic dipteros on a platform fronted by a deep pronaos. It was built in tufa with marble columns and capitals. In appearance, some of the columns are distinctly reminiscent of the Artemision in Ephesus, suggesting that Croesus contributed to their building. The cella was unroofed; it is possible the sky played a role in the process of divination. The temple had a small naiskos at the west end, where the bronze image of Apollo was kept. The victorious Persians removed it to Ekbatana, together with other portable temple artefacts such as the giant metal knuckle bone weighing 93kg, one of a pair, an ex-voto from Aristolochos and Thrason. The bronze of Apollo was later returned by the Seleucids, the knuckle bone was found in Susa in 1901 and is now in the Louvre. As for the Branchidae priests who had surrendered to the invader, they followed the Persians back home, fearful of the reaction of the Milesians, and were resettled in Sogdiana somewhere southeast of the Aral Sea. For over a century the spring dried up and the oracular function with it.

With the arrival of Alexander the Great the oracle revived (and predicted his victory at the Battle of Gaugamela). With the Persians on their knees and King Darius disposed of, Alexander hunted down the descendants of the Branchidae and exterminated them, a deed that pleased the Milesians greatly. The oracle was now restored to life and a new temple went up, the one we see today. It was built on a vast scale under the patronage of the Seleucids. Its administration was in the hand of prominent Milesian families (with occasionally hereditary posts). The chief priest (prophet) was in charge of organisation, of planning extravagant festivities and of interpreting the inchoate babbling of the prophetess in her trance. He then passed on the text to be put into verse and handed over to the postulant. We must assume that the prophet had a house close by, since inscribed elements of it were later used to build a church.

During the Roman era, Galatians and pirates proved worrisome but, on the whole, being part of the Roman province of Asia was good for Didyma, until the Goths struck in the mid-3rd century. The temple was fortified with a heavy wall and repaired: the holy water miraculously reappeared; a grateful inscription was set up in the pronaos. When Julian the Apostate visited on his way to fight the Persians, he found Christian chapels nearby to vent his anger on. The oracle wrongly predicted victory in his eastern enterprise, from which he never came back. A few years later, Emperor Theodosius banned any form of divination and with that the days of the Didymaion came to an end.

A 5th-century basilica, built with the spolia of the house of the prophet, went up inside the temple's inner court. It incorporated the Hellenistic naiskos in its west section but was destroyed in the next earthquake. A new, smaller church took its place, the walls of the cella were strengthened and the former temple became a tiny walled city, a fortified kastron, with a bishop and no public buildings: everything fitted inside the inner court, including the necropolis. It was known as Hieron, and later Jeronda.

Visiting Didyma

The site may have lost the subtle atmosphere that so charmed Richard Chandler in the 18th century, but it is still impressive. German archaeologists have been working hard to understand the structure and have re-erected large parts of it. It looks magnificent and is now a prime tourist attraction. The temple you see today (*see plan*) is Hellenistic, larger (110m by 51m) than its predecessor and unfinished, but still an Ionic dipteros, built in local marble from Latmos and in limestone. It was built on a high crepidoma at the centre of its temenos, where later the small village developed.

The entrance is via a monumental staircase leading to a pronaos with three rows of columns. Note the decorated capitals in the corners. The roof was in marble and coffered. At the centre of the wall opposite the entrance, a huge door had a very high threshold; outsiders could see the inner court open to the skies, with the naiskos in the distance beyond the laurel trees. Here at this door, the priests communicated with the postulants.

The next room, only accessible form the inside, was supported by two columns and had three doors to the east. It is believed that the 34 ivory tusks donated by Ptolemy XIII Theos in 41 BC were used for the decoration of these doors. They would be opened presumably on special occasions, allowing access to the inner court via a grand staircase. The function of this room is debated. On either side of it were flights of service steps; two leading to a room higher up or to a terrace, and two dark, stone-lined passages to the inner court.

The surface of the inner court, the cella of the temple, is on a level with the spring. There is no difference in level between the inside and the outside, which explains why the complex later functioned so well as a fortress, surrounded by massive walls over 25m high. The stark inner surface of the surrounding wall was interrupted by pilasters with griffins and vine tendrils in the capitals. The structure was still unroofed (probably too big to be spanned). Moreover, this was the garden of Apollo, with a laurel grove under the blue sky, a true temple within a temple, an ideal world removed from the squalid outside; later on, this inner surface was paved. At the far end was the naiskos, larger than the Archaic one (14m by 8m; 10m high) but roughly on the same plan. Here was kept the bronze statue of Apollo (that eventually fell victim to Christian zeal) and perhaps the spring. Beneath a marble slab in the floor, a foundation deposit, a single deposition of remains of sacrifices and of gold and silver objects has been found. It may be the original one that was placed under the Archaic temple. A close examination of the graffiti has given a precious insight into the planning and building of the temple, showing the use of geometry in the design of the profiles of the mouldings. This monument was burnt down by the Christians.

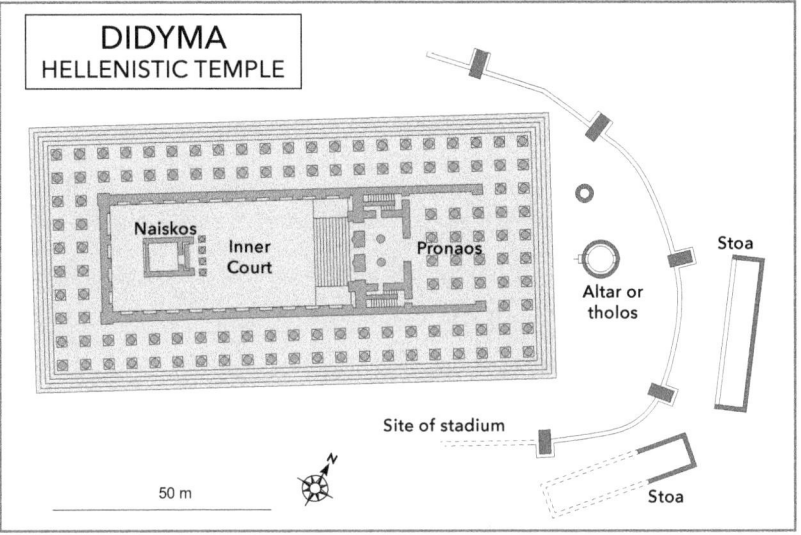

Outside the temple to the east, a semicircular terrace with a portico featured statues (of which only the bases remain) and votive offerings. In the centre, a circular structure, 8m in diameter, has been variously interpreted as an altar or a tholos. The well-known Medusa lying nearby comes from a 2nd-century AD frieze that ornamented an architrave. Steps gave access to the top of the terrace. The stadium was nearby. Fifteen metres wide and 60m long, it used the steps of the crepidoma as its north side while the south side was purpose-built

THE ORACLE OF DIDYMA

The oracular function at Didyma (attested from the 6th century BC) lay with the prophetess (just as in Delphi). She was not local and communicated with the divinity either by bathing in the holy water or by filling a bowl with it and using it like a crystal ball. To make herself receptive she needed to fast for three days before any pronouncements. This must seriously have curtailed her productivity: there was probably no more than one oracle per week. Most of the known responses concern Milesian affairs, suggesting that the oracle had a preponderantly regional function, advising on divisive issues such as the setting up of new colonies. However, the oracle did also have an international dimension, receiving visits from the king of Bithynia, the Seleucids and the Rhodians. In Roman times, the emperors Hadrian, Trajan and later Julian were prophets here, though probably only in an honorary capacity. In the 2nd century BC, games (athletic but also including the performing arts) were held every four years. That explains the presence of a stadium at Didyma.

THE SACRED WAY

A Sacred Way linked Miletus and Didyma, beginning in Miletus at the Delphinion and ending in a monumental construction at the east side of the temple at Didyma. Sections of it have been uncovered over time and the course of this 16.4km-long route is now known. Seven to ten metres wide, it covered a more ancient road dated to two centuries earlier and edged by burials. The Sacred Way, eventually paved, was punctuated by shrines, statues and other landmarks where pilgrims would stop. From the 5th century BC it was in the hands of a group of priests from Miletus, the Molpoi (the singers). They would lead the chanting and the sacrifices. Trajan, in gratitude for a favourable oracle (he had visited with his father who was then proconsul in Asia and had been predicted his imperial destiny) made some improvements. He added milestones and, by dint of cutting through hills and filling depressions, eased the gradient. It seems that the processional function of the road carried on into Christian times.

If you want to walk it and you have the stamina, it will take you five hours. It is best to find a guide at the village of Akköy first. In the ancient past it was possible to take a short cut, starting from the port of Didyma, Panormus, immediately to its northwest and from there head for the temple (1hr). That stretch of coast is now very built up and finding one's way would be difficult.

PRIENE

Perched on the slopes of Mount Mycale, now the Dilek Dağı, Priene (*map B, 5; open daily 9–8; charge*) is the darling of the tourist trade because, like Pompeii or Aphrodisias, it is 'frozen in time', allowing visitors to experience the past by walking in it. But Priene did not die in a natural disaster (like Pompeii), nor did it fade away when imperial support was withdrawn (like Aphrodisias). Instead, Priene died a lingering death, with many ups and downs. The model Hellenistic city that we see today conceals a long past and an even longer trail into the future, taking the history of Priene well into the 13th century AD.

HISTORY OF PRIENE

It all started with the Meander and the commercial possibilities it afforded. According to the latest thinking, there was an early settlement somewhere near or beneath the modern town of Söke, at the extreme east reaches of Mt Mycale, mirroring Miletus on the opposite side of the bay. If the Greek colonists settled here they would have found Carians, and possibly evidence of an earlier Mycenaean presence. This proto-Priene (Priene 1), then called Aneon, is now beyond the reach of the archaeologists' spades under a thick layer of silt. A series of earthquakes prompted relocation a few kilometres west, near the harbour of Naulochon. The location of this Priene 2 has not been firmly established. The only evidence for the existence of an Archaic Priene is an electrum coin dated to the 6th century BC and bearing the image of Athena. There is disagreement on the causes of the last move. Possibly the coast was silting up, or perhaps there were social tensions, awkward foreigners (the Persians). Archaic Priene was still by the water, a harbour city. But Naulochon in due course started silting up: when Strabo (*12,8,17*) wrote about it, in the 1st century AD, it was no longer operational and a new move was planned. In the 4th century BC the city relocated higher up and this time it had two harbours (also retaining its old harbour for good measure).

For all its talk as a city of sages (it had been ruled by Bias one of the Seven Sages), the blueprint for the new Priene was not very clever. Normally, Greek cities were re-founded for expansion but Priene, with its topography and difficult access, was cramped from birth. The grid pattern, which was strictly adhered to, was not designed for steep slopes, requiring the building of artificial terraces; moreover, the narrow streets and the frequent flights of steps would have been a hindrance to wheeled traffic. An advantage, however, was that by moving west, closer to Mt Mycale, Priene reaffirmed its important role in the Panionium (*see box overleaf*).

When the move was planned, the land was under Persian rule, and the local satrap was Mausolus. His liking of things Greek is well known and it could easily be that he had a hand the planning process. Work started c. 370 BC and received new impetus when Alexander the Great offered to finance the Temple of Athena. His contribution was readily accepted (unlike at Ephesus); the inscription recording the deed is now in the British Museum in London.

Later history is uneventful: neither the Attalids nor the Romans took much interest in this city that could not grow, and no new buildings went up. Rome was particularly heavy-handed, imposing a large tribute when the town was already exhausted after the Mithridatic Wars. Meanwhile, the Meander went on working and the harbours silted up.

Priene did not die completely; in fact, it actually picked up after the demise of the Roman Empire, a time when having a good wall circuit and a defensive position came in handy. Byzantine Priene was half the size but it had a bishop who used the abundant spolia from the pagan buildings for his cathedral. The grid was lost under encroaching buildings and houses, a chapel and a cattle pen were built in the old theatre. The Arab incursions of the 7th–8th centuries prompted a move to the acropolis, which was strengthened. Things improved in the 10th century, when Priene was the Byzantine fiscal unit of the Meander Valley. Later it was for a few years in the hands of a local strongman, Sabas Asidenos, who built a fort on top of the Temple of Zeus before bowing to the superior might of the Nicaean Empire. By the end of the 13th century, Priene was in Turkish hands.

The site was 'rediscovered' by British merchants based in Smyrna in 1673. Excavations, mainly German from the end of the 19th century, alerted the local population to the possibility of free worked stone and, after the unearthing of a coin hoard, of treasure, prompting some freelance archaeology. To this day about a third of the city has been explored, giving priority to the Hellenistic town (which is what you see today). As a result, the later development of the town is not well understood.

THE PANIONIUM

Situated in the Yarımadası Dilek Milli Parkı (*open Mon–Sun 9–8; charge*), the ancient Mycale Peninsula is an environmentally sensitive area of the northern Meander delta. Its backbone is a ridge running east–west, created by the collision of two tectonic plates; as a result, some of its limestone has been turned into marble by volcanic activity. The peninsula is separated by a narrow channel from the Greek island of Samos, which is geologically similar. In antiquity the wild fauna, panthers and such like, could be seen swimming back and forth. These days, the park is considerably more tame. Tourists will find beaches and shady picnic spots; there are trails to explore and interesting Mediterranean flora to discover. In antiquity the site hosted the Panionia, the festival that brought together the Ionian colonies at regular intervals to celebrate their shared identity. The festival cannot have passed off without a pang, however, stirring up unpleasant memories of its origin.

Back in the 8th century BC, Priene, Myus, Miletus, Ephesus, Colophon, Lebedus, Teos, Erythrae, Chios, Phocaea and Clazomenae all clubbed together to bring about the demise of Melia which, according to Vitruvius writing much later, was also an Ionian colony. The victors took over the Melian territory and built a sanctuary to Poseidon Heliconius, in memory of the town of Helice in Greece, where the cult had been established and which was claimed by the first colonists of Priene as their ancestral home. This was about the time when, according to sources, Priene was experiencing the social tensions which eventually prompted a relocation (*see above*).

The Temple of Poseidon Heliconius (also known as the Panionium) was intended as the cult centre of the newly established Ionian League. Politically the league was toothless, since the individual cities pursued their own courses. The regular gatherings, which included religious events and athletic competitions, were meant to produce a feeling of camaraderie that would bind the Ionian colonists together. The games, with officials from Priene presiding, were still being celebrated in Roman times, although with reduced importance. Only a couple of interruptions are known: in the 5th century BC, because of the raging war, they were moved to Ephesus, and later, under the Persians, were cancelled altogether. Alexander the Great reinstated them on Mycale. Both Herodotus and Strabo give indications of the site of the temple, on the basis of which Chandler explored the area around Güzelçamlı in the 18th century and identified the place from an inscription (now lost) that was built into a church. At the end of the 19th century, Theodore Wiegand found eleven tiers of a theatre, with no stage, built against a hill nearby. Further up, a sacred enclosure with an altar dated to the 6th century BC were later identified.

Visiting Priene

After the ticket booth on a side road uphill west of Güllübahçe, you enter the city from the east, through a gap in the wall circuit. Priene's walls 2.5km long with a few posterns and widely spaced, small towers, did not lend themselves to active defence; they relied more on sheer mass, being thick and heavily built in blue/grey limestone from the Mycale peninsula. The best stretches are preserved on the acropolis higher up to the north, more heavily defended, with a wall walk and bastions. The huge round bastion at the highest end is a later addition.

The Stadium and Lower Gymnasium

The **Stadium** was the exercise ground of the nearby Lower Gymnasium. Built on a slope with a huge retaining wall, the stadium, 185m long and 20m wide, is one of the few buildings in town that completely ignores the grid. Most of the rest is immaculately laid out orthogonally; when the slope was too steep, flights of steps took their place, with water drainage facilities underneath. The stadium, dated to the 2nd century BC, replaced an earlier structure; it was edged to the north by a terrace and a Doric stoa; rows of marble seats for judges and dignitaries can be seen. The rest was of wood. A construction of Corinthian pillars marked the starting point of the races. At some point, a 50cm wide wall was built in front of the lower row of seats, prompting the suggestion that the stadium was used for animal fights.

Crossing the stadium along the stoa, you enter the **Lower Gymnasium**, one of two in Priene. The other one, near the theatre, was much older, one of the first buildings to go up, but very little is left of it. The Lower Gymnasium was built in the 2nd century BC, the gift of a local magnate, replacing a housing development; its south and west sides were supported by heavy retaining walls. The building consists of a square peristyle yard with Doric columns, some 6m higher than the stadium. The open-air central area was a palaestra with changing rooms to the west. On the north side, a long passage provided light and ventilation to the elaborate five rooms behind and to the space for a statue display. At the centre was a 9.5m by 6.5m room with marble columns and walls and seven wooden benches on stone supports; it was the core of the establishment. The inscribed names of the adolescents sent here to study and train mean that this was an ephebeum, a standard Greek institution meant to prepare the new elite. It was a Spartan regime for the young boys, at least going by the facilities on offer for bodily care, to which the other four rooms were devoted. Only cold baths were available (though the marble panelling and lion-head spout might have made the experience more bearable in winter).

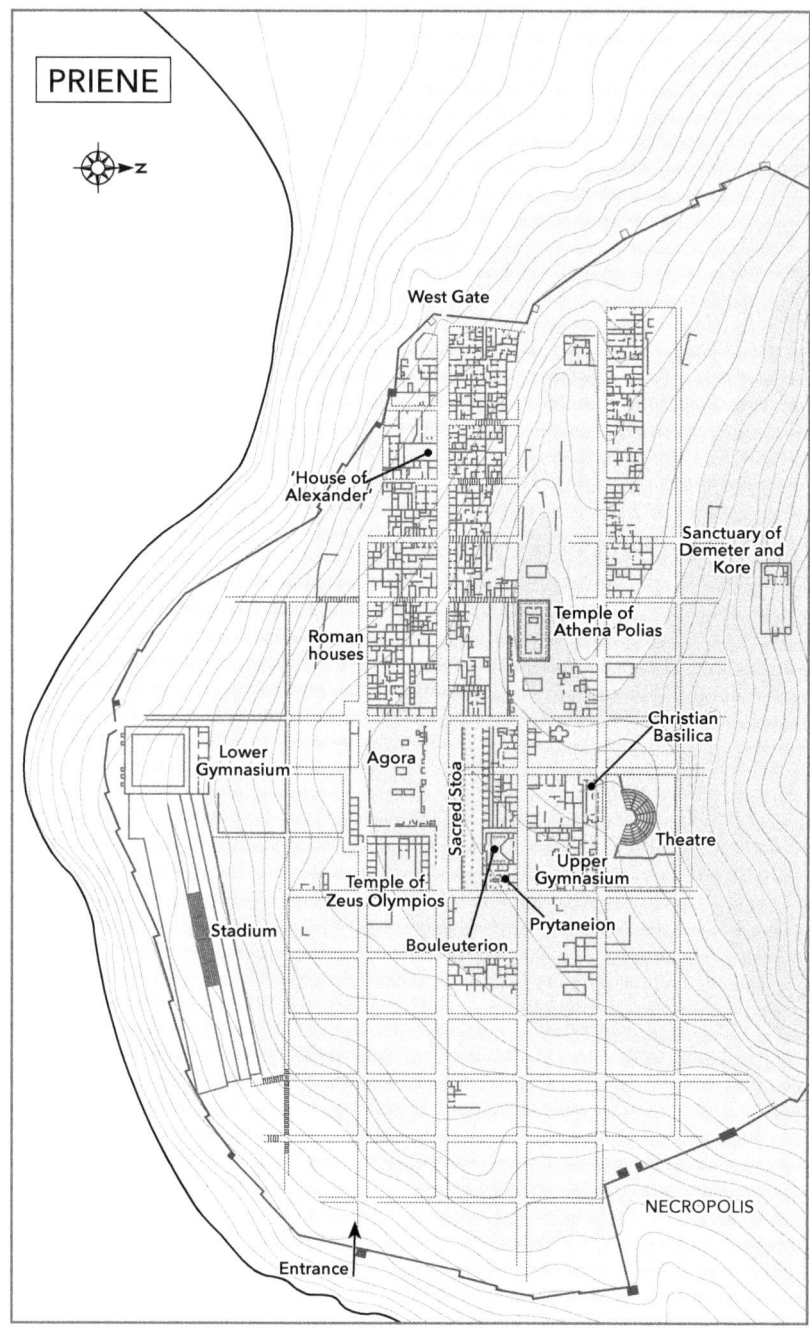

PRIENE

West Gate

'House of Alexander'

Sanctuary of Demeter and Kore

Roman houses

Temple of Athena Polias

Christian Basilica

Lower Gymnasium

Agora

Sacred Stoa

Upper Gymnasium

Theatre

Temple of Zeus Olympios

Stadium

Bouleuterion

Prytaneion

NECROPOLIS

Entrance

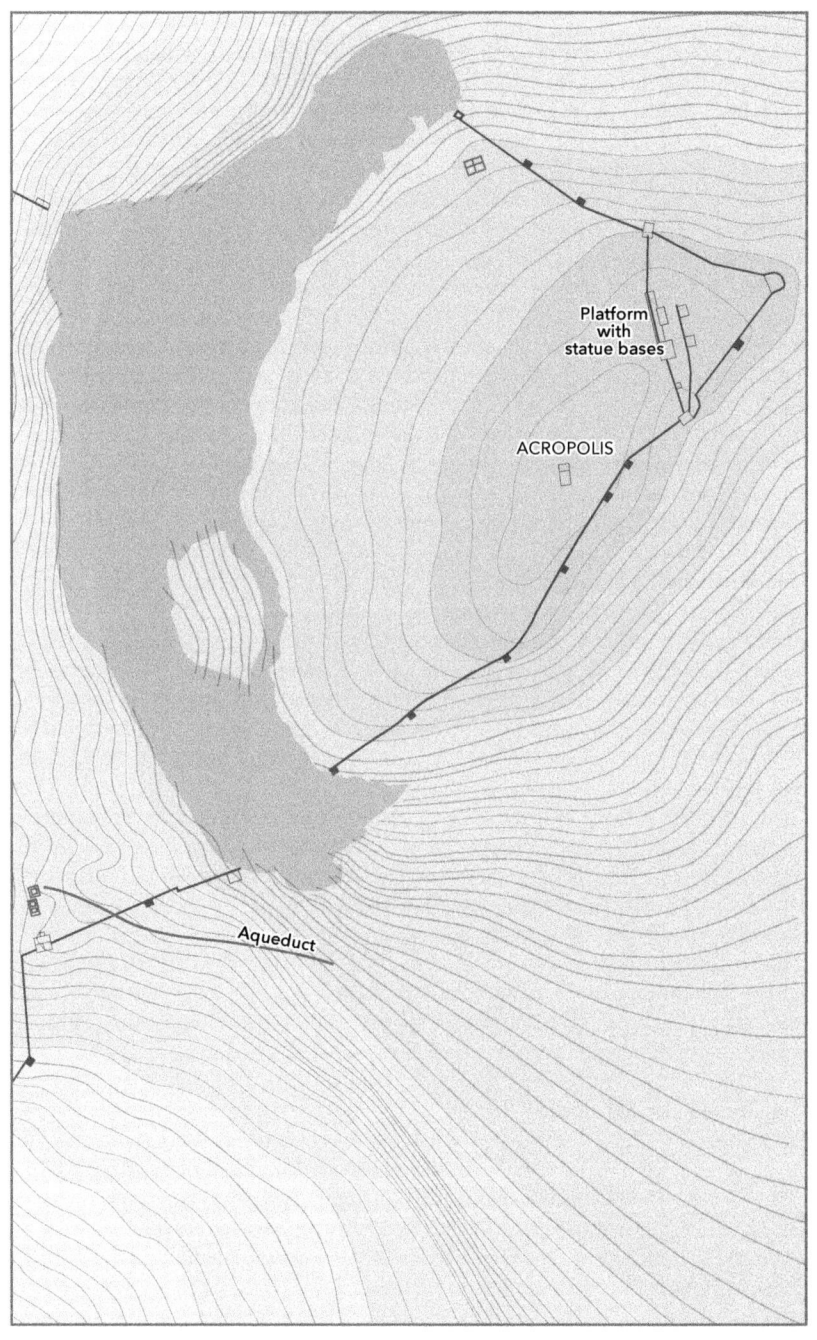

Platform with statue bases

ACROPOLIS

Aqueduct

The Agora area

The gymnasium was connected to the agora by a steep flight of steps. The agora played an important part in the life of the town since it housed the Temple of Zeus Olympios and gave access to the prytaneion and the bouleuterion. (The temple of Athena, Priene's main deity, was a separate focus to the northeast.) The massive Agora is dominated to the north by the 2nd-century BC **Sacred Stoa**. This held the city archives; here an inscription dated AD 10 marking the acceptance of the Julian Calendar was found. Below the stoa along the north side of the Agora there might have been commercial premises. Nothing much remains of the partially excavated **Temple of Zeus**, a small Ionic prostyle which was preceded, according to an inscription, by an earlier temple to Asclepius. Massive Byzantine defences were built on part of it. Proceed through the stoa (the gift of a Cappadocian king according to an inscription) to the **Prytaneion**, a courtyard structure possibly dating from the Roman period. The sacred flame was kept in the southeast room near the entrance. The **Bouleuterion**, a well-preserved small building, was found under a thick layer of charred tiles. Built in marble in the form of a rectangle open to the south, it could sit 640 people. A marble altar occupied the centre. The floor was of beaten earth. The tiled roof was supported on pilasters. Light came in from the south wall through windows and arches.

The 'House of Alexander'

Proceed to the west, where a number of Roman houses have been investigated. Originally each insula or block, the basic unit of the grid, was meant to have eight houses. As time progressed, social differentiation becomes apparent. In Roman times houses are less uniform and a single one can take up a whole insula. On the whole they conform to the standard plan of the peristyle house, the interior layout well-known from Pompeii. Decoration is muted, at best stucco imitating marble; latrines and baths are scarce.

The so-called 'House of Alexander' is on the way to the west gate. According to an inscription, the great man and benefactor of the city had his own cult centre in town: the Alexandreion. The 1899 excavations have failed to come up with a definitive answer. This clearly is no ordinary dwelling and the finding of a small marble statue of a young man looking like Alexander has prompted speculation. Could this be the house where he stayed in 334 BC? It seems that the house belonged to a religious society; ritual meals for 24 people could be served here. It was altered in the 2nd century BC when it was split into two halls, possibly corresponding to the worship of two heroes. In the Roman period there is no sign of any activity.

The Temple of Athena

The Temple of Athena Polias is to the northeast. This is the most ancient structure in Priene and the most prominent, especially now that five columns have been re-erected. In 1868 it was standing to a man's height but was unfortunately plundered as excavations began. Begun c. 350 BC, it was the work of Pythios, a Carian architect who had written a manual on temple building and the training of architects. Vitruvius much admired him; he hailed this work of his as an example of order and mathematical harmony, the epitome of felicitous proportions achieving a purity not marred by an intrusive decoration programme. The temple took a long time to finish; the west section was left incomplete for 200 years. The building was integrated into the city plan from the beginning but in a way it is separate, isolated on its massive 7m-high terrace, a beauty to behold. It was entered from the east and has been reconstructed as an Ionic peripteros some 37m by 20m with 12m columns, entirely built in Mycale stone on breccia foundations. Capitals inspired by the Ephesian Artemision find here their classical form. Inside, the 6.5m tall statue of Athena Polias, the gift of Orophernes, a Cappadocian ruler, stood on a marble-paved floor against a red and blue background. Opposite the entrance, an altar, like Pergamon's but much smaller, has been identified. From the extensively robbed remains it seems that it had a colonnade running all around and was connected to the temple by a stone paved surface. According to an inscription it was in due course dedicated to the cult of Augustus, meaning that Athena had to share with the imperial cult. In the 2nd century BC a tall stoa was constructed south of the temple, in a style comparable to that of the Sacred Stoa (*see above*). It hemmed in the temple, reducing its visibility, and blocked the direct line of sight uniting the temple with the altar of Zeus at the centre of the agora.

The Sanctuary of Demeter and Kore

The Sanctuary of Demeter and Kore is outside the planned town to the north, though still inside the walls. In a commanding position, it is the highest building in town. Among her many attributes, Demeter was also connected with death and therefore had no place in the heart of a city. The sanctuary sits in a 4th-century BC temenos some 45m by 17m. The entrance on the east side was marked by the statues of two priestesses, Timonassa and Nikeso. Nikeso is now in Berlin (the head and one arm are missing). The temple on the west side has an unusual plan, not Greek. It is oriented north–south and has none of the usual features. At the north end, a high stone bench held votive offerings and statues. Scholars are still poring over the rest. Outside, to the southeast, a square sacrificial pit lined with stone has been identified; it was covered with planks and would have received the blood from animal sacrifices, offered to propitiate the gods of the underworld. The altar set up at the east end of the temenos is Roman in date.

The worship of Demeter and Kore included the celebration of mysteries. It is difficult to know where this took place: the temple seems too small and unsuited for the purpose and yet the customary seating provisions are absent from the temenos.

The Theatre

Priene's Hellenistic Theatre (the cavea is the oldest in Asia) is on the way back to the entrance. The centre of the cultural and civic life, it would have been used for general assemblies for which the bouleuterion was too small; a water clock (of which the base has been found) was used to regulate the length of the speeches. The theatre is built on a slope and faces the plain. Originally it stretched much higher up the hill towards the acropolis. Much has been lost as the marble seats have been plundered to make staircases in private homes, leading to erosion of the cavea. At the bottom, the orchestra and the first row of seats were separated by a high wall from seats at the back. These special seats, five of which have backs, elegant arm rests and shaped legs, were for distinguished citizens; the altar in the middle was sacred to Dionysus, the patron of the arts. At the back, the populace used a passageway doubling as a drain to reach their seats. The presence of a number of square holes has been connected to the use of a cloth awning (velarium).

The evolution of performance practice, from Greek to Roman times, has been successfully investigated here. To start with, the action was in the orchestra, with the backdrop of a long, narrow building used as stage wings and also for storage and props. Later the stage moved to the roof of this building. To provide a backdrop, a second storey was added. At the same time the special seats for the officials had to move up to the fifth row of the cavea. The Romans further elaborated on this structure, adding depth to the scaena, which over time took on the familiar shape with columns, niches, arches and statues.

The Basilica

Priene's Christian basilica is south of the theatre and is dated to the 6th century, according to stylistic comparisons with the purpose-made Christian relief. The building, a three-aisled basilica 26m long, had an arched roof on pillars with a synthronon at the east end. The apse could not be seen from the outside as it was built into the adjacent baths. Most of the building material was spolia from the Athena Polias temple. Comparisons have been made with the contemporary church built in the inner court at Didyma and pulled down in the 1910s. But while the latter occupied a pagan space to mark the power of Christianity, at Priene the basilica respected the temenos of Athena and was built outside it.

The recent identification of a relief showing a menorah suggests the presence of Jews in the community but the synagogue is yet to be located with any certainty.

The Acropolis of Priene

For those brave enough to face the steep climb, there remains the Acropolis. It is best tackled from the east side along the line of the walls, past the aqueduct coming in from the north and which supplied Priene by gravity. You will be rewarded, after you negotiate the scarp, with fine stretches of the remains of walls and towers and magnificent views. You will be standing where Richard Chandler stood in the mid-18th century although, in his day, walls, gates and towers were all still standing. Towards the top of the acropolis, an artificial platform, 12m by 5m with statue bases cut in the rock, is thought to have had a ritual function for the commemoration of Telon, the mythical ancestor of Priene.

MAGNESIA ON THE MEANDER

Magnesia (*map B, 3; open 9–5; charge; on the main road, signposted*) is a place that seems to have had a fair amount of troubles in its longish life, though you would not imagine it now, in its present rural setting.

HISTORY OF MAGNESIA

According to Orhan Bingöl, Magnesia began as Mandrolyteia, in an unknown location on the north bank of the Meander, close to where the delta then was, at the mouth of the Lethaeus, a tributary of the main river. Apparently the founders were Aeolian Greeks and it is a fact that the city never became part of the Ionian League (*see p. 122*); it never felt Ionian. Trouble first occurred c. 700 BC with Lydia over one Magnes, a poet and a favourite of the Lydian ruler Gyges. The artist had not behaved well when in town (apparently singing poetry to some of the local women) and the population had responded in kind (the women's male relatives are said to have seized him, stripped him and shaved off his hair. The story appears in the Universal History of Nicholas of Damascus (1st century BC). His source appears to have been the 5th-century BC historian Xanthus of Lydia). When Lydia occupied Old Magnesia, as it was then, they paid for it. Later, after an unwelcome visit by the Cimmerians in 651 BC, Magnesia fell under Persian rule c. 530 BC. Magnesia's ambiguous position came to the fore in this period: not an Ionian city, but not quite Aeolian either (the Aeolians were more to the north and fading anyway). According to Strabo (*14,1,41*), writing much later, Magnesia was not even pure Greek (too coarse, too Asiatic).

In 464 BC Themistocles, the brilliant general and victor of the battle of Salamis that averted the Persian threat, was exiled by the Athenians. He found refuge here, a guest of the Persians. He was allocated an income and a female member of his family found employment as priestess in a temple dedicated to the cult of Cybele. However, as Thucydides (*1,138*) and other later historians relate, when asked by the Persians to take up arms against Greece, he declined and committed suicide. His funerary monument was erected in the agora. After falling under Spartan rule, Magnesia felt uncomfortably close to the Meander and its floods. The city was moved to a higher location, 3km north on Mt Thorax (Gümüş Dağ), close to the temple of Artemis Leucophryne, 'she of the white brow' and the sacred cave of Apollo Hylai, mentioned by Pausanias (*10,32,6*) and now believed to be near the village of Argavlı near Söke (a recently-discovered statue of Apollo is seen as supporting evidence; it is now in the museum in Aydın).

The new town, the one we can visit today, just off Route 525 south of Gümüşyeniköy, was laid out on a grid with the agora off centre, close to the temple of Artemis Leucophryne. After it submitted to Alexander the Great, Magnesia did well for itself, backing the up-and-coming Roman power in the Mithridatic Wars. It became a free city in 88 BC, overshadowed by nearby Ephesus, with whom relations were frequently tense, but still able to profit from the Meander trade route and flourishing agriculture. It remained unwalled until the time of Emperor Heraclius in the early 7th century, when it became necessary; the walled settlement was only a fraction of the Roman city. It was built with Hellenistic spolia. In the 10th century it was the home of St Lazarus, the wonder-worker of Mount Galesion, an ascetic who who spent a lot of his time on a pillar when he was not founding monasteries. The end of Magnesia is undocumented.

The ruins of Magnesia

Archaeological exploration started at the end of the 19th century when Karl Humann saw the theatre being demolished seat by seat and the blocks taken away to be sawn up to build a bridge. By then, the northern walls had been destroyed and the railway had cut through the west side of the site. Earlier on, 43 pieces of a panel frieze showing Greek warriors fighting the Amazons had been removed from the Temple of Artemis (presumably by Frenchmen since they can now be admired in the Louvre); the rest, to a total length of 175m, is in Istanbul and Berlin.

Excavations of the **Temple of Artemis Leucophryne** have established that the present building was erected on top of a 6th-century BC structure possibly dedicated to Cybele. It one was one of the major works of the architect Hermogenes, who also built the Temple of Dionysus at Teos; Ionic in style, it was a pseudo-dipteros with eight columns in front and fifteen at the sides. The above-mentioned frieze ran all the way round. The building was praised by Strabo and by Vitruvius, not so much for its size (a mere 41m by 67m, ranking third after Didyma and the Temple of Artemis in Ephesus), but for its harmonious proportions. It was completed to the west by an altar, 15m by 23m with a frieze representing the assembly of the gods. By its steps were two rows of 22 iron rings for tethering sacrificial animals. The complex was the centre of the Leucophryna, an international festival held every four years. Games played their part in it, but it was also an occasion for reminding everyone of the inviolable status of Magnesia. This had its foundation in a myth according to which Delphic Apollo had granted it special status. An inscription archive in the stoa of the **agora**, to the west of the temple, shows that this privilege was widely acknowledge in the Greek world.

The **Temple of Zeus Sosipolis**, 'Protector of the City', roughly in the middle of the agora and still in good shape in the 19th century, was later plundered for lime burning. It was the starting point of the solemn procession leading to the Temple of Artemis. The **stadium**, first mentioned in 1820, has recently been cleared. One of the best preserved in Anatolia, it was 185m long, U-shaped with tribunes, and had a seating capacity of 40,000. A toilet block complete with sewer channel, of the standard Roman sort and accommodating 32 people, was unearthed nearby.

The **theatre** (presently in large part covered for preservation) is not far from the agora on the west slopes of the hill. Built of local limestone and marble, it replaced an earlier Hellenistic structure. Adjustments were made in imperial times to turn it into an arena for water displays.

AYDIN & TRALLES

A short drive east of Magnesia is Aydın (*map B, 4*), a modern, bustling town that should not detain you too long (one of its past attractions—*see box*—is now no more), unless you want to visit the local museum on Batı Gazi Blv., which has finds from the region including Roman mosaics from Orthosia (near Yenipazar, to the east) displayed on screen and animated. Aydın, at an altitude of 60–80m, developed on an alluvial fan of the Tabakhane Suyu (the ancient Eudon), an affluent of the north bank of the Meander. The short stream starts at 1500m and follows a precipitous course at an incline of 20–30m/km. Over time it has eroded the mountain, creating the cone of conglomerate on which Aydın sits. However, the original settlement was higher up to the north, on the slopes of Mt Messogis (Kestane Dağ), on a plateau cut by cliffs and gorges. This settlement was known as Tralles.

FEASTING AND DANCING IN AYDIN

Aydın is a big town with a six-lane motorway (of which the locals are very proud) connecting it to İzmir. Its past incarnation, a kilometre away from the city centre in Tralles, is slowly being unravelled, though exploration has not yet divulged a great deal. So far we have a number of walls but no town plan. Modern Aydın, however, has a past of its own, more recent but very colourful, which Suraya Faroqui has exhumed from the city archives. Ottoman archives are a notoriously difficult resource to use. They are far from exhaustive, require knowledge of the Ottoman language (which is somewhat remote from modern Turkish) and they are written in the Arabic script. Moreover, they were not compiled for the purpose of recording the sort of social information we might be interested in today. The Kadi Registers in Aydın, however, record the local sale and manumission of slaves. A study of these records has shown that many of these people were black.

A document dated to the beginning of March 1576 goes a step further. In it the sultan requires his local administrators to avoid the disturbances of the previous year, when black slaves had come together for three days of revelry, disrupting public order. The revellers, it appears, had been bold enough to stand up to their slave masters and even 'encourage' them to allow their slaves to take part in the festivities while at the same time putting pressure on their black peers, both slaves and freedmen, to participate. We know little about the structure of the festival, but given the disparate origin of the slaves, it is unlikely that the choreography can be traced to any specific African festival. However, the organisers must have been familiar with urban ways because the festivities were presided over by an elected *kadi* (judge), a *bey* (provincial governor) and a *kethüda* (guild official). According to Suraya Faroqui, the set-up is reminiscent of European medieval fairs with their kings, queens and abbots. Alternatively, though, it might refer to the events in Cairo of 1446, when 500 or so black slaves rebelled and set up a miniature court outside the city. They gave themselves all the trappings of the ruling Mamluks, with a sultan, a vizier and provincial governors, and for a while made a living assaulting caravans. They were defeated by internal dissension.

We know that in Aydın there was dancing and feasting (and perhaps the trouble originated in the procurement of food). Women do not appear to have participated, otherwise there would probably have been accusations of immorality. Other places like İzmir and Istanbul have records of black festivals. One, the Feast of the Calf, incorporated some features of the Kurban Bayramı, the Feast of the Sacrifice, a very important Muslim holiday. But both İzmir and Istanbul were by this date cosmopolitan places, with harbours open to the world. It comes as much more of a surprise (possibly to the sultan as well as to us) that things of this sort should have been going on in the depths of the Meander Valley.

TRALLES: THE HISTORY
Tradition has Tralles as a foundation by Greek colonists from Argos or from Thrace, though recently unearthed Carian inscriptions have suggested to I.J. Adiego a Carian presence. Tralles is first mentioned in the *Anabasis* (*1,4,8*) as the place where Cyrus the Younger held hostage the wife and the children of a disloyal Greek commander. The town followed the usual development from Hellenistic to Roman city—and just in time, it seems, since the emperor Augustus offered generous financial aid when earthquake struck in 27 BC. He was at the time busy in Spain; even so, he managed to send out a fact-finding committee and, in due course, enough money. Out of gratitude Tralles renamed itself Caesarea. It developed into a well-established centre of the arts. On of its inhabitants whose name we know is Seikilos, a musician who had a tombstone erected for his wife Euterpe, with lyrics and music to go with it. This is the earliest example of Greek musical notation and has been dated to the period 200 BC –AD 100. The stone has had an eventful life; today it can be seen in the National Museum of Denmark in Copenhagen. Recently various arrangements of the funeral song have been made—some are available on CD—but unfortunately it is very brief: barely four lines long and lasts 30 seconds.

At the time of Hadrian, Phlegon, one of his freedmen originally from Tralles, became a historian: from his prolific output only the 'Book of Wonders' partially survives. A compilation of ghost stories, including tales of pregnant men, giants and sex changes, it was studiously copied by the amanuenses and finally went into print in 1568 in Greek and was promptly translated into French. It is said to have inspired the modern Gothic movement. Later still Tralles provided Anthemius, one of the architects of Hagia Sophia in Istanbul.

Late antique Tralles was probably a city in decline since the emperor Constantine felt free to remove statues for his hippodrome in Constantinople. Glassworking seem to have been an important local industry. When Christianity arrived, it was of the heretical variety. Monophysites concentrated here and on Mt Messogis a temple was replaced by a huge monastery. Tralles was not poor but it must have foundered at some point, since information about it resurfaces only much later.

In 1280, at the time of the refoundation of Tralles in the wake of the Battle of Manzikert and the ensuing troubles, Andronicus II, then a junior Byzantine emperor residing in the provinces, had a look at the plateau and its imposing ruins and decided it would make a good defensive position for the Greek population harassed by the Türkmen in search of winter pastures. His idea turned out to be a very bad one, since Tralles had relied for its water supply on the 4th-century aqueduct. When that was damaged by the besieging Menteşe, the new town had to depend for water on access to the Meander, which at the time was off limits to them. According to the contemporary historian Pachimeres, 10,000 of the 36,000 settlers died; the rest were enslaved and deported.

After the demise of Tralles a new town, first called Güzelhisar and later Aydın, after the Aydınid dynasty, developed lower down. In the mid-14th century, Genoese merchants were still doing business there. Aydın was eventually incorporated into the expanding Ottoman dominion.

The ruins of Tralles

The presence of ruins at Tralles (*open 8–5; free*) was long known to be a fact: Richard Pococke in the 18th century counted 50 rows of seats in the theatre and saw a double portico and various other buildings. Some of those stones ended up in Bey Cami in Aydın. Plundering, however, began in earnest in the 1840s with a massive recutting of friezes and reliefs to use as tombstones. The agora was devastated. Later in 1856–66, a lot of building stone was lost to the Smyrna–Aydın railway and, in due course, to reconstruction work following the 1892 earthquake. In more recent times, the whole area was in the hands of the military, which was a form of protection in a way, until they started digging (*see below*). Now they have moved out but have not cleared the whole area.

These days Tralles is marketed as a 'little Ephesus', which is certainly an overstatement as there is no known plan of the city and, so far as one can tell, no intention to piece one together. The ruins are presented as unrelated stumps in a beautiful setting. The breathtaking views over the Meander Valley and beyond, and the lush vegetation, are possibly the best things that Tralles has to offer.

The **Üç Gözler** ('Three Eyes', meaning three arches) will catch your attention first: it is part of a late 3rd-century gymnasium, probably the bath house, to judge by the number of terracotta pipes around. Nearby are the latrines, which could accommodate 65 people, and remains of the **colonnaded street** with monolithic marble columns; shops in the vicinity have been partly rebuilt and so has the arsenal. At the foot of the acropolis hill to the northeast are the theatre and the stadium. In the **theatre**, 150m across and originally all of marble, one of the first Hellenistic theatres with a decorated proscenium (the friezes are now in Istanbul and Berlin), German excavators in 1888 discovered a T-shaped tunnel over 2m below the orchestra, identified as a Charonian tunnel, a device allowing actors to stage otherwordly appearances. It was obliterated in 1946 by the military, when they dug a broad trench across it.

EAST OF AYDIN

Tralles marks a break in the urban development of the Meander Valley in antiquity. Hellenistic and Roman rulers could be relied on to bring a civilised—in other words, 'urban'—way of life to the deep interior but here, just as in nearby Pisidia, a graveyard of towns and good intentions, it did not last. Even those settlements that were set up to be metropolises, such as Hierapolis and Aphrodisias, did not survive long after the demise of their main backer, the emperor, a million miles away. Hierapolis tried to reinvent itself as a Christian pilgrimage centre but even St Philip, whichever saint of that name he may have been, proved ineffectual at stopping earthquakes and controlling unruly waters. Theses cities, the object of long and sustained archaeological excavations, have now come back to life as grade one tourist attractions. Of the other smaller centres, only Nysa has been partially investigated. As for Orthosia (at Donduran Köyü near Yenipazar), Harpasa (signposted from Esenköy; it is worth going that far to have a look at Arpaz Kalesi) and Mastaura (on the way to Beydağ from Nazilli, near Bozkurt), they are known from sources and a handful of coins. There are scattered remains, though; you might like to explore among the olive groves.

NYSA

Situated 3km due north of Sultanhisar, today in a fine rural setting, Nysa (*map B, 4*) had a reputation as a centre of learning in the mid 1st century BC, when the young Strabo studied there. Amasya, in the throes of the Mithridatic Wars, was probably not safe at the time, though the fame of the school of rhetoric and the presence of celebrated grammarians and Stoic philosophers may also have played a role. In Book 14, Strabo gives a vivid description of the town as it was then, the result of a Hellenistic amalgamation of two or three settlements. It would seem that Nysa flourished in the Roman period, when it minted its own coins and sent a couple of its sons to Rome as senators. The land was fertile and the town itself was on the main east–west route, though that later shifted south. Christianity certainly reached Nysa, but so did the Arabs and their raids spelled the beginning of the end for the town. Traces of later occupation, which is said to reach in places into the 13th century, were obliterated by the first excavators. They came in the early 1900s and found ruins that were quite shallow and inviting. What we see today is a layout of the city centre that Strabo would have known. The buildings at any rate are in the same place, though they were restored and improved in later times.

Nysa lies on the lower slopes of Mt Mesogis, the eastern reaches of the Aydın Dağları, in an endless olive grove cut by many ravines. It occupies a challenging position across one of them, a site which was used very creatively by the ancient town planners with the help of some clever engineering. The town is said to be planned on an orthogonal grid. City walls have not been yet traced by the Turkish excavators, who have now been exploring Nysa systematically since the 1990s.

Taking the road to the north into the mountains from the west edge of Sultanhisar, you arrive, after a couple of kilometres, in the area of the **gymnasium**, dated to the 2nd century AD. It is a large structure (no public access) with a cistern and a palaestra surrounded by vaulted pillars decorated with theatre masks. Somewhat absent-mindedly, the excavators have built their dig house in the northeast corner of the known perimeter of the feature. To the north you can see the ruins of the **library**, dated to AD 130 (about the time that Celsus had his erected in Ephesus; it may replace an earlier building. Like Celsus' it houses the sarcophagus of the patron. Of the building, which was also used for meetings and official ceremonies, only part remains, on two storeys with niches lined in marble and stucco decoration where the scrolls would have been. There are no traces of an eye-catching façade.

The **stadium**, now a ruin, occupied the ravine. The structure, a narrow U shape, is over 250m long. It straddles a seasonal stream, then called the Thebaites, now the Çakırcak Çayı. Over time, the bottom has collapsed, making the stadium and the seats at the sides difficult to make out. The best place to see rows of seats is at the north end. At both ends of the stadium the ravine was spanned by a bridge. The north bridge continued east in a **colonnaded street** which has now been excavated and partly re-erected over 100m; according to the excavators this was the main east–west axis of the city. Further north, the **theatre** sits in a natural hollow with the ravine continuing to the east; graffiti show that the theatre was still used in the 6th–7th centuries. With an estimated capacity of 10,000, it is a fine structure which has now been fully exposed. Much of the skene has been preserved, part of it *in situ*. The reconstruction shows a three-storey extravaganza of columns, niches, aediculae and statuary to a total height of over 25m. It is unfortunate that the podium frieze, with scenes of the life of Dionysus and which was discovered intact, has been recently defaced.

To the east of the theatre is another **Roman bridge**. It spans the ravine and the stream, extending for quite a way and creating a platform over which the modern road runs. The area is supported by an impressive two-tier substructure in mortared stone. The idea was the same as in Pergamon, where the Selinus, cutting across the temenos of the Kızıl Avlu, had to be dealt with. Here you can walk along the remaining 150m of the vaulted 'tunnel' (provided the Çakırcak Çayı is dry). The modern road next cuts across a **civil basilica**, identified when the road was enlarged; it is believed that the forum was to the east. The **bouleuterion** can be reached by heading cross-country to the south. This small assembly room, with a capacity of 700, was rebuilt in the 2nd century with a generous contribution from a wealthy local, Sextus Antoninus Pythodoros, in memory of his mother. The reconstruction shows a semicircle with twelve rows of seats, set in a square building 27m by 23m covered with a tiled roof supported on a wooden frame. The south wall on the inside was very elaborately conceived, with statues, niches, columns, bucrania reliefs, a true theatre skene fronted by the circular floor space with an opus sectile pattern. On the outside, beyond the paved street, stood a propylon with Corinthian columns. The complex was bordered to the south by a portico and to the east by a row of shops, both with elaborate mosaic floors. The **agora** to the east is late Hellenistic with subsequent modifications. The square structure 113m by 150m was surrounded by a colonnade (double on the north and east sides) with shops all around.

ACHARACA

Not far from Nysa to the west at Salavatlı (due north on a secondary road between Kösk and Sultanhisar) was another landmark mentioned by Strabo (14,1,44): Acharaca. He clearly did not occupy all his mornings with rhetoric and all his afternoons with grammar, but as a budding geographer made the time to get around. More than one place styles itself as the entry to the Underworld (the Charonium) and by implication as the place where Pluto ravished Kore (Persephone), to the despair and fury of her mother. Places with a strong sulphurous smell, such as the Plutonium at Hierapolis, stood a fair chance of being listed as a contender. At Salavatlı, the recent find of a long inscription stating that it was placed originally in the temple of Pluto and Kore has now settled the location of Acharaca. The precise whereabouts of the opening to the Underworld have not been identified. It may have been in a cave, now collapsed. The local river, the appropriately-named Sarı Su (yellow stream), is full of sulphur; the smell is in the air. Architectural remains of a temple have been found on the river's east bank. The natural attributes of this spot led to the development of a cult centred on healing (though sulphur emanations can be deadly) and on the celebration of the Theogamia festival commemorating the union of Pluto and Kore, in which Nysa may have played a part. The addition of Byzantine architectural elements to the temple suggests that it may have become a Christian church. Eventually, however, neither Nysa nor Acharaca were able reinvent themselves as places with a relevant role to play in a world with different values.

PAMUKKALE & HIERAPOLIS

North of Denizli, Pamukkale (*map C, 3*), the 'cotton castle', a UNESCO World Heritage Site rising from the northern bank of the Lycus (Çürüksu), is a stunning sight; try to experience it first from a good distance, to see it towering in its magnificence, with the ruins of Hierapolis on top and the stark white travertine on the slope, the distance hiding the problems that beset it. There are plenty of these, as would be the case for any beauty spot, the result of a rare combination of ecological events, which receives over 2 million visitors a year.

Geologically Pamukkale is young. The building up of its calcite plateau and later of its memorable pools, began tens of thousands of years ago, a combination of the earth moving, the crust fissuring and water percolating. Earthquakes are nothing new in the Anatolian peninsula, where tectonic plates meet and collide with disastrous results at times. Here, as the Eurasian and the African plates meet, the Anatolian Plate, squeezed between the two, is forever escaping west, stretching the crust. Because the area is the meeting point (at Sarayköy, a few kilometres to the west) of four grabens (Gediz, Menderes, Küçük Menderes and Lykus), the crust is particularly thin and has been fractured. The Pamukkale Fault stretches some 30km to the northwest to Buldan; with it comes a network of anatomising fissures giving the percolating water access to the mantle and its high temperature. This same water re-emerges some 50 years later, still warm (35–100°C) and charged with all the minerals it has accumulated during its time underground by dissolving whatever rock formation it made its way through, be it marble, limestone, conglomerates or recent alluvium. On contact with the atmosphere the water cools, sheds its load of gases, and deposits a carbonated rock, soft at first but which hardens over time. This is the travertine, which is stark white at Pamukkale while at Karayıt close by, it has a red tinge because of the prevalence of oxides. Much later in historical times, possibly when the earth once again shook in the 7th century AD, the travertine mound on which Hierapolis sits was fractured. The Hierapolis Fault runs approximately along the main street of the archaeological site, the Plateia. With that event water circulation was disrupted and much of the archaeology was buried under a layer of travertine, in places two metres thick.

This background makes Pamukkale ecologically a very sensitive and volatile area, often at odds with the requirements of modern mass tourism and other economic imperatives. In the 1960s a number of hotels were built on the ridge overlooking the pools on the slope. They tapped the water of the natural hot springs for their own swimming pools, starving the travertine basins below which promptly started turning grey with algae. The hotels were eventually demolished c. 2000 with the exception of one, run by the Denizli municipality. Its swimming pool is the flooded civic agora of Hierapolis, with its fallen capitals and columns: microbial growth and mechanical damage clearly show environmental degradation. It is a fact that while Roman Hierapolis had a sewer system running beneath the Plateia in the 1st century AD, the system today is far less well organised, with makeshift cesspools that readily leak, thus polluting the water. Past mistakes such as diverting the spring water, covering the archaeology with tarmac roads, have now been remedied but much remains to be done. The use of replica pools alongside the real ones is a very short-term solution since bathers will use soaps and creams and carry their own micro-organisms with them, which will eventually find their way into the water system and pollute it. Removing wheeled traffic from the walled precinct of Hierapolis is also a step in the right direction. Unfortunately such good intentions are negated by the plans to fill the Severan theatre (*see below*) with thousands of people for music festivals twice a year. No amount of restoration work on an ancient structure can handle that impact.

The main trouble is that there is no figure for the carrying capacity of Pamukkale and Hierapolis. Environmental plans, studies and assessments have come thick and fast but there seems to be no agreement on what intake of visitors this unique site can tolerate without damage: conflicting interests are too powerful. Pamukkale village has, at the latest count, 27 hotels to fill. The prospect that the number of visitors may have to be limited is not something anyone apparently wants to think about. Responsibilities on the ground are shared between different bodies, entailing fragmentation and lack of an overall vision, while rules are not consistently enforced.

A HISTORICAL OUTLINE

Archaeological investigation has not so far shown signs of occupation prior to the Hellenistic period. The very same reasons that prompted the Hellenistic development would have been relevant earlier on; evidence may have been obliterated by the later works. First and foremost, the site is on a trade route linking Lydia and Phrygia: the north gate leads to Sardes, the south gate to Laodiceia. In addition the water, abundant and warm, would easily have fostered a culture of healing that is still alive today. The water's mineral content varies from spring to spring. Some is toxic, so one should be careful; the spa waters (both for drinking and bathing), however, are advertised as being beneficial for a long list of ailments. And there is yet another legacy of Pamukkale's tormented geology: the chasm in the middle of the plateau where the Romans in due course built a temple to Pluto and Kore. It exudes a distinct smell of sulphur and made claim to be yet another entrance to the Underworld. It is very likely that in ancient times there was some form of cult associated with this very spot.

The founding of a city here, in the 2nd century BC or earlier, was part of the Hellenistic drive to harness the landscape. The name Hierapolis (though some would like to attribute it to the presumed sanctity of the place) may be a tribute to Hiera, the Amazon wife of Telephos, the mythical founder of Pergamon. That would make Hierapolis a Pergamene foundation. However, there are other contenders, such as the Seleucids. Little is known of Hellenistic Hierapolis apart from some tumuli in the north necropolis and industrial installations that produced Pergamene style pottery, preserved under the north agora. Its size was roughly that of the Byzantine town. The presence of a mystery cult of Dionysos Kathegemon has been mooted. As Peter Thonemann puts it, the unstable hydrography would have provided fertile ground for the generation of myths, both pagan and later Christian, induced by a sort of waterborne anxiety.

When it came into Roman hands in the late 1st century BC, Hierapolis was remodelled, with the construction of a theatre, a temple to Apollo and an agora in the centre of town, as well as a stoa and a gymnasium. The orthogonal grid (retrieved from satellite images and observations on the ground) may have been laid out at this time. Shortly afterwards, following an earthquake in AD 60, the main axis of the town was widened and monumentalised. To the north, a new commercial agora was backed by a second theatre on the eastern slopes. Large public baths went up. An aqueduct coming in from the east improved the water supply. Not all of this was provided by local money: showcasing cities was something Roman emperors were keen on during periods of peace and prosperity, when barbarian incursions were not an immediate threat At the centre of a prosperous agricultural and wine-producing region, with a thriving weaving and dyeing industry (a gift of the mineralised water), blessed with a good supply of building stone, with good trade and a steady influx of pilgrims (either keen to improve their health, to attend the Pythian games or to consult the oracle), Hierapolis, still unwalled and with a substantial Jewish community (attested by inscriptions and epitaphs) did very well.

In due course, Christianity arrived, resulting in the abandonment of the Temple of Apollo in the 5th–6th century. The lime kilns were put to work and Christian basilicas went up. The walling of the city dates to the 4th–5th century, but though walls were thrown up in a hurry and reduced the size of the city both at the north and the south ends, times were still very good. In 370 Hierapolis was the residence of Emperor Valens; shortly afterwards, the St Philip Martyrion complex to the east of town offered a new focus to Christian pilgrims. Decay set in in the mid-6th century when structures went up in flames and were not rebuilt (e.g. the main building in the above-mentioned complex) and when the urban grid was encroached upon. The Persians, who visited in 616 (and the Arabs in due course), cannot have helped, nor did the earthquake that followed. It created the Hierapolis Fault and dislocated the geology. The spring that had created the travertine deposits on which Hierapolis sits, believed to be somewhere in the vicinity of the theatre in the centre of town, was disrupted and water started flowing on the surface uncontrolled, depositing travertine. The resurgence of Ephesus in the 10th–11th century kept trade going but the town by this time was in terminal decline. The Crusaders described it as a 'destroyed city' in 1190. By 1204 it was lost to the Seljuk ruler Gıyaseddin Keyhüsrev I, the 'Shadow of God on Earth'. Oil presses suggest a lingering interest in agriculture. Ongoing archaeological excavations, in the hands of an Italian team, began in 1957.

A walk through Hierapolis

You can approach Hierapolis (*open Nov–March 6am–6.30pm, April–Oct 6am–midnight; charge*) from the north or from the south by road; alternatively it is possible to walk uphill from the village of Pamukkale through the artificial pools, but here you have to proceed barefoot and the loose gravel can be a nuisance. Whichever way, there is a fair amount of walking involved, so do not pick a very hot day.

The Byzantine Gate

Starting from the south entrance, you will come into the site through the **Byzantine Gate**, which has a good stretch of city wall on either side. This was buried deep in concretions, created by the opening of the Hierapolis Fault in the 7th century, and has therefore survived well, though it had to be freed using pneumatic drills. The course of the wall can be followed on the east and north sides, while it is lost to the west, probably the result of the building of the hotels in the 1960s.

You are now on the **Plateia**, the main axis of the town, a great project of Sextus Iulius Frontinus when he was proconsul of Asia and resided in Ephesus. A former senator and a man of vision, Frontinus epitomises the typical Roman administrator at a time when the empire was on the ascendant and money apparently plentiful. Not only did he reorganise the region's road network (as proven by the inscribed milestones) but he also enlarged the city.

Around the Museum

Four hundred metres on along the Plateia is a large **church** (Chiesa a Pilastri), dated approximately to the 6th century. It would have had a vaulted roof supported by pilasters of two different sizes and divided into a nave and two aisles. The Hierapolis Fault runs longitudinally through it. The **Civic Agora** lies immediately afterwards to the west. This, the main meeting point of the ancient town (now a swimming pool; *open Nov–March 8–5.30, April–Oct 8–7.30; charge*) has not yet been fully explored. It was a colonnaded rectangle on two storeys (Ionic below and Corinthian above), some 141m by 88m and dated to the early 1st century AD. Beyond it to the west is the **Hierapolis Archaeological Museum** (*open summer Tues–Sun 8.30–7; winter 8.30–5.30; charge*), originally a huge Roman thermal complex dated to the 2nd century and over time buried under a four-metre blanket of medieval building. Built mainly in travertine with occasional marble facing and naturalistic stucco decoration, it also had a sizeable palaestra. The vaulted ceilings were of travertine. The 4th-century earthquake damage was repaired by scavenging columns from the nearby Temple of Apollo, painting dados to imitate marble instead of using marble facing and rebuilding the vaulting in brick rather than stone. This structure collapsed in the next earthquake. A Byzantine tower went up. However, it was still in use in the 13th–14th century when the former bathing complex was occupied by well-to-do Seljuks—at least according to the imported pottery and the coinage they left behind. The museum has a fine collection of statuary and reliefs from the town and the surrounding area.

Around the Temple of Apollo

Opposite the museum are the remains of the Temple of Apollo and ancillary buildings. They were fronted on the Plateia by a **monumental fountain** or nymphaeum, for ritual ablutions prior to entering the sacred space; it is dated to the 3rd century, possibly a replacement of an earlier fountain. It was quite a grand construction, with a basin measuring 21m by 11m fronted by a wide staircase. The backdrop was a two-storey structure built into the wall of the temple precinct and featuring five exedrae, niches, columns and statuary. An Amazon frieze halfway up ran fo the entire length.

The **Temple of Apollo** complex, dated to the early 1st century AD, consisted of three buildings straddling a natural deep crack in the rock, surrounded by a marble colonnade part of which has been re-erected. Systematic dismantling and plundering of the area started in 5th century; later, after the opening of the Hierapolis Fault, it was buried under concretions. The Temple of Apollo was the central building, with six Ionic columns at the front (according to the coins) and a high podium. To the north stood a temple to Pluto and Kore, guarded by the images of Cerberus and of a snake. The mysterious goings-on in the **Plutonium** to the south, which gave off foul smells and deadly gases, were described by various authors in antiquity, from Strabo to the physician Asclepiodotus, who bravely ventured into the hypogeum until he found a stream that he could not cross. This was an entrance to the Underworld and sacred to Pluto. Modern exploration has shown that after crossing a small, vaulted, stone-paved chamber, one would have reached a gap at the back through which one could see a deep cleft in the rock with a fast-running stream. All this is now blocked

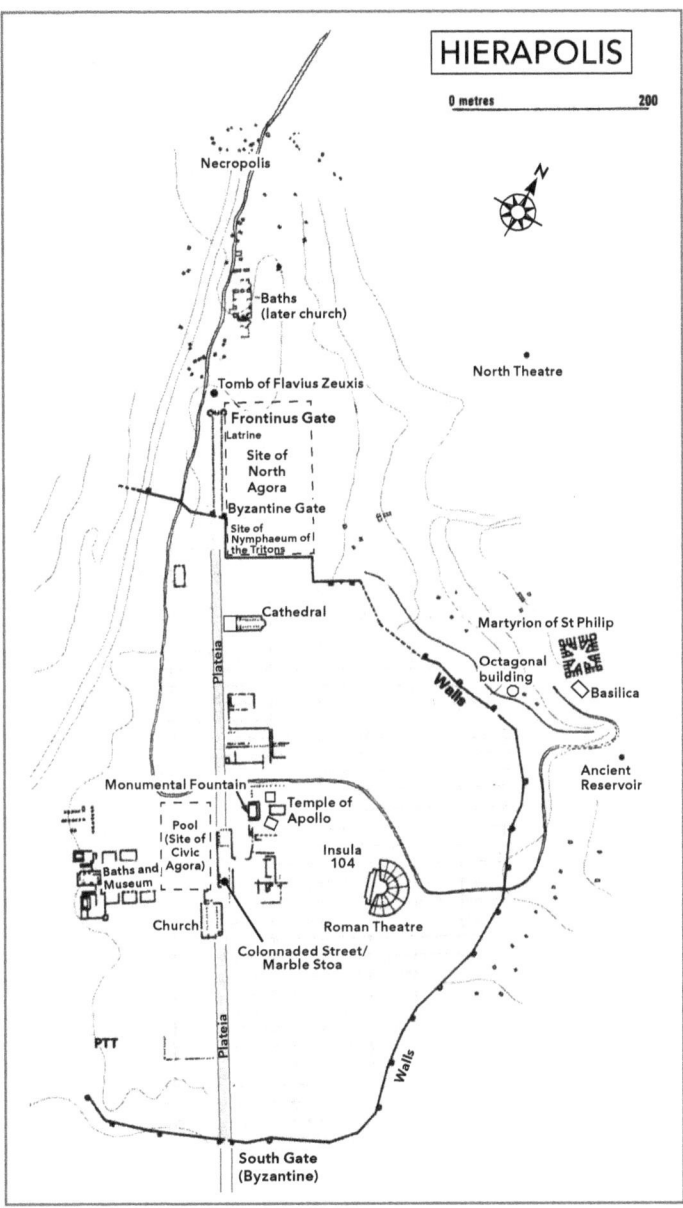

HIERAPOLIS

0 metres — 200

Necropolis

Baths
(later church)

North Theatre

Tomb of Flavius Zeuxis

Frontinus Gate

Latrine

Site of
North
Agora

Byzantine Gate

Site of
Nymphaeum of
the Tritons

Cathedral

Martyrion of St Philip

Octagonal
building

Basilica

Plateia

Walls

Ancient
Reservoir

Monumental Fountain

Temple of
Apollo

Pool
(Site of
Civic
Agora)

Insula
104

Baths and
Museum

Church

Roman Theatre

Colonnaded Street/
Marble Stoa

PTT

Plateia

Walls

South Gate
(Byzantine)

up and off limits to visitors. Even so, the gases (carbon dioxide in high concentrations with sulphur and other noxious fumes) escaping through the purpose-built vents in the temple structure, still catch the throat and makes the eyes smart.

The cult is certainly older than the building (which is dated to the 3rd century) would suggest. Apollo was worshipped here as Apollo Lairbenus, a Phrygian deity whose mother Cybele was equated to Leto, Apollo's mother. In other words, we are dealing with an ancient Anatolian cult which over time was appropriated as a tourist asset by the Roman administration. The oracular function rested with a number of deities, including Apollo, Pluto and Poseidon. Those who officiated were the castrated priests of Cybele, the Galli from Pessinus (*see Blue Guide Central Anatolia*). They could go into the Plutonium and re-emerge unharmed if they held their breath for long enough.

Exploration of the immediate surroundings suggests that near the entrance to the Plutonium were a small circular temple, a water feature and a viewing stand from which to follow proceedings (which may have involved a liberal use of fire, at least to judge by the abundant charcoal recovered in the pits). Ritual sacrifice by gassing, of large animals like bulls, is also a possibility. Oracular pronouncements were probably uttered by the priests, in a trance-like state induced by spending just enough time underground.

In the immediate vicinity, towards the theatre, is **Insula 104**, one of the few domestic quarters investigated at Hierapolis. It contained a couple of two-storey high-status dwellings, centred around a courtyard with frescoes, opus sectile floors, red breccia and banded travertine columns, and a latrine paved with mosaics. After damage in the 4th century, the buildings were restructured as storage space and workshops for making small objects out of stucco and marble chippings; the complex was eventually destroyed in the 7th-century earthquake. By then building techniques had deteriorated, with pisé (compacted earth) being used for the upper storey. Later developments show that the area, like the rest of town, became rural.

The Roman Theatre

The Roman Theatre is set directly on a rocky slope, with some substructures at the top end to complete the cavea. It does not fit into the grid but it is tilted to face the temple complex, with which it was strongly connected. Every four years the Pythian Games were held here, which was probably the main reason for building a theatre here, especially considering that Hierapolis already had one, Hellenistic in date, to the north (*see below*); obviously a more central location with a closer connection to the temple was deemed beneficial. The original structure was probably Augustan, with a row of marble seats for distinguished guests at orchestra level. At the time of Severus, the seating pattern was replanned, elevating the spectators 1.5m higher, out of the reach of wild beasts. The orchestra was reduced in size; the skene and stage were made of marble and travertine. The royal box higher up was enlarged. Further alterations were made in the 4th century to enable water performances to take place. The capacity has been estimated at 12,000–15,000. After a ban on theatre performances in the 6th century, the structure, damaged by earthquakes, was pillaged and the supporting vaults were taken over by squatters. On the whole, the quality of the building material (travertine and locally-sourced marble, with some use of the Dokimaion variety, sourced a good distance away) is not very high while the workmanship is inferior to that found in Nysa and Aphrodisias. That said, a large proportion of the collapsed skene has been retrieved and reconstructed on paper, indicating that it must have provided a stunning backdrop to the action. It was three storeys high with a profusion of reliefs and the usual array of podia, columns, niches, aediculae and statuary centred around two main themes: the Roman imperial family and the appropriation of a Greek past through an iconography rich in Greek mythology. It would certainly have been a way for the town to ingratiate itself with the emperor, by showing that its Anatolian baggage had been shed. The structure you visit now has been heavily restored, with reinforced concrete and the insertion of steel bars to cope with the demands of its present use as a venue for grand public performances.

Upper Plateia and beyond the Byzantine Gate

Return to the Plateia and continue north to the **Cathedral**, which was connected to the main street by an atrium flanked by two wings. The church itself (its ground plan well visible from the air or Google Earth) had a nave and two aisles and the central nave was overlooked on either side by a gallery with Ionic arcades. In the apse stood a synthronon with seven steps. The style is of the mid-5th–6th century. It had a baptistery, with red breccia columns, to the south. It was probably abandoned after the 7th century, following the earthquake. Spolia from it were used to build a high-status grave in the grounds immediately to the south. The structure demonstrates a survival of ancient pagan customs since it has libation conduits enabling mourners to share funerary banquets with the deceased.

Further north you reach the edge of the Byzantine walls. The **Nymphaeum of the Tritons**, a late Severan structure, stood just past the corner of the wall. It was built in local stone and against the back wall of the north agora. The basin was 57m long and 4.7m deep with a marble balustrade in front shaped with exedrae. At the back stood a two-storey extravaganza of columns, niches and statues with a frieze of nymphs, musical tritons, river gods and Amazons running halfway up. It collapsed in the 4th century, a fair amount of it into the basin.

Beyond the Byzantine Gate are the **latrines**, part of a development willed by Frontinus when he became proconsul of Asia. He set about making the Plateia the commercial heart of the town by widening it to 9m and adding pavements on either side, over two metres in depth; beneath the street a cloaca ran all the way to the south gate, fed by conduits from the side streets. In this north section evidence shows that the Plateia was lined on either side by pilasters and engaged half columns. The intervening space was built up to create shops and workshops. The 27m long latrine complex, whose monolithic columns supported a travertine roof, was a natural addition to the scheme.

The **Frontinus Gate**, a triple archway flanked by two massive towers, marked the end of the Plateia. It bore two inscriptions, in Latin and in Greek, giving the name of the sponsor, a freedman of the emperor Domitian, and of the proconsul Frontinus. In due course the name of Domitian was chiselled away. To the east is a large space (170m by 280m) marking the **site of the North Agora**, dated to the 2nd century AD and built on top of a necropolis and a Hellenistic industrial development after the ground was levelled. Its function is unclear. The central area was not paved, suggesting it may have been used for sporting events, while around three sides ran a wide stoa with a double colonnade and polychrome marbles and friezes. Its east side had a basilica with an elaborate, two-storey façade with pillars linked by elegant arches; it was entered halfway along its length via a massive propylon. After earthquake damage in the 4th century, the agora was abandoned and quarried for stone and lime. Over time it was covered by a 3m thick blanket of alluvium, brought by a torrent coming in from the southeast.

Frontinus' development was carried out at the expense of the necropolis, still in use in the early 1st century AD as the Tomba Bella, a heroön, testifies. It was later incorporated in a large peristyle town house. The 1st-century AD **Tomb of Flavius Zeuxis**, a merchant who made 72 trips to Italy, shows how active traders were in Hieraopolis. Further to the north, a **baths complex** went up; it was later transformed into a church, hence the unorthodox orientation.

Of the **North Theatre**, which stood further east up the slope and was oriented to face the agora, very little is left: its travertine seats were systematically removed. It has not yet been fully investigated and its relationship with the other theatre remains unclear.

Christian Hierapolis

After the demise of the pagan religion, entailing the end of oracles and games, Hierapolis re-invented itself as a major Christian destination by claiming to be the place where St Philip had died. A new set of buildings went up to the east of town, outside the walls, in a prestigious, dominant position, around the 5th century. In town a processional way cut across an insula to reach the walls through a monumental gate flanked by towers. It continued on a stone bridge over a turbulent stream (the very same that obliterated the North Agora) and led to a complex consisting of a bath house, a martyrion with accommodation for pilgrims, and a church. The present path north of the theatre roughly follows that course. Little remains of the buildings themselves, which were already in a ruinous state by the 11th century, though a recently excavated grave has shown that pilgrims were still coming from as far as France, seeking healing and salvation in the 14th century.

The **octagonal bath house** was just beyond the bridge to the north; beyond, up a flight of steps, was the **Martyrion**, a geometrical *tour de force* in the form of a Greek cross inscribed within an octagon and set in a square. It had a church in the centre and 28 rooms to accommodate pilgrims on all four sides. The plan, making prominent use of the octagon, for early Christians a symbol of eternity, is a variant of Gregory of Nyssa's description of a domed octagonal space in his letter to the bishop of Iconium in 380. The question remains of the identity of the St Philip to which this place was sacred. Saints of that name include St Philip the Apostle, who was present at the miracles of the Feeding of the Five Thousand and the Wedding at Cana. Then there is a deacon named Philip and an evangelist (so called on account of his vigorous preaching), though these are also possibly the same person. It was long thought that St Philip's bones were buried in the martyrion, under the central dome. However, a new feature has lately come to light 40km to the south, close to a fountain. Here in the 5th century, a three-aisle **basilica** with marble capitals and an opus sectile floor was built around a much earlier tomb dated to the 1st century AD.

This had been incorporated into a larger marble structure with two pools sanctified by crosses and fed by water running close to the grave. The holy water here was no longer the thermal water but clear, spring water from the hills, sanctified by the closeness to the holy burial. So St Philip had two churches, one up the hill and one down here, just as is represented on a bread seal (used to authenticate the bread distributed to pilgrims) now in the museum in Richmond (USA). The tomb at the second site, near the spring, was found empty, however. It is anyone's guess where the bones of St Philip are: apparently they were claimed by Constantinople in the 6th century, for the rebuilding of the Church of the Holy Apostles (no longer extant). Could they now be in the Chiesa dei SS Apostoli in Rome, which makes a claim to be its successor? A tomb chest under the sanctuary there certainly purports to hold the mortal remains of St Philip.

LAODICEIA AD LYKUM

Hemmed in by two streams, the Asopus (Kuzgun Deresi) to the west and the Caprus (Botlarık Deresi) and the railway line from Goncalı to Denizli, Laodiceia (*map C, 3*) sits in a very good spot on a plateau of porous stone and consolidated gravel and is protected by a scarp all around. It was the project of a Seleucid ruler who, sometime in the 3rd century BC, turned the pre-existing village into a town and named it after a female member of his family; it may have been walled then. Very little is known of Hellenistic Laodiceia, a trading place on a good through route from Pergamon to Antalya and east–west from Apamea to Ephesus; it seems that communications were rerouted here at the expense of Colossae (*see below*). It was famed for its cloth, deep black and woven from the fleece of the local sheep, fine, glossy and soft, according to Vitruvius, attributes all due to the local water. It came under Pergamene rule in 188 BC and was incorporated into the Roman province of Asia in 129 BC. That brought a mixed bag of benefits: it found itself drawn into the Mithridatic Wars, where though it made its choice wisely it still suffered, and was later caught up in the Roman civil strife. Peace came with the establishment of the Empire. The town was beautified with public buildings, of which we see some of the ruins today. Apparently trade was so good and the local populace so well off that, according to Tacitus (*Annals 14:27*) imperial money was turned down after the massive earthquake of AD 61. Christianity came early, through the good works of one Epaphras, a disciple of St Paul from Colossae. He apparently found a strong Jewish community, well attested in the epigraphy, which may have helped him or hindered him; it is impossible to know. St John of the Apocalypse was certainly not impressed; he berated the lukewarm faith of some of the local people (*Revelation 3:14–21*). Even so, Laodiceia was one of the Seven Churches of Asia (*see below*), a bishopric and the seat of a council in 380.

It appears to have suffered a long, lingering decline. At some point after the 4th/5th century it was walled. The well-made circuit, homogeneous and not using spolia, followed roughly the contour of the land; it was apparently pierced by four gates, to Hierapolis, Ephesus, Aphrodisias and Syria, though further investigations are needed. The deeply-buried arches of the Ephesus Gate (all gate names are modern) can be seen on the west side of the enceinte. Sources mention Laodiceia as a bishopric up to the 11th century; it appears to have survived the assaults of Sassanids, Arabs and earthquakes. The Turks devastated it in 1097 and again about a century later, but in 1190, once more in Byzantine hands, it graciously received the Holy Roman Emperor Frederick Barbarossa, who was on his way to Syria on crusade (he was to meet his untimely death on the journey); to give the emperor a fitting welcome, some officialdom must have been present in Laodiceia. Indeed, the emperor was so impressed by his reception that he prayed on his knees for the prosperity of the inhabitants. Beyond that there is very little to go on in the archaeology. Laodiceia has always been investigated as a Roman town with little regard to what happened in later times—or earlier ones for that matter. In the 14th century, Ibn Battuta visited in the course of his travels and found a mixed community with a clear dress code (pointed hats marked out the Greeks). Meanwhile in the hamam, Greek slaves were plying the 'oldest profession'—with the approval of officialdom, one presumes, since young ladies belonged to the *kadi*, the Muslim judge.

One of the very early travellers to venture here, with the backing of the British ambassador and braving the dubious reputation of the deserted ruins, was Thomas Smith, a learned chaplain from Smyrna, who came in April 1671. Guided by his Bible, he was searching for the Seven Churches of Asia (Ephesus, Pergamon, Smyrna, Laodiceia, Sardes, Thyatira and Philadelphia). He correctly identified Laodiceia, though his 'church' by the stadium later turned out to be a bathing establishment. When the accounts of his travels were translated from the original Latin into English, they spawned a fashion among the European colony in Smyrna for autumn excursions to the Seven Churches circuit. After Smith came others like Pococke, Chandler and Laborde; their accounts speak of impressive remains. Unfortunately one person's atmospheric ruins are somebody else's ready-made, pre-worked stone: a lot of Laodiceia disappeared to Denizli and into the building of the railway.

Visiting Laodiceia

Laodiceia today (*open mid-April–Sept 8.30–7; Oct–mid-April 8–5; charge*) has set itself a new challenge. It is now billed to become an alternative to Ephesus, enticing visitors from Pamukkale and Aphrodisias and persuading them to stay in the area a little bit longer. Excavations, until recently quite low key (probably for lack of funds), have taken a new turn. The city is being uncovered and rebuilt at the same time, which explains all the cranes and scaffolding in the background. The aim appears to be to set up Classical features for tourists rather than to understand the development of the town.

There are two roads into Laodiceia, from the east and from the south. From the east, past the dig house and close to the location of the Syrian Gate, you follow the main east–west axis of the town, which appears to have been laid out on a grid. This continues into a long marble-paved **colonnaded street** beneath which ran a sewer and, in separate terracotta pipes, a water supply system for the city. On the north side is **Temple A**, in travertine with marble facing, sacred to Zeus or to Apollo and partly re-erected; some fallen architectural elements can be seen through the glass flooring. It sits high on a podium and is fronted by four twisted columns; on its south side it had a colonnaded portico with niches and statues. Beyond the temple are **two theatres** resting on a natural slope, the western one smaller, possibly an odeion of Hadrianic date. They have both lost their skene and a number of seats. The larger one has not been dated. However, since Cicero (here on a visit to administer justice) watched gladiatorial games in Laodicea when he was governor of Cilicia in the 1st century BC, he may well have sat here, unless there was an earlier structure. Between the theatres is an apsidal structure that may have been a church.

Laodiceia is quite short on church structures considering that it had several centuries of Christian life, was a bishopric and one of the Seven Churches. In 2011, a large building with massive columns was located using ground-penetrating radar. It has been dated to the early 4th century. The building, with mosaics and an opus sectile floor, also had a baptistery; it may be a church. Further news and details of this important discovery are awaited.

Where the two main streets cross is a **nymphaeum**, one of the six fountains in town which had in the past been investigated by a French team. Originally a c. 3rd-century construction, it had a basin with ornamental columns and statues flanked on the east and west sides by two semicircular fountains. Later the basin was covered and, according to some, turned into a baptismal font. Water for this and other fountains, as well as for the baths and for general use, was supplied from the Başpınar spring near Denizli, 8km distant, via an **aqueduct** of imperial date. Early travellers were able to trace its entire course, on arches and cut into the rock. Today only a number of arches remain to the south of the city, where the ruins of the *castellum aquae* can still be seen. This structure, with vents for regular access and cleaning, shows signs of incrustation due to the hardness of the water.

Walk to the south for the **stadium**, an impressive structure 350m by 60m with two rounded ends and the long sides slightly curved for better visibility. Built at the time of Vespasian, it could accommodate 20–30,000 spectators. The baths nearby were intitially mistaken for a gymnasium attested in the epigraphy. The inscription mentioning the emperor and his wife Sabina suggests a Hadrianic date. They fronted a wide agora with a bouleuterion at the north end.

COLOSSAE

Since 2005 Colossae (*map C, 5*), between Denizli and Honaz, the third city of the Lykus Valley, has had a tourist development plan: the beginning of the end of Colossae's troubles may be at hand. Older than Hierapolis and Laodiceia, with a name that strongly reflects an Anatolian influence, it has suffered a cruel fate. As recently as 1991 it was dubbed Laodiceia's predecessor and dismissed as a dead-end, Hellenistic development. Even its precise whereabouts, which mattered so much to biblical scholars searching for the Colossians of St Paul's epistle, have hardly ever been fixed, at some point shifting west as far as Rhodes, the site of the famous Colossus, because of the assonance. In addition, when the area was under Ottoman rule, it seems that the sultan's writ did not reach this far, discouraging antiquarian travellers from exploring: it was apparently just too risky.

Unlike the other two cities of the Lykus Valley, Colossae had a military role, as a base defending the pass through the Taurus mountains to Antalya as well as safeguarding east–west communications. When times became troubled, with the Arab incursions, the settlement turned truly defensive and moved to the slopes of the mountains 5km south. By then it was known as Chonae, which in due course became Honaz. The ruined fortress at the top end of the town, up the slope, was originally Byzantine; the Seljuks and the Ottomans enlarged it to accommodate 10,000 soldiers. If you climb right up to it, the commanding view of the valley will illustrate why they did so. In 1739 it took 40,000 Ottoman troops to dislodge Soley Bey Ogle, a famous rebel who had gone to ground here with 4,000 followers and 11 cannons.

After it was abandoned, the original site was thoroughly plundered to build the fortress, the new town and the Akhan caravansaray 6km east of Denizli, as well as for stone to use as grave markers and animal pens and to turn into lime. Stray finds such the Horus now displayed in the garden of Hierapolis Museum, found their way into museums under the label 'Laodiceia', which was better known. No wonder *Murray's Handbook for Travellers* of 1908 dismissed Colossae out of hand: 'Nothing to see'.

Recently, the careful collation of epigraphic, historical and numismatic evidence has in a way rehabilitated Colossae though, on location, there is still not a great deal to see. If you visit the original site, an accumulation of debris, a mound said to date from the Bronze Age signposted in the plain east of Denizli, you will need some imagination. The site is in a fertile valley with abundant water. It was famed for its wool and cloth, the *colossinus*, the colour of cyclamen (Pliny, *21,51*). At the time of the Persian domination it was large enough and rich enough to play host for several days to Xerxes and his men on their way to Sardes in 481 BC (*Herodotus 7,30*) and to Cyrus and his 30,000-strong army (including Xenophon's ten thousand mercenaries) on their way east in 401 BC. This means that Colossae had the required resources in timber, space and food, and an efficient bureaucracy to take care of the logistics. The limited evidence suggests this was a land of large estates with abundant hunting for the Persian ruler to reward his followers with; one of them murdered general Tissaphernes at Colossae. The foundation of Laodiceia was probably a commercial blow but Colossae retained its strategic importance. It minted coins, had a treasury in Roman times, was a seat of the imperial cult and was visited by the emperor Hadrian on his Panhellenic Tour of AD 129. By then there was a Christian community, the recipients of the Epistle to the Colossians which St Paul wrote c. mid-1st century AD. In due course, Colossae became the seat of a bishop and later of a metropolitan, meaning it was a separate see from Laodicea. The development in the 4th–5th century of the cult of St Michael (a warrior angel leading troops against the devil), who had a grand cathedral here, and the healing spring in the area of the necropolis north of town, were contrary to St Paul's advice regarding the cult of angels (*Colossians 18*), but in tune with the times and the Anatolian culture, as the tradition of angel-worship at Germia shows (*see Blue Guide Central Anatolia*). Colossae suffered greatly during the Iconoclastic period, as both the local *strategos* and the bishop were opposed not only to icons but also to holy sites and anything that could suggest idolatry. The cult of the archangel Michael and the of healing spring are still alive today, however, though against a Muslim background.

APHRODISIAS

Tucked away at an altitude of 600m, backing onto the Taurus mountains, Aphrodisias (*map B, 6*) stands out in the graveyard of antique towns that characterises this part of the world. Like the other settlements, Aphrodisias was situated in a fertile, well-watered valley. It was not on any trade routes of importance, nor was it in a strategic location. Its identity was not truly Carian but in its early days was subject to Phrygian and Lydian influence. Certainly investigations in the area, at Herakleia Salbace, Apollonia Salbace, Tabae or Antiochia ad Meandrum, would help to put Aphrodisias in its proper context, which must be sought in the locality here as well as in the broader context of the Roman Empire. It might also reduce the steady trickle of coins from the unguarded sites that keeps appearing online.

What differentiates Aphrodisias from the other dead cities is that it outlasted all of them, gaining international appeal and finding favour with a dynasty of Roman emperors (the most important, founding dynasty), finally ending its career as the main Christian centre of Caria until it was taken over by the Seljuks. At some point the Byzantine name Stavropolis ('City of the Cross') was changed to Geyre, a corruption of Caria. A career such as this inevitably produced a lot of lasting architecture and an equally vast collection of inscriptions. Work at Aphrodisias has been ongoing since the American-educated Turkish archaeologist Kenan Erim, as a young man, saw pictures of villagers using column capitals as coffee tables at the local *kahvehane* in the late 1950s and was inspired to start a sustained research programme. It is still going strong, an international effort under joint American and Turkish leadership. The village has been moved to the west but Kenan Erim's grave is here, not far from the museum.

HISTORICAL OUTLINE
Regional surveys of the Aphrodisias area show a pattern of early, dispersed settlement with elements such as tumuli suggesting the presence of a ruling elite of wealthy landlords. Finds point to Lydian and Phrygian contacts and influence. In the town itself, the elevation to the southeast, the Pekmez Hüyük, not a natural mound, has been investigated and has shown mudbrick structures and finds with traits linking the site to the west in the Bronze Age. The other elevation, known as the acropolis, 100m to the west and against which the cavea of the theatre rests, is more difficult to excavate because the

early levels are now below the water table. The other focal point of the area was to the north, where investigations below the later temple of Aphrodite have uncovered evidence from as far back as the 6th century BC of worship of a deity, possible Cybele to judge by the waterspout with a lion's head and the figurines, and centred around a salt water spring if we believe Pausanias (*1,26,5*). Aphrodisias is in an earthquake zone and it is not surprising that if there was a salt-water well here in antiquity, it cannot now be traced. As a pilgrimage locus, something of a backwater in rural Caria, the settlement sails untouched through the waves of Hellenistic urban foundations. It acquired urban status later on, sometime in the 2nd century BC, but apparently not as an afterthought of Hellenistic dynasts. It has been suggested that the impetus may have come from the local people themselves, at a time when Seleucid power was on the wane and the area was in the hands of distant Rhodes. This might have created a power vacuum that encouraged the ruling elite to apply for *polis* status. Such status would have enhanced the appeal of the sanctuary, widening its catchment area, and would also have ensured that the body of citizens could make their own laws and follow their own customs. Indeed, one can see an effort in that direction as the canonical image of the goddess takes on the characteristics of the Artemis of Ephesus: the same stiff pose, arms forward, a goddess of sky, land and sea, with a plethora of zodiac signs and even the same sacred bird, the dove. It is still a recognisably Greek Anatolian figure with no signs of a Roman connection, and so it remained. The goddess also still maintained her warlike attributes since Sulla, the Roman general, visited in 82 BC to offer a double axe and a gold crown (Appian, *1,97*).

Later on, another important visitor followed but on a different errand: Julius Caesar. His votive offering, a golden Eros, shows clearly what he had in mind: not a goddess of war but a goddess of love. Aphrodisias was reborn as the cult city of Caesar's trophy ancestor, Aphrodite herself as Venus Prometor, the mother of Aeneas and grandmother of Iulus, from whom Caesar's family, the Gens Julia, claimed descent. It is not clear what drove Caesar here, unless the place had already shed its original name, Ninoe. According to Plutarch, Caesar had been toying with the idea of founding a new Rome in the Troad, to build on the Troy connection. Perhaps his journey here was all part of that plan.

Ultimately the area was incorporated into the Roman Empire. A letter written by Octavian (Caesar's adopted son and later emperor) dated to 39–38 BC and proudly displayed on the archive wall of the theatre, stated 'This one city I have taken for mine out of all Asia'. From this time on things went well for Aphrodisias, although whereas for citizens of other cities of the Roman province of Asia, the empire offered opportunities for social and political advancement, there are no signs of any Aphrodisians in Rome. They appeared to have stayed at home, suggesting to some that Aphrodisias was a good place to enjoy obscurity in comfort. With Octavian's embrace came undoubted privileges, such as exemption from taxes and liturgies (compulsory public service) as well as asylum rights and possibly funding (Aphrodisias had a competent organiser with money of his own in the guise of the locally-born Zoilus, the emperor's freedman), as well as the opening or discovery of marble quarries c. 30 BC within walking distance of the town. This last was probably the most important thing. Aphrodisias is some distance from the sea and there is no way marble could be transported there from the coast. Over the next three centuries, Aphrodisias was beautified with its own stone and turned into a city devoted to the cult of Aphrodite, ancestor of the founder of the Empire.

Things appear to have come to a halt in the 3rd century, a time of troubles when there is a sudden lull in the epigraphy, all-important for a site like this, which seldom appears in historical accounts. Later, in the 350–360s, city walls went up, but these were still relatively quiet times and the work was not done in a hurry. The necropoleis around the city were systematically dismantled and rebuilt into the wall and spolia from the theatre, then under renovation, were also used; concurrently various restorations and alterations were carried out in town. By then the economic privileges may have been revoked but Aphrodisias had become capital of the province of Caria, the seat of the imperial governor. It had a bishop by the 4th century, at which time Christianity was pervasive enough to dislodge the former cult and turn its temple into a church, in a process requiring skilled engineers and considerable sums of money. Stavropolis, as the Byzantine city was known, was an important ecclesiastical administrative centre eventually reduced to its kastron, i.e. the former theatre, fortified and covered in houses. This is probably what the Seljuks found.

Being remote from communication axes and having no large settlement nearby, Aphrodisias gently collapsed and was left to crumble where it stood. The new village of Geyre that took its place was built out of spolia that were retrieved when the village was moved. The ruins have always been apparent but protected by remoteness. Earthquakes, altogether quite frequent, are responsible for most of the damage, though Texier, who visited in 1835, was sufficiently alarmed to suggest that the French government should intervene: the first excavator, in 1904, was a Frenchman, the railway engineer Paul Gaudin.

So far, about one third of the city has been excavated, exposing the centre of town with its public buildings. Other phantom buildings that appear in inscriptions such as a banqueting hall for the entire citizenry, an archive building and gymnasia, remain to be found.

Visiting Aphrodisias

The site (*open 8–7; shorter hours in winter; charge*) is entered from the east. The museum (*closes at 6.30*), with a new extension housing the reliefs from the Sebasteion (*see below*), is possibly best explored at the end of the visit, at which time the statuary and other carvings will make more sense. While the majority of the site is on a Hippodamian grid, this eastern part of town appears to follow an earlier Hellenistic layout, which might explain the orientation of the Sebasteion. The Temple of Aphrodite and the theatre are also off the grid: the first because it followed an earlier building, the second because of practical constraints.

The Sebasteion

From the entrance you can get to the **Sebasteion (1)** (a modern name referring to the deities and heroes worshipped here) past the dig house. A project possibly conceived c. AD 14, the building is unique in its conception: a long narrow corridor linked to an important artery of the town to the east. It is certainly more cramped than the one in Pessinus, which is contemporary (*see Blue Guide Central Anatolia*). The erection of a sebasteion reflects, according to R.R.R. Smith, the anxieties of the local elite at the death of their main supporter, the emperor Augustus. Alternatively, it could have been built slightly later, as a sign of gratitude to Tiberius for renewing the city's exemptions and privileges. In either case it would seem that the sponsors, two local families, found it difficult to find a plot of land anywhere in town for their project and had to make do with this: a 14m-wide alleyway. Blind three-storey façades rose to a height of 12m on either side, above a ground-floor portico. The end result must have been a trifle claustrophobic. Over the portico, two storeys supported panels in high relief carved with images of emperors, gods, heroes and conquered nations. At the back were rooms of shabby construction with earthen floors and poor illumination. It is not known what they were used for.

At the east end, on a podium and preceded by a flight of steps, a temple very much in the style of the contemporary imperial temples in Rome closed the vista but not the passageway, which remained open on either side. At the west end a monumental columnar screen or propylon connected the Sebasteion to one of the main arteries of town. The propylon set the tone for celebrations, with the statues of Venus Prometor or Genetrix, of Aeneas, of Atia, Augustus's mother, and of Livia his wife.

It seems that the model for the Sebasteion was the yet-to-be-located Porticum ad Nationes in Rome that Pliny mentions (*36,39*). This would certainly seem to be the case, judging by the defeated nations represented here, which include nations that had not been defeated, like the Ethiopians, and some fairly obscure ones such as the Trumplini, an alpine tribe from the Val Trompia north of Brixia (modern Brescia). However, porticoes in the Roman fora had a variety of functions: judicial, educational and commercial. Here it was not until the 4th/5th century that the back rooms began to be used as shops and manufacturing centres; a number of Jewish graffiti testify to the presence of an active Jewish community. By then an earthquake had already toppled part of the north aisle of the Sebasteion. The temple at the east end had been dismantled, leaving six columns supporting an architrave to close the vista.

The change of use of the Sebasteion reflects the waning of the imperial cult and goes hand in hand with the ascendancy of Christianity. The reliefs were allowed to stay but a certain amount of censorship was applied. Images of pagan gods and of sacrifices were erased while the rest was respected as a monument from the past. The number of chiselled-off figures is very small but removing them was a coordinated action requiring the setting up of scaffolding and the employment of skilled workers. In the process a few exposed genitals and breasts were also obliterated. The complex

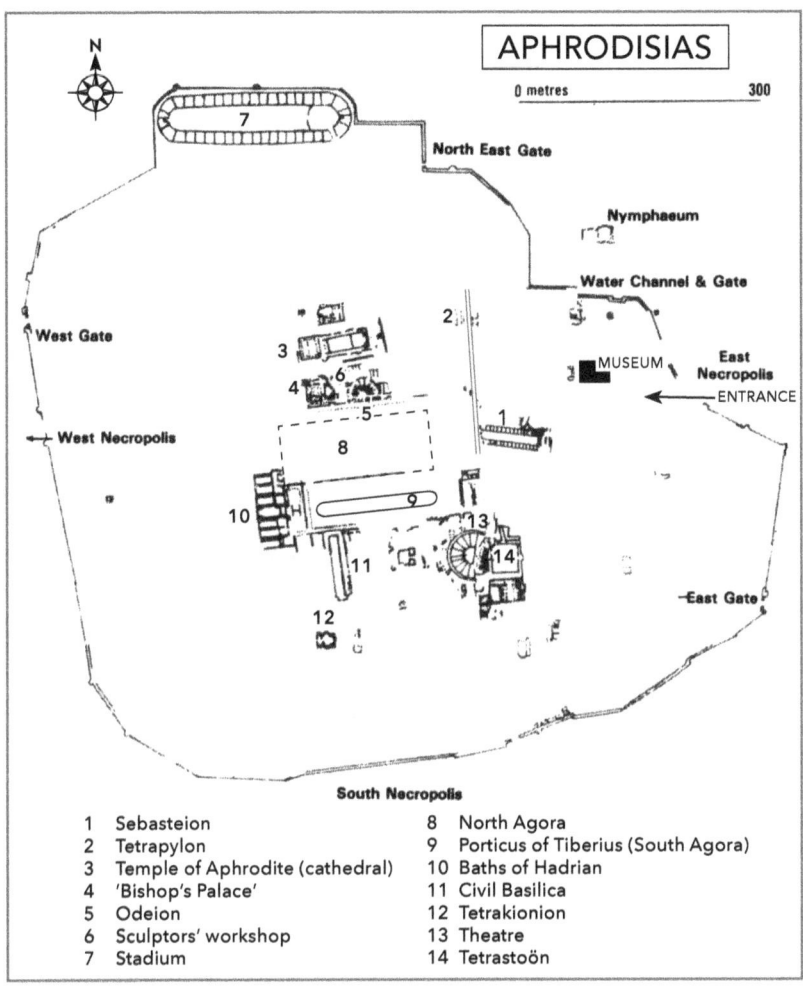

APHRODISIAS

0 metres   300

1   Sebasteion
2   Tetrapylon
3   Temple of Aphrodite (cathedral)
4   'Bishop's Palace'
5   Odeion
6   Sculptors' workshop
7   Stadium
8   North Agora
9   Porticus of Tiberius (South Agora)
10 Baths of Hadrian
11 Civil Basilica
12 Tetrakionion
13 Theatre
14 Tetrastoön

came down around the 7th century in an earthquake. The reliefs shattered but their fragments were protected by the topography: they filled the empty rooms and the deep passageway.

The Tetrapylon and Temple of Aphrodite

Follow the road due north for the rebuilt **Tetrapylon (2)**, a well-known Aphrodisias landmark. A 10m by 11m structure with 16 marble columns and arcuated lintels, coffered ceilings and a 2nd AD date, it was conceived to provide a great ceremonial entrance to the temenos of the Temple of Aphrodite. In due course, a relief with a small Eros and a bust of Aphrodite were chiselled away and exorcised by a Cross on the west pediment.

The **Temple of Aphrodite** (**3**), slightly off the Hippodamian grid, was paid for by Zoilus (*see above*), who was also a priest here, and by private donations. It is a replacement of an earlier temple on the same site and seems to have taken some time to build, from the mid-1st century BC to the time of Tiberius. A pseudo-dipteral structure with 13 columns at the sides and eight in front, it was literally turned inside out when it was transformed into a cathedral, on a basilical plan, at the time of Leo I (457–71). The 13 lateral columns stayed put and six were added on either side to lengthen the nave. An apse and later a synthronon were added at the east end. A fair amount of the temple was reused as spolia in the process. A colonnaded atrium and a baptistery were added at the west end. The roof was of wood. The work incurred considerable expense: there is the possibility that some of it was paid for by imperial patronage, bearing in mind that a visit in 443 by Emperor Thedosius has been mooted. The building was renovated in the 10th–11th century and abandoned in the 12th after a fire.

The 'Bishop's Palace', odeion and sculptors' workshop

To the south is the so-called '**Bishop's Palace**' (**4**), a high-status residence with reception rooms. The 4th-century fresco of the *Three Graces* that it contains seems entirely unsuitable for a bishop; this may in fact have been the governor's palace. It was occupied up until the 12th century, well after the population had moved into the fortified theatre. To the east, a smaller structure, variously called the bouleuterion or **odeion** (**5**), probably fulfilled several functions. It had a capacity of 1,700, far too large for a meeting hall of city councillors. It is perhaps more likely to have been used for festival performances, public addresses and musical events. It was originally built on a grand scale, with a south wall three storeys high and looking like a theatre skene, with five openings, a profusion of statues and an opus sectile floor in the orchestra. Later, after it had lost its roof, an inscription suggests that it also served as a palaestra, possibly for wrestling competitions. It fell out of use in the 6th century and was turned into an infants' burial ground.

In the vicinity, the **sculptors' workshop** (**6**) is a reminder of what Aphrodisias was best at: sculpture (portraits and mythological scenes). The shop was active between the early 3rd and the end of the 4th centuries, when it was built over with domestic structures and an olive press. Certainly Aphrodisias's artists, who signed their work, have left enough pieces around the Empire (including in prestigious sites such as Hadrian's Villa at Tivoli) to prove that they were in high demand and willing to travel. From the remains here it seems that the incumbents specialised in small mythological figures and portraits of notables, as well as in repairing and recycling. The so-called 'fisherman', a reworking of a Hellenistic theme whose torso is in Berlin while the head is in the museum here, shows what the local artists were capable of.

The Stadium

At the far north is the **Stadium** (**7**), a 1st-century structure with some later modifications. The first mention of athletic contests in Aphrodisias is from that time, so there is possibly a connection. The stadium, with an estimated capacity of 30,000, had a royal box and tunnel entrances on either side. In the 4th–5th century an arena was fenced off at the east end, probably not for gladiatorial combats, which had been banned by Constantine in 325, but for spectacles involving wild beasts, which continued in Aphrodisias into the 6th century. One can safely assume that the Christian population attended them. In due course the stadium was incorporated into the city walls, possibly by reworking a portico on the north side. You can have a look at the city walls here; they date from the mid-4th century, a time when Aphrodisias was a provincial capital and a certain amount of money was being spent on various projects such as the refurbishment of the Basilica and Tetrastoön. It may be that, at the time, rather than being a defence requirement, the addition of city walls was meant to project an image of prosperity, strength and a long history. The 3.5km long circuit, in places standing 9.5m high with nine gates and 23 towers, looks older than it really is because of its isodomic construction with regular, uniform ashlar blocks on the outside and newly quarried small marble blocks on the inside. The core was of mortared rubble with deep string courses. The larger blocks were sourced in the necropolis, which explains why there are no monumental tombs left, only their foundations. The defence work also incorporated part of the archive wall of the theatre, which was being renovated at the time.

The Agorae and Porticus of Tiberius

Following the road to the south you will come across two agoras. The **North Agora (8)** has not been fully explored. Originally built c. 20 BC, it was therefore part of the Hellenistic town. It apparently had a fountain and an altar in the middle and a double portico all around. To the south, another agora or **Porticus of Tiberius (9)**, with a very distinctive, elongated water feature in the middle, was a place of relaxation and—according to palaeobotanists—the locus of the palm grove mentioned in an inscription. With its stoas, the *euripos* (long pool) with statues all around, and the *xystum* (sports ground), the Porticus of Tiberius evoked the setting of well-to-do Roman villas like the Villa dei Papiri at Herculaneum. To the east it was accessed by a monumental gate of the 2nd century AD in the style of a theatre skene flanked by two square towers. In the 5th century this was turned into a nymphaeum.

This part of town had always had drainage problems. It was crossed by a stream, the Dandalas, which originally supplied the inhabitants of the acropolis with water. Over time it became marshy so, in the 5th century, the ground level between the pool and the colonnade was raised. It all toppled in the 11th century in an earthquake and was later built over.

To the west are the **Baths of Hadrian (10)**, which may have used the Porticus of Tiberius as an extension; the complex certainly lacked a swimming pool and a large enough palaestra. The baths, a series of vaulted halls with marble flooring, were still functioning in the 6th century. The entrance from the north was monumental with a tetrastyle set around a small square pool.

The Civil Basilica

To the south and accessed via the Porticus of Tiberius, is the **Civil Basilica (11)**, a cross between a Hellenistic stoa and a meeting hall, the legal and commercial heart of the town. When it was inaugurated, in the second half of the 1st century AD, it would have been twice as tall and twice as wide as any building in town. It was modelled on the basilica in Ephesus, which is larger (but then Ephesus was also a much bigger commercial centre). At Aphrodisias this extravagant building was part of the image of a favoured imperial city. One hundred and thirty metres long and 30m wide, it was divided into a nave and two aisles by two rows of columns. The nave had a clerestory. The floors were covered in mosaic and the ceilings, in wood and stucco, were barrel-vaulted and coffered. The place had its complement of statues, including the blue horse and rider that you can admire in the museum. Modelled on a Greek myth relating the death of Troilus, the youngest son of Priam, killed by Achilles, this was a widespread topos for heroes. Germanicus sported it on the cuirass he wears in the bronze statue of him from Amelia in Umbria. Here in Aphrodisias the artwork has suffered the ravages of time but even so the life-size horse, made of the local blue marble with grey streaks, at full gallop, off the ground and flying through the air, is a piece of virtuoso carving. What is missing is Troilus, pulled by the hair and lifted off the saddle by Achilles. Of the saddle, a cloth imitating a feline skin, only the paws are left. It was probably made of metal and was fixed with 45 metal pins. The original base of the monument was found in the city walls, suggesting that the basilica was not its original location.

Plastered across the entrance to the basilica, on thin marble slabs, are the two edicts of Diocletian intended to solve the financial problems of the Roman Empire. There were many of these: cumulatively the documents contain a total of 4,000 words (*see box*).

The Tetrakionion and Theatre

At the south end of the basilica was another piece of the kind street furniture that so delighted the local Aphrodisians by giving their city an apparently imperial aspect. This one is known as the **Tetrakionion (12)**, a four-columned arrangement built at a road intersection, modelled on the one that breaks the Arcadiane in Ephesus in half, or on the one in the centre of town at Palmyra. It was in due course incorporated into a Byzantine triconch church, where it probably supported a dome.

The **Theatre (13)**, on the route to the exit, is an excellent place to end your visit. Originally late Hellenistic, it was still in use in the 6th century, for a variety of spectacles to entertain the populace and impress visitors and for civic functions. Graffiti show that the Blues and the Greens, the factions that created havoc in the Hippodrome in Constantinople, were powerful here as well, though these were probably not horse-racing factions but the expressions of urban strife. As did the amphitheatre in Dürres, Albania, so too did the theatre here in due course acquire a chapel dedicated to St Michael, with good-quality painting. The theatre cavea was quite large, with a seating capacity of 8,000, although it had been curtailed at the north end to make room for the south agora (*see above*). After the impressive skene came tumbling down in an earthquake in the 7th century, its spolia were used to build houses in the cavea and to strengthen defences, making the theatre, now the core of the Byzantine kastron, the longest-lasting monument in Aphrodisias.

Immediately east of the theatre is the **Tetrastoön (14)**, a commercial building.

DIOCLETIAN'S MONEY

When Diocletian became emperor in AD 284, he inherited an empire that was bankrupt and had suffered several decades of misrule and turmoil. He set about reforming the way it was run by acknowledging that it was too large for a single ruler. The creation of the Tetrarchy, with two emperors (the *Augusti*) and two co-emperors (the *Caesares*), may have been conducive to better administration but its immediate effect was to increase expenditure, as courts, official residences and armies multiplied. The trouble was that there was no new money to be had. The Roman Empire at the time was fighting to stand still, not to expand as it had in the old days, when newly conquered land paid for itself.

Diocletian knew all too well that unhappy soldiers could be a major source of trouble, potentially destabilising society. Soldier's pay was an important element in the imperial economy because of the sheer amount of coinage changing hands, as soldiers looked for goods and services in the local markets. Coinage was needed to pay them and to advertise the accession of a new emperor; it was also a powerful propaganda tool. But coinage was precisely the problem. It had been regularly debased by preceding rulers, who had come thick and fast in the turbulent 3rd century, some of them lasting only a matter of days. As a result, the *denarius*, which at the time of Nero had a 94% silver content, was now a copper alloy coin with 0.5% of silver (and sometimes not even that, but a tin wash to make it look like silver). As for the gold coins, they had either disappeared from circulation or had been mercilessly clipped. Diocletian's approach was twofold. His Currency Edict of 294 aimed at restoring faith in the currency system by promising gold and silver coins as pure as at the time of the Empire at its height (which was not possible as there was no gold or silver to mint them with), and pegging the value of the new bronze coin to the gold coin at an unrealistically high level. The result was a renewed bout of inflation. The Price Edict, which followed in 301, was intended to control inflation by fixing maximum prices for a number of goods and services, an attack on unscrupulous merchants who ripped off soldiers. The document, with its emotive opening lines, was meant to be applied throughout the Empire, though the 40-plus copies known mainly originate in the East, the area that Diocletian ruled. The Edict listed some 1,400 prices for goods and services, with some odd lacunae. It mentions barbers but not hairdressers, veterinarians but not doctors. It sometimes looks like a list drawn up in haste. We learn from it that the most expensive commodity was a lion (150,000 *denarii*) while ten doormice could be had for 40 *denarii*. The Edict did not enjoy a long life. There was no effective government machine to enforce it and inflict the death penalty on transgressors. Moreover, market forces proved stronger than the will of the emperor. When Diocletian abdicated and retired to his villa at Split in Dalmatia, the Edict was rescinded. In some places it was taken down and its slabs reused as spolia. In places where it was structural, like at Aphrodisias, it was left in place for the archaeologists to find.

PRACTICAL INFORMATION

TOURIST INFORMATION

The area includes a number of very popular sites that rank high on the list of 'things to see' in Turkey. All-inclusive organised tours can be booked from as far away as Istanbul. Your hotel may well have the information or if not, will direct you to the nearest tourist office. This applies both to destinations south of Selçuk (Miletus, Priene and Didyma) and east up the Meander Valley (Pamukkale and Aphrodisias). In Didyma, the Didim Tourist Information Centre (*open Mon–Fri 8–5*) is opposite the Belediye Café on Yalı Cd., by the sea near the harbour. Denizli has tourist offices at train and bus stations. Pamukkale's tourist office is in the village. Hierapolis has a visitor centre at both ends of the Plateia.

GETTING AROUND

By bus: A number of destinations can be reached by bus but bear in mind that the road from Aydın to Denizli has not been upgraded and can often be clogged with traffic.

The newly refurbished Denizli Otogar is just south of the train station. It caters for local and long-distance buses. In summer it runs dolmuş trips to Pamukkale, 20km away (direction Karahayıt). The same transport can drop you off at Ören Yeri for Laodiceia (c. 1km away). You will have to think how to arrange your way back.

Aphrodisias is trickier to get to by public transport. There is a dolmuş from Nazilli that will drop you at Karasu on Route 585, where you will have to wait for a different one to reach your destination. Accommodation at Karasu and in Aphrodisias is limited. To visit as a day trip, you will need to join an organised tour. They normally allow you two and a half hours on site, which is barely enough. For both Laodiceia and Aphrodisias, it is advisable to take your own snacks and drinks.

For Tralles you can take a dolmuş from Aydın and walk the rest of the way (15mins).

By train: From İzmir Basmane railway station, a train service links İzmir to Aydın, Nazilli and Denizli. The train is more comfortable but less reliable and slower than the bus.

WHERE TO STAY

For the sites that are close to the sea, an obvious choice of accommodation is **Kuşadası** (*map B, 3*), a popular resort (you will need to book in summer). The Sentinus Hotel on the edge of town to the south (Sümbül Sk, *sentinushotels. com*), close to the sea, may be a good choice in the height of summer to get away from the crowds. On the other hand, if you want to join them, try the Anzac Golden Bed Pension (*anzacgoldenbed.com*), which offers a fine view from its roof, or Cennet Pension (*cennetpension.com*). Both are in the middle of town and both are small, so don't just turn up late in the evening, you need to book in advance.

Close to **Priene**, the Priene Pansyion at Güllübahçe (*T: 256 547 17 25*) is also open to campers.

Söke (*map B, 3*) can be a good base as it has a spread of modern accommodation such as the Hotel Akalin (*T: 256 512 77 93*) and the Derici Hotel (*T: 256 512 77 93*), both not far from Route 525. There are other options as well.

For **Didyma** you can choose between the Medusa House (*medusahouse.com*), a pretty house lost in greenery close to the temple, and a number of impersonal outfits to the south close to the beach.

People tend to spend just one night in **Pamukkale**. The place is too far out for a day trip but once you have seen the ruins and luxuriated in the warm pools, there is not much else to do unless you come for one of the two Summer Festivals of Music and Culture (*see below*). Places to stay are quite abundant and so are the visitors. Try the Alida Hotel (*alidahotelpamukkale. com*), which has a distinct Asian flavour, a clear reflection of the strong pulling power of the site. The Artemis Yürük Hotel on Turgut Özal Cd. (*T: 258 272 26 74*) will offer you a budget alternative, as will the Kervansaray Hotel (*kervansaraypension.com*), where the rooms are rather small but where there is a pool and a glorious terrace for a healthy breakfast. If you wish to spend time in Pamukkale to take the waters, the Colossae Thermal Hotel in Karahayıt (*colossaehotel.com*) is truly colossal—as indeed is the pool that goes with it.

For **Aphrodisias**, you will need to stay in Karacasu, where the choice is more limited. Try the Aphrodisias Dandalos Hotel (*aphrodisiasdandaloshotel.com*) near Istiklal Cd. or, a cheaper option, the small and friendly Elmas Pansiyon on Tavas Cd. (*T: 532 295 71 68*).

WHERE TO EAT

Kuşadası (*map B, 3*) has plenty of eateries, mostly concentrated around the harbour. If you want a treat, go to the Castle Restaurant, which has a well-deserved reputation for seafood and interesting Turkish soups. Alternatively, sample the stuffed calamari at Kazim Usta nearby. In **Didim** (*map B, 5*), you can join the locals at the Didim Şehir Lokantası, close to the Belediye.

At the two big supersites, Pamukkale and Aphrodisias, fast food seems to be ubiquitous. The clientèle is truly international and so is what is on offer. It is probably best to stick to Turkish food, though. In **Pamukkale**, the Venus Hotel (with a fine garden) is a good choice. The Ünal Restaurant at the north end of town, between Değirmen Sk and Kuzey Sk, has a reputation for *mantı* and interesting soups. Aphrodisias is not very well served. **Karacasu** (*map B, 6*) has a few places: the cheap and cheerful Sirin Pide Salonu in the middle of the village and the Anatolia Restaurant for grilled fish and kebaps nearby.

WHAT TO DO

Sample the **cherries** at Honaz (*map C, 5*), the cherry capital of Turkey, where there is a festival dedicated to them in early June. Alternatively, try one of the many variety of **strawberries** (32 are available, apparently) at Sultanhisar near Nysa (*map B, 4*) in May. The celebration comes with an Art and Culture Festival. Follow this with the **Folk Dance Festival** in July and the **Music Festival** in September, both in Pamukkale (*map C, 3*) in the restored Roman theatre.

CARIA

South of the Meander Valley is Caria, a great rump of rock with bad communications both east–west and north–south. A broken terrain, a land of thin soils, averaging higher altitudes than the land to its north and sparsely populated, Caria was not part of the Greek primary wave of colonisation. The Greeks certainly knew of the Carians that Homer (*Iliad*, 2:867) called 'uncouth of speech', clearly barbarians. They knew of their wine, olive oil and honey, they raided the land for slaves and recruited mercenaries there. And yet Caria in antiquity has a Greek side to it. Even so, Herodotus, who was born in Halicarnassus in the early 5th century BC, considered himself a Greek born in a Greek city and as any Greek he qualified Carian speech as 'barbarian' (8:135). Later on in the 4th century BC, the inhabitants, even those on the coast, could still be qualified barbarians; they were therefore enslaved, which is the treatment meted out by the Spartan commander Lysander to the people of Cedreae, a town allied with the Athenians on the Ceramic Gulf.

Hellenisation occurred to a great extent under the Hekatomnids, a dynasty that saw the setting up of Greek-style cities as a mission. The Carians were 'encouraged' to abandon their villages and live instead in urban centres complete with theatres, gymnasia, stadia, agorai and all the trappings of a Greek city state. But one does wonder: was there a body of free, male citizens? Were the fundamental values, those codified by Plato in the *Republic*, such as justice, wisdom and moderation, part of the deal? The Hekatomnids, for all their good intentions, originated as Persian satraps and then, when Persian control slackened, became local dynasts: they ruled subjects, not citizens. Dealing with a heterogeneous population, the Hekatomnids pursued a twin policy of Carianisation and Hellenisation. Their Caria was the land to the west of a line running due south from Tralles along the valley of the Çine Çay, the ancient Marsyas. According to Ronald Marchese, Greekness in Caria was a veneer and an aspiration. It was used to foster local values and customs but also basically because it looked good. It was a second-hand Hellenism, an import from Samos or Rhodes, just off the coast, rather than directly sourced from Greece. It was unevenly and thinly spread, petering out as one moved inland. Aphrodisias, the capital of Caria in the late Roman Empire, is a good case in point. How Carian was it and what was the reason for the choice? Security? The presence of all the right buildings for a provincial capital? Its trajectory through history is so unique, that in any case it can hardly be representative.

The presence of leagues has been much touted as evidence that the *poleis* were politically united. However, the 5th-century BC Delian League was an instrument of Athenian domination, then at its apogee. As for the Chrysaoric League, first attested in 267 BC, it was primarily a religious body with no political role. It involved getting together for festivities and games and much of the time was occupied in squabbling over control of the sanctuary at Labranda; to quote Vincent Gabrielsen, loyalties to the league were internally fragile and externally—*vis à vis* other powers i.e. the

Seleucids and Rhodes—they were divided. The fact is that after the Classical world unravelled there were no cities left in Caria. The place reverted to type, in other words to village settlements, and was plunged until comparatively recently into relative obscurity. There was a legacy, though. Because of urbanisation, agriculture had been encouraged, leading to soil erosion and ultimately to the silting up of the Meander, whose deep estuary was transformed into a braided, sluggish delta. The forest cover was lost, turning upland Caria into a land of sheep pasture.

It is tourism that has brought life back to Caria, and with it have arrived some decent communications and an interest in its archaeology. In this field much remains to be done, especially on the coast (particularly at risk because of uncontrolled tourist developments). The following chapters of this guide cover the sites up to and including the Bodrum Peninsula.

MYUS

On the western rocky reaches of the Latmian massif, now the Beşparmak of which more below, facing Priene, Myus (*map B, 5; open 8–5 daily*) was one of the original Ionian *poleis* claiming an Athenian connection via its founder, a natural son of the last king of Athens, the mythical Codros according to Strabo (*14:1,16*). Strabo was writing about 1,000 years later and by then Myus was no longer.

What had seemed to be a brilliant spot, deep within the Meander estuary, turned into a nightmare as the river carried down more silt, the harbour went out of use and the open sea turned into marshes and a breeding ground for mosquitoes. Water management was clearly a problem as Vitruvius's (*1:14*) mention of frequent floods suggests. The town's development never really took off; Myus remained the smallest of the twelve Ionian foundations, never really a political community. According to Herodotus (*5,36,4*), 200 Persian ships could be accommodated in the harbour in 499 BC but the fact is that five years later at the battle of Lade, the culmination of the Ionian revolt, Myus was only able to contribute three vessels to the cause. The Persian victory was short-lived but it looks as though Myus did not go on to benefit from the ultimate defeat of the Persian foe in the Greek mainland and in Ionia in 479 BC.

Myus's low status turned it into a bargaining chip, at least in the popular lore. First it was assigned to Themistocles as his provider of the *opson*, the relish or garnish that livened up the staple diet of bread and barley (the *sitos*). The brilliant general, the victor of Salamis, had fallen out with the Athenians and had fled to the Persians. Together with Myus for the *opson*, he was assigned wine from Lampsacus (today's Lapseki in the Dardanelles) and from Magnesia, where he took up residence. The town supplied him also with bread and an annual income of 50 talents. Later, according to Athenaeus (*3:78*), Myus was given to Magnesia by Philip, King of Macedonia, in exchange for the figs that had been supplied to his army. Both stories should be taken with a large pinch of salt. They are gibes, probably reflecting the perceived low status of Myus in society at large, and should not be taken literally. For a start, at the time of Themistocles's flight to Magnesia, Myus was part of the

Delian League and under Athenian control: it was not in the gift of the Persian king to bequeath it to anyone. As for the second reference, Athenaeus was writing much later, around the 2nd century AD, and in a lightweight context, that of dinner-party talk. Myus was by then apparently a good target for a cheap joke. Already by the time of Strabo, the end of the 1st century BC, the inhabitants had admitted defeat and taken their belongings and the statues of their gods to Miletus and one hears no more of them. The abandoned town was used by the Milesians as a quarry for building stone. Its position on a rocky outcrop inspired the Byzantines to build a castle there.

The ruins

Visiting Myus today, south of the cotton fields of Söke near the village of Avşar, in a land of scrub and fig trees, is a good day out, one that requires sturdy shoes and sunscreen. There is nothing left of the town to suggest that it ever was a harbour. The ruins are certainly unprepossessing, yet evocative.

The town was built on terraces carved out of the rock. Those could not be taken away, nor could the rock-cut cisterns and tombs. Everything else has been pillaged. Of the two temples (one to Apollo Terebinteus, the lord of the turpentine tree; the other sacred to Dionysus, built in white marble, according to sources), only stray blocks and column fragments remain. The Germans took an interest in the site from nearby Miletus, which explains why some of the finds, such as the chariot race frieze believed to have belonged to the Temple of Dionysus, and the votary of Hermonax and of his wife with boustrophedon writing, are in Berlin. The **Byzantine castle** dominating the site was known as Melaundion in the 11th century, when it was the chief fortification of the area. It was taken by the Saracens in 1079 but was again in Byzantine hands in the 13th century, at the time when the Byzantine emperor had been ousted from Constantinople by the Latins and when the Lascarids, whose portion of the empire was based in Nicaea, were taking a sustained interest in the defence of Anatolia. Melaundion was then an important administrative centre, in spite of being under pressure from the Seljuk emirs. Some 90m by 35m, it was built of rubble masonry with towers, a curtain wall with blind arches and fancy brickwork, vaulted rooms and two main gates, one to the north and one to the south. .

THE LATMOS REGION & HERAKLEIA

Now a national park, with stunning fauna and flora and a subtle atmosphere, the Latmos massif overlooking Lake Bafa (Bafa Gölü; *map B, 5*) has long been difficult of access. When she visited in the early 1950s, Freya Stark caught a boat from the southern shores of the lake, heading northeast towards the Beşparmak Mountains (the 'Five Fingers', a reference to the five peaks), the ancient Latmos, a Carian name. She had ample time to contrast the gentle Ionian landscape with this rugged, forbidding granite and gneiss massif, denuded and smoothed by millennia of erosion, strewn with huge tumbled boulders and culminating at 1375m in the Tekerlek Dağ ('the Wheel' in Turkish, an allusion to its rounded shape).

The Latmos region is an excellent choice for trekking, mountaineering or just for taking a day off with a picnic, either on foot or by donkey, and enjoying the fine setting. You will need a guide for this. The area is now being developed, very much with tourism in mind, and guided tours are available. You will be able to visit the Monastery of the Seven Brothers (Yediler), north of Gölyaka, and see the rock paintings. Herakleia and Latmos are both accessible by road north of Bafa. The best time to go is from April to June.

HISTORICAL OUTLINE OF THE LATMOS REGION

Caria begins here: that was true also at the time when the lake was a sea inlet, eventually blocked by the silting of the Meander at a date which is quite variable, from the 3rd–5th centuries AD. Miletus controlled the south shore with the town of Ioniapolis and the marble quarries used for the Didyma temple. Whoever controlled the route to Bafa and the Bafa Pass to the east had the access key to Caria. According to some, the past geography was the reason for the foundation of the now-deserted town of Latmos, which may have had a harbour, now possibly underwater. Alternatively, the new foundation may have been a refuge site for coastal Carians pushed inland by the colonising Ionians, or it may have been a way for the locals to hide from the marauding Cimmerians in the 7th century BC.

The town of Latmos, immediately to the east of Herakleia, is known in some detail from the work of Anneliese Paschlow Bindokat and her team. As Strabo (*14,1,8*) tells us, it was the predecessor of Herakleia and appears in the written sources from the 6th century BC; in the 5th century BC it was part of the Delian League as a tribute-paying polity, a non-Greek city. In the 4th century BC Latmos was part of the satrapy of Caria, therefore in Persian hands and fortified; it minted its own coins. By the early 3rd century BC it had been abandoned and the population moved to the newly-founded nearby town of Herakleia (though at this point it was called by a different name). The reasons for the move remain unclear. It seems that c. 290 BC a Carian dynast, one Pleistarchos, wanted a bigger, more showy town by the sea. Clearly, because of its topography, Latmos could not expand, though there was still empty space inside its walls. The move was possibly inspired by the refoundation of Ephesus by Lysimachus, a way to link one's name to an important project. What is certain is that the new town was originally called Pleistarcheia, though this was in due course changed to Herakleia, apparently in honour of Antiochus III of the Seleucid dynasty, who claimed descent from Herakles.

The new town was set out on a large scale with an immense wall circuit that is today its chief glory, as it has survived the centuries largely unscathed, one of the best examples of Hellenistic defensive architecture. The town itself has been little explored and is partly overlaid by the village of Kapıkırı; some of it is under water due to fluctuations. The visible ruins postdate the time of the foundation. As for Latmos, it was not completely forgotten. While some of it was quarried for building stone for Pleistarcheia, the land was used as a necropolis for the new town, with rock-hewn graves. Later, a small Byzantine settlement developed. The territory of Herakleia is thought to have extended from Myus to Amyzon in the east (*see below*) and to have included some arable land as well as the rugged mountains. The economy was based on the production of olive oil and honey and the exploitation of the iron resources in the mountains, an activity that only ceased in the 1970s. It is in the heights that the region got a new lease of life, when practical considerations made living by the sea a bad choice.

From around the 7th century AD, the Latmos massif became a 'monkery' (to use Chandler's expression). Monks and hermits from Sinai and the west Arabian coast settled here, living in caves, attracted by the remoteness and possibly the relative security of the area. From there they fanned out to Priene, Miletus, Magnesia and Tralles. They founded monasteries on the mainland and on the islands; at least 13 are known by name. The community lasted until the end of the 13th century. When they settled here, the area was certainly not uninhabited. Painstaking recording work has shown that the massif was criss-crossed by a dense network of roads and paths, some paved, some cut in the rock, extending for a total of c. 120km, with spring houses along the route stretching from Myus to Çukurköy on the eastern reaches of the Beşparmak. These roadways, like the cave paintings that have been found, some possibly prehistoric, cannot be dated precisely; however, the Hittite hieroglyph inscription shows a presence in the area as early as c. 1300 BC.

LATMOS

You may be forgiven for missing out Latmos altogether, at the foot of the Beşparmak, since it is perfectly camouflaged among the rocks and invisible from the water to the south. Bear in mind that it is barely one kilometre east of the landmark Byzantine castle on the southernmost reaches of Herakleia, and some 500m up a valley. To catch a glimpse of this elusive town, stop by the road after leaving Herakleia, as soon as you can see the outside city walls to your left. Take any of the paths uphill and you will soon come across huge worked stones, the remains of the city walls. Beyond, it is a scramble among the olive trees.

The town has a roughly rectangular shape some 700m by 500m, about the size of Priene. The wall circuit, with forts and towers in an elegant isodomic style typical of the Hekatomnids, has been traced in its entirety. Sections several courses high can be seen. The town was cut in two by a cross wall separating the citadel to the north with a roughly rectangular inner fort with four corner towers. The remains of a Byzantine chapel incorporating Hellenistic spolia mark the agora. In its southeast corner is the so-called Tomb of Endymion (*see box*). The town, all on a slope, was built on terraces. The retaining walls have regular embossed blocks in a style reminiscent of Labranda's. Many houses have been identified; a number cluster around the chapel and belong to the later occupation of the site. The one- or two-room constructions nestle in the spaces between the boulders and are built of irregular masonry and covered with tiled roofs. They differ very little from the traditional, timeless Latmian architecture that was prevalent in the region until the age of concrete took over.

ENDYMION

The myth of Endymion is inextricably linked with the Latmos mountains. It is thought to derive from an amalgamation of an earlier Carian deity, the focus of a cult on the Latmos massif, with the weather god that the Greeks appropriated as Zeus Akraios. According to the legend, Endymion was a beautiful youth, possibly a shepherd, who captivated Selene, the moon goddess. She obtained for him the gift of eternal youth by having him put to sleep for ever in a cave on Latmos. She bore him 50 daughters and one son. The myth has caught the imagination of countless writers, from Sappho to Keats, and inspired many artists. In the Latmos region two monuments are attributed to cult of Endymion, mainly because they are partly hewn out of the rock, mimicking the cave in which he slept. Selene, on the other hand, has a very minor place in the legend and no cult at all in the area. Of the monuments, one is in Herakleia, the other one is in Latmos in the southeast corner of the agora. The latter is supposed to be Endymion's tomb (though as he had been granted eternal youth, this presumably also entailed everlasting life). The monument was until quite recently in a very good state of preservation, mainly because of its remoteness; it was surrounded by a temenos some 12m by 20m. Measuring approximately 7m by 5.50m, the structure is part hewn in the rock and part built in well-cut ashlars. The cover consists of several monolithic gneiss blocks well over 4m long, just, but not completely, covering the thick side walls. The entrance is in the middle of the west wall. The style of the building, a heroön rather than a grave since it is in the agora and not outside the city walls, is reminiscent of the Hellenistic graves at Labranda, suggesting therefore that it was constructed before the town of Latmos was abandoned. Inside are two rooms, one of them cut into the living rock.

In Christian times the legend was sanitised, with Endymion still cast as a shepherd but also as a budding astronomer, which would explain his interest in the moon that he had ample time to study while tending his flock in the wilderness of Latmos. Alternatively, he is presented as a mystic and in some cases an early version of the Pantocrator. There is no accounting for the power of the Latmos mountains.

HERAKLEIA

Herakleia (*map B, 5*) offers a complete change from the eerie feeling of Latmos and its buzzing bees. The town, also called Kapıkırı, is alive and ready for tourists. The ruins are dotted around among the modern buildings and interspersed with large boulders

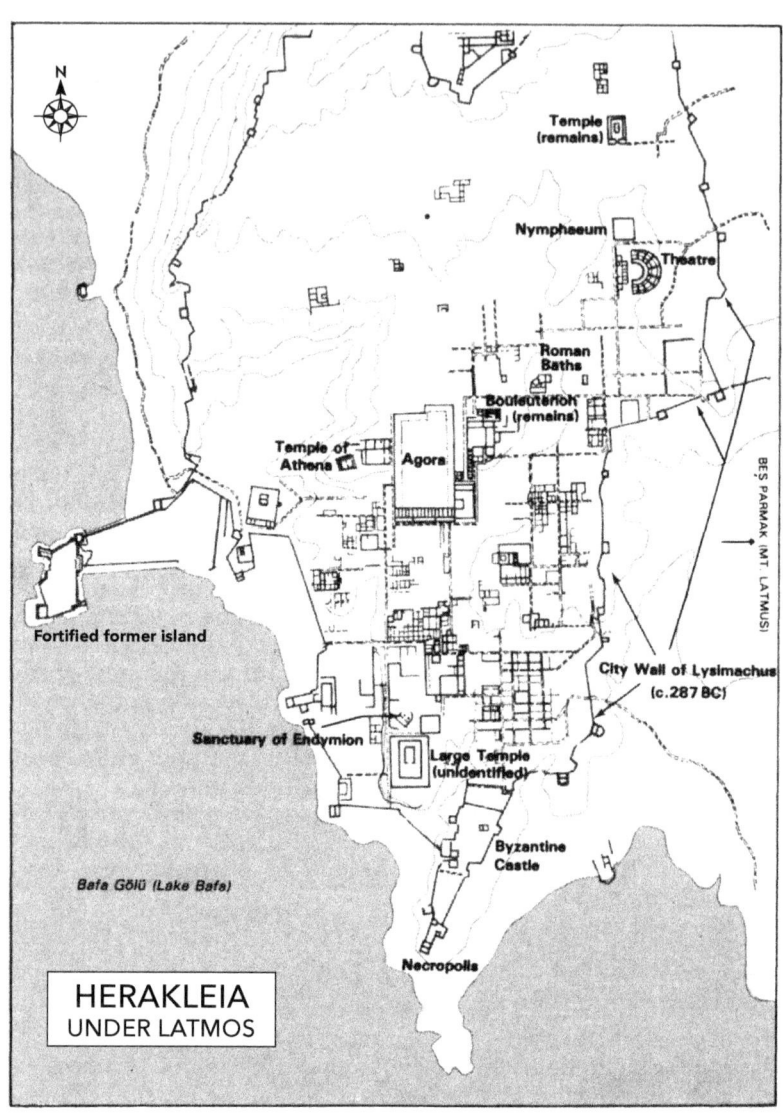

tumbled from above which give the place a dramatic look. The settlement is said to have been laid out on a grid. Start with the **agora**, where the school house is. A Hellenistic feature some 60m by 130m, it was supported by a massive terracing wall, still extant at the south end, which supported a row of shops. The cella walls of the **Temple of Athena**, not aligned to the city grid, are to the west on a spur. Hellenistic in date, this temple, in antis with a pronaos, was identified by an inscription.

Traces of the **bouleuterion** can be found among the olive trees in someone's back garden to the east of the agora. To the north, the scant remains of the **Roman theatre** facing west, of baths of the same period and other structures, possibly temples, have been identified. To the west by the water is an island which was fortified by the Byzantines and was then joined to the mainland by an isthmus with a wall now submerged by the changing water levels.

To the south along the coast, on a rise, is a **sanctuary to Endymion** (*see box above*), partly built in the rock, facing west and not aligned to the grid; its front porch, with five columns flanked by two pilasters, has not been satisfactorily explained. The fortified harbour is thought to have been by the rocky peninsula stretching south, where later the Byzantines built a castle and graves were cut in the rock.

A good pair of shoes will get you around the **city wall** of Herakleia (all 6km of it) up into the rugged slopes of Latmos. The wall is certainly Herakleia's chief attraction because of its pristine condition, possibly the best example of Hellenistic defensive technology. It is dated stylistically to the 3rd century BC, the time of Pleistarchos, the minor Hellenistic ruler busy carving himself a space in history between Lysimachus' Ephesus and the up-and-coming Seleucids of Syria. The circuit encloses far more land than the city Pleistarchos founded could ever occupy, an ambitious plan but doomed to fail since Pleistarcheia, later Herakleia, was destined to become a backwater. With 65 towers, numerous gates, posterns and wall walks, it was built on the bare rock hugging the heights, making the most of the steepness of the terrain. The wall survives to the second storey and in places to the tiled roofs; windows and slits for archers can be seen. The structure suggests that they were built to cope with advanced torsion artillery techniques. One simply wonders at the size of the garrison required to man it.

AMYZON

One should not be put off by the difficulty of getting to Amyzon (*map B, 6*; now Mazin Kalesi, Mazin being the Turkish rendering of Amyzon), on a secondary road from Gafarlar, 30km south of Koçarlı. The site, at 650m on the northern flanks of the Tekerlek Dağ, is stunning and wild, with fine views and scents. Presently work is being done to attract tourists. A recent survey has produced a good crop of coins and evidence of a theatre, a nymphaeum and an agora. Perhaps Amyzon's time has finally come: the latest archaeological investigation dates from the 1970s and much has been lost in the meantime.

Amyzon (a name which is either Carian or Luwian) is hardly mentioned in the written sources. Strabo (*14,2,23*) dismisses it as not even a city in his time. Earlier on, according to the inscriptions, its politics oscillated between the Seleucids and the Ptolemies. Its main feature was an important Temple of Artemis and Apollo, which offered the right of asylum. In the troubled times of the waning of Byzantine power, the temple terrace was fortified with a wall and twelve towers. Amyzon was then the seat of the suffragan bishop of Aphrodisias. The location was still inhabited in the 15th century, when the Ottomans transferred the population to Koçarlı.

The main feature of the site are two terraces in local blue-veined limestone, set at right angles. The west terrace, 168m by 62m, has not been much investigated. The east terrace, 62m by 74m with huge retaining walls on three sides, supports the temple, a Doric prostyle. It was accessed from the east via a propylon with Ionic columns on both sides. The present ruins date to the time of Idreus, according to his dedicatory inscription on the architrave of the propylon; the style of the remains is reminiscent of Labranda. The grand setting for the rebuilding of the temple (stray finds of terracotta figurines and of fragments of friezes found during excavation suggest the presence of an earlier, Archaic temple dated to the 6th century BC but not underlying the new temple) marked the reorganisation of this inaccessible mountain community by the Hekatomnids into something resembling a Greek city. The attempted rebranding did not quite work; Amyzon remained an isolated mountain community and later efforts by the Romans, who built a theatre here, were no more successful. Amyzon is a place with no water resources; no trace of an aqueduct has been found. It has been suggested that the so-far undated vaulted underground chambers in the larger west terrace may have been cisterns. Dotted around are impressive stretches of a 3rd-century BC city wall, in places seven metres high.

BARGYLIA & IASOS

Situated on the edge of the Güllük Körfezi, anciently Mandalya Bay, these two sites have had a diverging trajectory, both in antiquity and more recently.

BARGYLIA
In an area groaning under tourist development on the east side of the gulf, the site of Bargylia (*map B, 5*), east of Boğaziçi, stands out as a surprising stretch of green land. And so it should be: the ancient city is a grade one archaeological site. On the other hand there have been no excavations and knowledge of the site has not progressed much since George Bean sketched a plan and made a list of the visible remains in the late 1960s. He identified city walls, a temple, an altar, a theatre an odeion, a stoa and an aqueduct (tentatively dated as Hellenistic and Roman) to the north, as well as Byzantine features (a church, a castle and other buildings) to the south.

Topography was the reason why Bargylia ever developed: on a promontory overlooking a narrow, sheltered inlet of the bay, known as Varvil Bay, now Ulelibük Bay. These days most of it has all turned into marshy land and the flamingoes of the Tuzla Kuş Cenneti (Bird Paradise) have taken the place of the Ottoman salt pans that explain why it is now called Tuzla (*tuz* = salt). The original name (Bargylia) suggests an old Anatolian origin, which is confirmed by the presence of some Archaic remains; its time as a city came after Alexander the Great. Later Seleucids, Macedonians, and Rhodians occupied it in turn. Philip V, the Macedonian king, wintered his fleet here in 201 BC and was almost trapped in the harbour, which by that time was already silting up. Bargylia clearly had a life in the Roman period. The chief goddess that appears on its coins, Artemis Cindyas, had to share her temple with Augustus. This particular Artemis had originally been worshipped in the Archaic town of Cindya nearby to the east, on the other side of the Milas–Bodrum road. Sometime in the 3rd century BC, the town ceased to exist and the population was incorporated into Bargylia. The Byzantines were the first to use Bargylia as a quarry for their church, castle and other buildings. Later, much worked stone was lost because of the closeness of the ruins to the sea. The rest went with illegal digging. These days there is not much to see as the vegetation has spread uncontrolled. The owners, who inherited the plot from their father, may not build or use it for any purpose that involves digging or building. They may sell it but with the same restrictions. At the time of writing they had recently put it on the market, which served to highlight the plight of many grade one archaeological sites in private ownership in Turkey. No one is doing anything to protect and investigate these sites, illegal digging is rife and the owners find their land worthless.

IASOS

A beautiful 1km-long rocky peninsula, shaped like a teardrop, stretches into the gulf of Mandalya to the north and west of Güllük. Iasos (*map B, 5*) is promised a bright future in the tourist literature: 'A must-see for yachtsmen'. Fortunately it is also accessible by land (sparingly signposted from main road). In a land of poor soil and with poor lines of communication inland, Iasos by necessity turned towards the sea. It owes its fortune to fishing and to the fine, sheltered harbour to the west, facing the modern village of Kıyıkışlacık. A grade one archaeological site, it has been a difficult one to investigate. The land is privately owned and under a blanket cover of mature olive trees. Excavations, for a long time in the hands of the Italians, have perforce been restricted. Even so, after 60 years of painstaking work, Iasos's trajectory through history is beginning to take shape. Work on site has been assisted by a study of the hinterland showing that the territory of the city of Iasos, extending to the Grion mountains to the northeast, was defined from the Archaic Period onwards by a limestone wall with some 20 towers hugging the heights.

HISTORICAL OUTLINE OF IASOS

In the course of investigations, early material from Crete and the Cyclades has been found, showing contact but leaving the nature of it uncertain, suggesting that the peninsula was a contact area between Anatolia and the wide world of the Aegean to the west. Later, in the 10th century BC, the Protogeometric necropolis and other layers of occupation underlying the later agora show a settled presence before the arrival of Greek colonists, according to tradition from Argos, sometime in the 9th century BC. With some initial help from Miletus, Iasos prospered. Fish was plentiful, probably spawning a trade in salt fish; good limestone and marble could be had from the quarries on the mainland; the possibility of a spot of piracy should not be discounted. Certainly, by the time the Spartans sacked it in 412 BC (Thucydides, 8:28), they had reason to be pleased with their efforts; in the words of the historian, Iasos was 'a place full of ancient wealth'. At the time Iasos was a member of the Delian League and was caught up in the rivalry between Sparta and Athens, with the Persians looming large. In the following century it was still in Persian hands and in the troubled times after the death of Alexander the Great it was contested by the Seleucids of Syria and the rulers of Egypt.

Incorporation into the Roman Empire, under which it was a customs station, eventually brought peace and prosperity (judging by the fine buildings and mosaics of that date). The city, however, had originally put up a fierce resistance and paid a heavy price for it. In the Late Antique and Early Byzantine periods, Iasos was still flourishing—at least, the numerous churches suggest as much, though perhaps it suffered from Arab incursions in the 7th–9th centuries, when signs of decline begin to appear, suggesting a reduction in population. The castle by the isthmus immediately to the north of the agora is the work of the Byzantines, with an 11th-century date. It suggests retrenchment, defending the mainland and giving up the peninsula.

The castle on the acropolis is later, c. 14th–15th century. It was the work of the Menteşe, the dynasty of emirs who preceded the Ottomans in the area. They also refurbished the harbour to the west and for a while ran a profitable alum trade. In due course, towards the end of the 16th century, the Ottomans housed their fleet in Iasos's harbour. When Richard Chandler visited in 1775, the place was deserted and strewn with spolia, just as it was some 60 year later, when Texier began the first systematic study of the remains. The great spoliation of Iasos—which is chiefly responsible for its unprepossessing appearance today— dates to the end of the 19th century when the city walls, the theatre and other standing structures were systematically demolished to provide worked stone for the quays in Istanbul. That is the price one pays for being so close to the sea.

Visiting Iasos

Because of the nature of the excavations, limited in scope by practical constraints, it has not been possible to recover the plan of the city. However it appears that the west and south sides, gently sloping from the high point of the acropolis to the sea, were residential with buildings on terraces cut in the rock in the period from the 6th century BC to the 5th century AD. Evidence for high-status Hellenistic and Roman villas has been recovered, with at the very tip of the peninsula the remains of the earlier **Sanctuary of Demeter and Kore**, with a propylon to the south showing it was meant to be approached from the sea. The east side of the peninsula was apparently deemed too rocky and steep for building.

On the **Acropolis**, the Menteşe wall circuit with towers overlays evidence of activity from the Prehistoric to the Classical periods which has not been yet investigated. The heavily spoliated **Theatre**, northeast of the acropolis and looking east, is Roman in date with a possible Hellenistic antecedent.

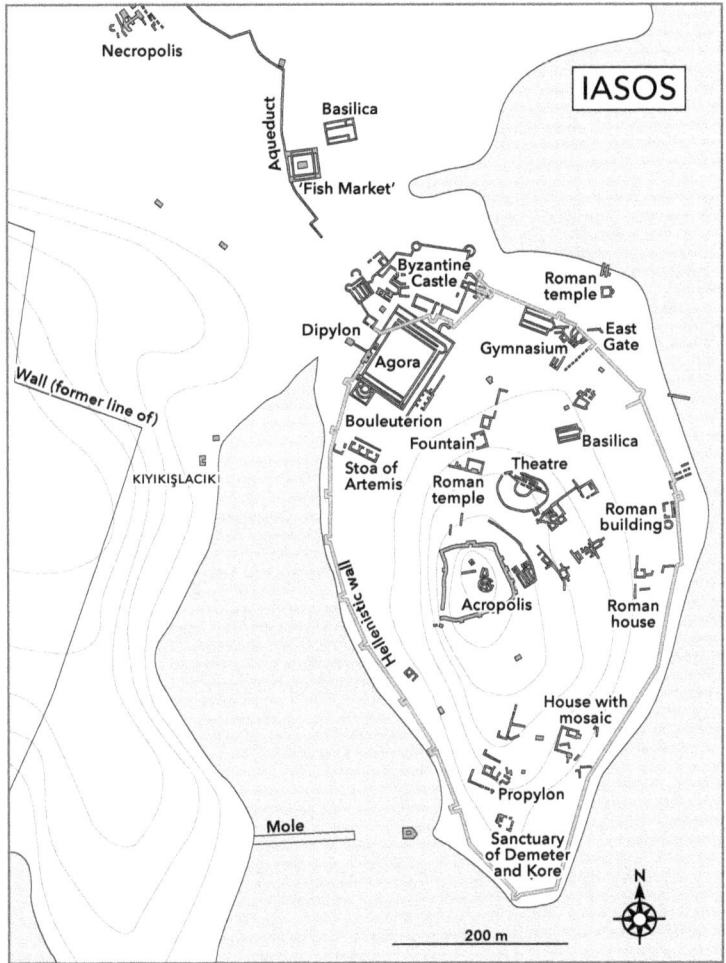

To the northwest, by the isthmus, the main focus is the **Agora** overlying a
Protogeometric necropolis. The Roman agora (107m by 87m), with double and
single stoas all around, occupies the spot of the earlier 4th-century BC agora.
It remained a functioning public space until around the 5th century AD, when it
started to be dismantled to provide building stone for churches and the middle space
became a necropolis. It was accessed from the west via a monumental Hellenistic
dipylon. Beyond the stoa at the southeast, a complex of three rooms with controlled
access and water features has been interpreted as a sanctuary to Egyptian deities with
a 2nd-century AD date. On the south side of the agora, next to the well-preserved
Bouleuterion of Roman date, a large building was dedicated to the worship of
Emperor Commodus (r. 180–92). It housed an earlier **temple** in its centre, possibly

dedicated to Artemis Astias. She shared with Zeus Megistos the position of main deity of the city; Zeus's temple has been identified in the northeast section of the peninsula close to the city walls.

The **city walls** that ran all around the peninsula were Iasos's chief glory as they were quite tall (having no help from the topography), had plenty of towers and were starkly white. So much so that Texier thought they were made of marble (in fact the material was good quality limestone). The Byzantines in their heyday reinforced the circuit by adding a tower at the entrance to the harbour, on top of the more easterly of the two piers controlling access. The walls are tentatively dated to the 4th century BC; they look Hekatomnid in style, though there is no clear evidence that Iasos ever came into their hands. On the isthmus in Roman times, when city walls ceased to be important, a section was demolished to enlarge the agora. Later, however, when defence again became a priority and the Byzantines built their castle on the isthmus, the north corner of the agora, at the time a burial ground, was clipped and the monumental entrance partly destroyed.

Christianity is documented in Iasos as from the first half of the 5th century, roughly as in the rest of Caria, a land that, not being on a main through route like Colossae or Laodiceia for example, was bypassed by the earlier preachers. Thus far **five churches** have been identified. The one on the acropolis, an area that may have been short of water (which would explain why it had a rock-cut cistern in the atrium), was rather large (23m by 13m) but made of inferior material. It was later turned into a tetraconch church with four apses and massive piers. Significantly, Christianity also marked its presence in the middle of the former agora, with a basilica right on top of a Hellenistic naiskos possibly dedicated to the cult of Artemis Astias. The other three churches on the peninsula, including one outside the walls, are only known through their surface remains. On the mainland, north of the Byzantine castle, the large 5th-century basilica with three naves and a polygonal apse, is awaiting full investigation. Its plan has been compared to the monastery church of St John Studios in Constantinople. Its opus sectile floor had been lifted from an earlier building.

By the remains of the aqueduct is the so-called '**Fish Market**'. It is certainly likely that a place like Iasos should have had a fish market, but it was definitely not this building, the entirety of which is a mausoleum, a tomb surrounded by a portico. The Turks, however, call it so (*balık pazarı*) and the name has stuck. It now houses an antiquarium (*open Wed–Mon 8–5*), which is well worth a visit although most of Iasos's earlier finds have ended up in Istanbul or İzmir. As for the tomb itself, of Roman date in well-cut ashlar, it was originally some 9m tall, including the podium with ten steps full of sunken slab-covered graves. Not much remains of the superstructure with Corinthian pilasters. The surrounding portico, of far inferior masonry, has been heavily restored and rebuilt. A good comparandum for the grave is the Gümüş Kesen monument in Milas.

Immediately to the west is the village of **Kıyıkışlacık**. It overlies a necropolis, indeed some of the houses incorporate a number of the monumental tombs. The village has also spread over an earlier feature that was visible when the first antiquarians visited. This was a 2.5km-long wall in large blocks of coarse limestone and schist, in the shape of a trapezium with circular towers and one main entrance. George Bean though it was the work of the aboriginal inhabitants of Caria, the Leleges of whom one knows very little. That would have implied a strong native presence in the area. After mature consideration and taking account that the inside of the circuit was quite empty apart from a couple of huts, it seems that, rather than a town, this was a military camp. The layout, with jogs and sally ports, and the scorpion slits in the towers for archers to do their deadly work from, are Hellenistic. The most likely builder of such a structure would be the Macedonian ruler Philip V, sometime in the very late 3rd century BC when he made an ultimately unsuccessful bid to expand in Anatolia and, as a result, was stuck here for a time with his army.

EUROMOS

North of Milas, Euromos (*map B, 6*) is conveniently located by the roadside on Route 525, a few kilometres south of Selimiye. The temple, surrounded by olive groves, has been a tourist attraction for quite some time. If the *bekçi* is in attendance you will have to buy a ticket.

When Chandler visited in 1764, thinking he had found Labranda, the old stones were being fed to the lime kilns set up *in situ*. Lime is an excellent fertiliser. Even so, enough has remained for reconstruction and these days the **Temple to Zeus Lepsynus**, identified by the inscription on one of the columns, is classed as one of the best Greek-style temples in Turkey (the requirement of a 'pure mind and a righteous soul' to enter it, as spelt out in the same inscription, has been waived). The temple cannot fail to impress, with its 14.5m by 27m stylobate and 16 standing fluted columns supporting part of the architrave. The style is Corinthian and the date is Hadrianic, first quarter of the 2nd century. It was never completed, as some unfluted columns suggest. As for 'Lepsynus', this epithet of Zeus is attested in the area, at Iasos for instance, so it may have been a local cult.

Work in the early 1970s revealed a bothros with a profusion of fragments of painted, terracotta relief slabs; these are characteristic of Archaic temples, where they were nailed to the wooden supporting structure to protect it. Analysis of the motifs (banquet scenes and a procession of gods on chariots pulled by winged horses, lotus flowers and palmettes) have suggested to Suat Ateşlier that the 6th-century BC Archaic temple complex was dedicated to Hecate, the goddess of childbirth and of the cycle of life and death, thought to have an Anatolian origin. The temple roof had gorgon acroteria almost a metre in diameter. To the south, signposted, is one of the necropoleis, with vaulted tombs of Roman date.

The story of Euromos does not end here, though. It was a city and the temple was extramural. Originally called Kyromos or Hyromos, the city Hellenised its name around the 4th century BC to Euromos, which chimed with the Greek word '*rhome*', meaning strength, but when Philip V of Macedon occupied it in the 2nd century BC it was briefly called Philippoi. Situated in a good agricultural region favourable to oil and wine production, Euromos struggled in a balancing act between Herakleia and

Milas, resorting to appealing for help to the Rhodians at some point. It survived into Roman times and was a bishopric later under Byzantium. Coinage is known from the 4th century BC.

Work on the remains of the city has only recently started. It was situated north of the temple and was surrounded by a **wall circuit** over 2.5m thick in huge, well-cut ashlars, Hellenistic in date. Stretches up to five courses high can be seen among the olive trees. Remains of towers have been identified. The circuit extended on both sides of the modern road. Inside the wall circuit an agora 50m by 70m with a stoa has been identified, with a possible bath house to the north. The theatre, dated to the 3rd century BC with an estimated capacity of 3,000, was situated on a natural slope well to the east where the land rises. It has been heavily robbed and not much remains of the skene nor of the seating.

STRATONIKEIA & LAGINA

Deep into Caria, on the way to Yatağan from Milas, a couple of sites are now vying for attention, though they have both been known for some time.

Dubbed a second Pompeii, the city of marble and the city of love, Stratonikeia (*map B, 6*) is alas an example of what happens when you pay attention to the archaeology too late. Built in the early 1980s, the Yatağan power station has been fed with the lignite extracted nearby, close to the village of Eskihisar which previously occupied the site of Stratonikeia. Large spoil heaps were created with no regard to the old remains; in 1985 a road was driven through, cutting the old city in half. Eventually, in order to expand the mine, the village was moved to the west (though some villagers have stayed put). In the last ten or so years, Yatağan municipality has been very active promoting the town as a tourist attraction, in order entice the crowds from the beaches to come inland for a day in the mountains. Turkish archaeologists have been busy uncovering and tidying up what is left.

Lagina, infected by the same fever, may fare better. While getting there involves going past the unappealing industrial town of Turgut, on the north side of Route 330, beyond that point the landscape is really beautiful and the ruins certainly worth the trouble.

A SHORT HISTORY OF STRATONIKEIA

On a plain between hills, Stratonikeia was a Hellenistic foundation, sometime after 268 BC when this part of the world came under the domination of the Seleucids. It may have replaced and enlarged an earlier Carian settlement called Idrias or Chrysaoris. The latter name has been suggested because of the involvement of the town with the Chrysaorian League (League 'of the Golden Sword') and the temple of Zeus Chrysaoris, supposedly in the vicinity (it has not yet been located).

The new name was in honour of a young lady called Stratonice who, according to Stephanos of Byzantium, writing in the 6th century AD, had first married Seleucus I Nicator and then had inspired a violent passion in her stepson, Antiochus. Seleucus had graciously allowed the couple to marry. Strabo (*14,2,25*) described the city as 'full of expensive buildings' and also noted that there was a strong Macedonian input, probably veterans after the occupation by Philip V. Certainly the Hellenistic city was planned on a grand scale, with all the appropriate public buildings; such profusion was a statement in itself, meaning that this was a Carian city fully partaking in the Greek world. After the Macedonians, it fell into the hands of the Rhodians. In 133 BC Stratonikeia became one of the headquarters of the revolt led by Aristonikos (identified either as the illegitimate son of Attalus III, the last Pergamene king, or the son of a musician). He had opposed Attalus III's bequest of the kingdom of Pergamon to the Romans and had apparently enjoyed the support of the lower classes, the slaves and the mercenaries. He lost, and in the process devastated the region, putting up a fierce and futile resistance in the mountainous district between the Lycus and the Marsyas rivers. His last holdout was southeast of Stratonikeia at Şahan Kaya, a mass of igneous rock up a narrow valley; it is unexcavated to this day but was clearly a strategic location, as the Byzantine fortifications reusing Hellenistic material imply.

In due course Stratonikeia joined the Roman province of Asia, only to be sacked by Mithridates VI for opposing him against the up-and-coming western power in 88 BC. After more upsets, during which its territory was devastated by the rogue Roman general Labienus, Stratonikeia settled down to an uneventful, peaceful period. Both Augustus and later Hadrian offered financial help to improve the infrastructure and to make repairs after earthquakes; for a while the place took the name of Hadrianopolis. Christian Stratonikeia is little known apart from some bishops' names and a few stones with well-made crosses belonging to a building yet to be identified.

When R. Pococke visited in 1743 he was impressed by the remains. He could trace the city wall, pseudo-isodomic in style and in local slate, all 2.5km of it. Later Chandler recorded some inscriptions. By then if not before, a village had sprung up among the ruins, using spolia as building material or simply as stools to sit on and socialise. The latest industrial developments have not been kind to the community or to the ancient remains.

Visiting Stratonikeia

The site, on Route 330, is immediately southeast of the modern village of Eskihisar. The acropolis, about which little is known except that it had its own wall circuit, is across the road to the south. During works in the 1980s a monumental fountain 41m long was uncovered by the roadside. It has been dated to the 1st century BC. Between the road and the theatre, in a commanding position on the north side of the road, are the remains of the **Temple of Augustus**, 15m by 21m with fluted Ionic columns. It has been compared in style to the Temple of Zeus at Labranda and some have argued that originally it could have been the temple of Zeus Chrysaoris but there is nothing to prove it. The **theatre**, originally Hellenistic, refurbished and enlarged in the Roman period, could accommodate 10,000. It now sits among the trees waiting for the skene to be completely exposed. Further north are the scanty remains of the **gymnasium**, the largest in Anatolia (105m by180m), dated to the 2nd century BC, one of the earliest public buildings in the town. It has produced a number of inscriptions detailing local events. Immediately to the east are the remains of a **hamam**, thought to be medieval in date, when Stratonikeia was occupied by a Seljuk emir.

The well-preserved bouleuterion marks the agora, not yet fully explored, which had a monumental entrance to the west. The **bouleuterion**, of which four rows of seating survive, was made of well-cut large blocks, quite an impressive construction. On the outside, to the north, look out for a copy of Diocletian's Price Edict (*see p. 157*) in Latin and, among the modern graffiti, for an exquisite relief of a vase and flowers with an Arabic inscription. Inside the bouleuterion, a number of Greek and Latin inscriptions record oracular responses, including one from the Sanctuary of Zeus Panamaros, yet another holy place thought to have been in the territory of Stratonikeia but not yet located. The building to the southeast of the bouleuterion is the 19th-century **mansion of Hasan Şar**, who was then the local ağa. It is being restored and will be the site museum. Here you will be able to see the intriguing Mycenaean stirrup jar associated with the site: unfortunately there is no information about the context in which it was found.

The paved **colonnaded street**, over 100m long, has recently been exposed and re-erected. It leads to the north gate. Some of the houses on either side have mosaic floors which were under restoration at the time of writing. The street terminates in a monumental semicircular fountain, located between the two arches of the **North Gate**. The sacred way to Lagina started here. Immediately to the east, a stronghold with two towers guarded the ravine nearby. Originally Hellenistic, it was refurbished and restored up until Byzantine times. Outside the gate was the necropolis, partly buried under the refuse created by the mining activities. Here a number of underground vaults have been identified, as well as several stelae of gladiators (now in Muğla Museum), adding yet another nickname to Stratonikeia's long list: 'the town of retired gladiators'. Nothing much remains of the city walls, though their course is known.

LAGINA

Lagina (*map B, 6*), earlier called Leyna, is a fine sight in a beautiful mountainous setting, a complete change from the industrial town of Turgut, with its marble quarries and open-cast mines. Take the turning at the Yatağan power station and drive north. The site is poorly signposted to the east of Turgut, on a bad road some 500m long. You may have to pay an entrance fee if the *bekçi* is there; otherwise it is unfenced.

Lagina was a site sacred to Hecate. There is no known settlement, though there are signs of occupation in the wider area that go back to the Bronze Age. Since the goddess is probably of Anatolian origin, only later incorporated into the Graeco-Roman pantheon, is it possible that beneath the late Hellenistic–Roman ruins there was an earlier indigenous sanctuary.

The Temple of Hecate had a wide catchment area extending across Caria. Its purpose was to create not so much a political unity as a focal point for the Carian people to celebrate their common ethnicity and religious beliefs. Festivals and games were held here at regular intervals: every four years in the case of the *Hecatesia Romaea*, instituted after the Mithridatic Wars; annually for the Birthday Festival and for the Bearing of the Key, a ceremony celebrating the translation of the key of the temple to and from Stratonikeia along the sacred way. Recently the local municipality has revived this last ceremony. Local girls dress up in Greek attire and perform the ceremony to an invented choreography (though it is doubtful that they walk the entire 9.5km-long road which the ancient ceremony entailed). There is not much left of the road in any case, since it has been severely damaged by the lignite mines.

The bonding of the Carians did not only take place here. Other locations where they could get together were the Temple of Zeus Chrysaoris, the seat of the Chrysaorian League, or the Temple of Zeus Panamaros; both are yet to be located. The Seleucids are credited with the building of the Hellenistic sanctuary to Hecate which was later sacked by Labienus, venting his rage here after he failed to take Stratonikeia in 40 BC. Emperor Augustus stepped in to finance the reconstruction, as stated by an inscription on the propylon. The temple continued to function until about the 3rd century, after which the site was abandoned; the Byzantine apsidal chapel with three naves is not precisely dated but it shows a desire to stamp out old beliefs. Built with spolia between the temple and the altar to the east, it used the stylobate and the colonnade as an aisle. It incorporates a relief of Serapis and elements of a naiskos dated to the 2nd century AD. Recently there has been a surge of interest in Lagina and Hecate by modern followers of occult religions.

Investigations at Lagina have until recently been minimal. Osman Hamdi Bey worked here for one season, just long enough to remove the temple and altar friezes to the Istanbul Archaeological Museum that he had set up and was busy filling. He left *in situ* one block belonging to the altar but this has now disappeared. Recently a Turkish team has been busy excavating and recording.

Visiting Lagina

The **Temple of Hecate** sits in a large trapezium-shaped precinct measuring 150m by 135m, with a Doric stoa on three sides. On the south side the steps may have been used as spectators' stands to watch the mysteries. On that side to the east was the entrance, with a monumental propylon. The temple, with a stylobate measuring 20m by 28m on a four-step podium, must have looked rather small. A Corinthian pseudo-dipteros, it faced east and consisted of a cella fronted by a deep pronaos with two Ionic columns. On the antae and on the temple walls were affixed a number of inscriptions (dedications, lists and decrees). Among them were two letters from the Roman general Sulla and a decree of the Roman Senate granting the temple the right of asylum for backing the Roman cause at the time of the Mithridatic

Wars. The remains of the altar, on a stepped podium to the east, are not sufficient to reconstruct its shape. Recent excavations have unearthed structures believed to belong to the priests' houses. Outside the precinct, 300m to the south, a sacred pool for purification ceremonies has been identified.

HECATE

Hecate is a goddess of many parts: she reigns over land, air and sea, as well as over the moon and the underworld. She was first described by Hesiod in the *Theogony*, a poem dated to the 8th century BC dealing with the origins of the universe. In the *Theogony*, Hecate is a descendant of the Titans, but other versions make her a daughter of Zeus, though she was never a full Olympian deity, possibly reflecting her non-Greek origins. She was perceived initially as quite benevolent and friendly to humanity. She could bestow success in a number of human endeavours: in sports, fishing, animal husbandry and business. Over time though, she took on a more sinister character, mingling with magic, sorcery and the unknown regions of the underworld, a character that appears to have persisted to this day.

Hecate is sometimes represented in triplicate, as three female figures joined at the back, possibly a reflection of her ritual, which involved celebrations at crossoads and junctions. Recently though, a little bronze Hecate has been unearthed at Lagina. Here the goddess greatly resembles the Artemis of Ephesus, with the multiple 'breasts', making Hecate a truly Anatolian goddess. Hecate is bound to remain elusive; she reflects human fears and those are numerous, from childbirth, for which she carries a lighted torch since she brings the child to light, to the dangers of soldiers at war and sailors on rough seas, as well as the threatening restless spirits that are everywhere in people's imagination; this explains why small sanctuaries devoted to her were located by the entrance doors of buildings that she was entreated to protect.

The Lagina reliefs

The reliefs of Lagina have been studied by Pamela Webb. Nothing much can be said of the altar for lack of evidence. As for the temple, it had a frieze running all the way around, of which about half is extant. It has been dated to the mid-late 2nd century BC. Webb identified a gigantomachy in a rocky setting, in the style of the Pergamon altar, at the west end. The north and south friezes are difficult to make out and do not appear to have a unified theme. At the front, the sculptural decoration celebrates the birth of Hecate's father Zeus, showing the infant with his mother Rhea reclining on a *kline*, a bed; all around them the Curetes are dancing and shouting, to cover the cries of the new-born baby. A woman carries a stone wrapped in swaddling clothes. She will give it to Chronos, Zeus' father, who did not want any children to threaten his dominion and therefore swallowed them at birth. (When Zeus became the chief god, he found all his siblings alive and well in Chronos's stomach, as well as the stone.)

GERGAS

Six kilometres southeast of Eski Çine, Gergas (*map B, 6*), up the valley of the Madran Çay and spread across two hills, has now become more accessible since the road from Çine to Yatağan has been improved because of the recent building of the Çine dam (at the time of writing still under construction). Even so, it is better to join a group with a guide than to wander off into the wilderness.

The starting point is the İncekemer Köprüsü, a bridge with slender arches (hence the name) spanning a ravine on the Çine Çay. Unfortunately it is destined to go under the waters of the dam, to the horror of the local press who immediately dubbed it 'Roman' (it is probably in fact Ottoman in date).

Since it was explored by a couple of intrepid Frenchmen in 1900, Gergas has changed little. There have been no excavations. The site—one would hesitate to call it a settlement, though the first explorers did see some ruins of buildings but they could not be dated—is particularly distinctive for being unlike anything else, and that in itself makes it worth a visit, quite apart from the enjoyment of a good day out. It has a name which is repeated at least 30 times across the site, on stones and artefacts, occurring variously as Gerga, Gergas or Gergakome, this last variant suggesting a village, in tall lettering in both Greek and Latin. Sometimes the script has been found in concealed places, perhaps for apotropaic practices. A couple of crude statues some 3m tall are to be seen lying toppled; shaped stones could be stelae. A few small structures have been interpreted as tombs or fountain houses. The most impressive monument remains the 'temple' entirely built of huge, well-cut stone elements. It imitates wooden architecture, with mortises and tenons. At the back is a recess for either a statue or a tomb. On the pediment across the front, a huge 'Gergas' screams for attention. For want of a better reference the masonry has been called Carian; it is certainly not Greek nor Roman nor later. Known Lelegian buildings and tombs from the Bodrum peninsula do not however provide anything so monumental, certainly nothing like the tall statues. While Gergas remains a mystery, speculation is rife.

ALABANDA TO BODRUM

West of Çine, on the high plateau where the Latmos Mountains slope towards the valley of the Çine Çay, the towns of Alinda and Alabanda, two Anatolian-sounding names, are not far from the river Marsyas (now the Çine Çay), a river flowing north into the Meander and the locus of one of the best known Greek myths about Apollo. Clearly music, at which the god excelled, did not soften or refine his disposition. When Marsyas, a satyr living in the woods in the area, challenged him at playing the flute and lost, the god tied him to a tree and flayed him alive. The river grew out of the tears of fellow satyrs, nymphs and of Marsyas' pupils. Now the river has changed a bit, there is a dam under construction and the clear waters might no longer be so clear.

ALABANDA

The ruins of Alabanda (*map B, 6*) are a few kilometres west of Çine, by a village variously called Araphisar or Doğanyurt, and in countryside reputed in the past for being excellent for horse rearing. The settlement, physically planned as a Greek city, was founded in the 4th century BC: foundation legends abound, involving mythical Alabandus and his amazing feats of war. More prosaically, Mausolus or another Hekatomnid ruler was the founder. The time was right and their desire to urbanise the Carians is well known. Later Alabanda may have become important as a halfway house between the Meander and Stratonikeia to the south. According to some, the location can be identified with Waliwanda, which would imply an earlier Hittite interest.

HISTORY OF ALABANDA
In the 3rd century BC the history of Alabanda followed the usual pattern. Initially in the hands of the Seleucids, it later became Antiochia of the Chrysaorians. The town went through a spell of Macedonian domination and was sacked by Philip V; later the region fell to Rhodes but Alabanda remained a free city. In the turmoil of the Roman civil wars of the 1st century BC, when generals such as Labienus roamed free in Caria looking for booty to support their cause, it lost its temple treasures; when it rebelled, Labienus put the inhabitants to the sword. In imperial times came peace and prosperity—and even luxury, according to Strabo (*3,26*), who is quite censorious about its culture of banqueting to the music of young ladies playing the harp. It cannot have been that bad, since Alabanda was the seat of the district court at the time. Pliny the Elder (*38,6*) praised its almandine, a variety of garnet used for seals and inlays.

The later history of the city is one of decline. Minting ceased c. 250, later there was a bishop and a church built with spolia, mutilated and placed face to face to exorcise the power of the ancient religion; other antiquities were reused as stelae in the Muslim cemetery. Plundering played its part in the obliteration of the city but there was also a problem with flooding. The local stream issuing from the hills ran uncontrolled into the plain, blanketing many ruins with a thick layer of silt (3m deep in places according to some). However, enough remained strewn around and visible since, in 1905, when Halil Edhem Bey, the younger brother of Osman Hamdi Bey and like him busy filling up the Istanbul Archaeological Museum, had to pick a site that would furnish antiquities, he chose Alabanda. That explains why some material is in the museum in Istanbul; it is only fair to say that he traced the wall circuit with towers and gates at a time when it was more visible. Otherwise up to very recently little research has been done; presently Turkish archaeologists are working there.

The site
The city plan is roughly known and up to a point conforms to Strabo's description (*14,2,22*). He says that the town is located at the foot of two hills so that it looks like

an ass carrying two panniers (full of scorpions, he goes on to add). There are actually three hills to the south and the easternmost was the acropolis. The town extended in the plain to the north. The **city wall**, in bossed ashlar blocks and filled with rubble with some 30 towers and six gates, best seen on the hills, is dated to the 4th century BC. The **theatre**, possibly originally Hellenistic but later enlarged, is set against the slope of the acropolis (which is carpeted with a fantastic bloom of irises at the right time of year). The analemma wall is a fine piece of masonry. Inside, much has been lost, though you can still admire the seats with lion's paws for the town dignitaries. The foundations of the skene have now been exposed and re-erected. To the east are the remains of the **temple to Apollo Isotimus** (equal in honour), which may mean equal to Zeus Chrysaoris originally and later, with the introduction of the imperial cult, possibly equal to the divine Roman emperors. The temple, with massive white marble columns, was Ionic in style and had a frieze representing the battle between the Greeks and the Amazons. It dates from the 2nd century BC. Recent excavations have uncovered an exquisite head of Artemis (with an impressive hairstyle), at present exhibited in Aydın Museum. In the vicinity, the foundations of another, smaller temple is believed to be the one mentioned by Livy (43,6,5), dedicated to Rome under whose protection the city had placed itself in the 2nd century BC.

Nothing much remains of the agora, known to have been a large rectangle with colonnaded stoas on at least two sides. It was situated immediately to the north of the most prominent ruin of Alabanda: the huge outer wall of the bouleuterion, standing in places to 9m high. Built in brown stone in huge regular ashlars, the structure had a roughly rectangular shape. The façade had four doors with a number of windows above. Inside, not much remains of the semicircular seating. Note the rows of square holes, possibly used to affix architectural decorations.

ALINDA

Alinda (*map B, 6*) is not far: keep west to Karpuzlu; the ruins are just beyond the west end of the village. Little is known of the earlier history of Alinda, a city that has yielded very few inscriptions. It makes a grand entry in history towards the end of the 4th century BC, with Alexander the Great. At that point the satrap in Halicarnassus was Pixidarus, the youngest of the Hekatomnids (*see box below*), who had seized power by throwing out his sister Ada five years earlier. She had fled to Alinda and one can presume that its fortified acropolis was the main reason for her choice. When the young, charismatic Macedonian general entered Caria in 334 BC, Ada went to meet him and to win him with her mature charms. She offered to adopt him as a son in exchange for his help to recover her due. Alexander accepted the challenge, expelled Pixidarus from Halicarnassus, reinstated Ada and moved on. In gratitude, Alinda was for a while renamed Alexandria ad Latmos. Beyond this episode, its history is a blank. It is known that it minted coins from the 2nd century BC to the 3rd century AD and judging by the remains, it seems that Roman Alinda enjoyed a certain prosperity. The Byzantine church within the extreme eastern section of the city walls shows a survival into late antiquity and possibly beyond, when Alinda was the see of a bishopric. It was still mentioned as city in the 10th century, by which time it was possibly reduced to the acropolis. Altogether Alinda looks more rustic and native that nearby Alabanda. No decorative element of any building is known; there are no statues, nor any name to link it to an artistic or intellectual life of any sort.

MAKING A SPLASH:THE HEKATOMNIDS

The history of Caria is dominated by the towering figure of Mausolus, the third generation of a short-lived but highly successful dynasty originally from around Mylasa but afterwards firmly embedded in the history of Halicarnassus. It all happened in just 60 years, from the appointment by the ruling Persians of Hekatomnus to the newly created satrapy of Caria (up to then Caria had been part of the satrapy of Lydia) c. 392 BC, to the death of his granddaughter, known as Ada II, who had married the last Persian satrap of Halicarnassus, Othontopates. After this, Caria fell into the hands of the successors of Alexander the Great, the diadochoi.

Satraps, that is local governors acting for the Great King in distant Persia, had up to the early 4th century BC been of Persian extraction. The appointment of Hekatomnus marks a departure and is not easily explained. It could be seen as a mark of weakness of the over-extended empire, beset by problems both outside its borders and within them, as satrapies became hereditary with the entailing loss of control of central power. Mausolus moved adroitly in this messy world. After his grandfather Hyssaldomos left his stronghold of Peçin Kale for Mylasa in the plain (*see Milas, below*), Mausolus developed his plans on a grander scale, moving to the sea and and increasing his own territory, becoming a player in the Aegean world, which at the time was dominated by the Persian-Greek rivalry. The newly-founded Halicarnassus (modern Bodrum), with an expanded population, was intended to be a window on the west and a suitable place to showcase not so much Persian power but the up-and-coming Hekatomninds. It is said that Mausolus himself was deeply involved in the planning of the refounded city and one can easily believe it, since he sited his own majestic tomb (the Mausoleum) in the middle of it; one could say that the city was built around it. Moreover, according to Vitruvius (*2,8,10*), he designed his palace on the Zephyron peninsula, where Bodrum Castle now is.

In all this there seems to have been little space for Carian feelings. While the Hekatomninds paid lip service to the Carian League and to Zeus Carios at Labranda, they acted as tyrants, moving people out of villages into towns, devoting vast amounts of resources to self-glorification and generally setting themselves apart from the rest of the population.

Although we have no information about marriage patterns in Caria, the mating of full siblings was a novelty this far west. The marriage of Mausolus and his sister Artemisia, and of his brother Idreus with his sister Ada, must have raised a few eyebrows in the Greek world that the Hekatomninds purported to admire. The practice has been variously explained. There are known Hittite instances that can be cited; the Persians practised it as a way of keeping property in the family and alleviating worries about the purity of the line. The Egyptians can also be brought in, through the floruit of sister-brother marriages in Ptolemaic and Roman times. As for the Carians, they possibly forgave everything, so thrilled were they that the Mausoleum had become one of the Seven Wonders of the World on a par with the Pyramids of Egypt and the Colossus of Rhodes. It is true that it does not quite make it onto every list, but to appear on six out of the eight known lists is no mean feat.

The site

The ruins of Alinda's **wall circuit** define its character as a city. The lower town may have had the trappings of a *polis* but it remained overlooked by a heavily fortified acropolis to the west, a set-up more suited to a tyrant than to a democratically chosen leader. According to McNicoll, the acropolis's defences were at some point 'neutralised' and dismantled; this could correspond to a change in the function of the city from strategic stronghold to something more peaceful. On the acropolis, the walls in local gneiss are very uniform in their architecture, with long stretchers and narrow headers throughout. A number of regularly spaced two-storey towers and gates have been identified. The acropolis walls are dated stylistically to the earlier part of the 4th century BC; it is not conceivable that Ada, fleeing from Halicarnassus, could have had the time or the financial means to build the circuit. The lower town walls are later, early Hellenistic.

The lower town, so far, has only been surveyed. There has been very little excavation. It is said to have been built on a grid plan, though there are not very many visible alignments. The most striking feature is the **market hall**, south of the agora, which has been compared to the one at Aigai. Some 100m long and 12m deep, it was originally some 15m high and articulated over three storeys. The south façade had twelve doorways giving access to shops with dimly-lit rooms at the back. The second storey was single long room (unless it had wooden partitions) divided lengthways by a double row of columns; it was lit by windows to the west and narrow slits in the long wall to the south. Very little survives of the top floor, which could be accessed via the agora. The building is believed to be Roman in date.

The **agora**, 30m wide and as long as the market, had a stoa all around of which few columns have been found. The remains to the east belong to the Byzantine church mentioned above. The **theatre**, originally Hellenistic with Roman modifications, is now blanketed with mature olive trees. It had 35 rows of seats and perhaps a stage buildings (awaiting investigation). The supporting wall in Hellenistic masonry and the arched entrances to the diazoma are a fine sight.

The **temple** is to the north on the highest point of the lower town. It was surrounded by a temenos with an entrance to the east. Today only the foundations, in local gneiss and granite, are left, which has suggested to some that the structure itself was in marble and was later plundered for lime to fertilise fields or make mortar with. A 12m by 17m structure with two pillars in antis, the temple was fronted to the east by a rectangular altar; it has been compared to the temple of Athena at Herakleia. To the northwest of the temple, some rock-cut features have been interpreted as a location for libation offerings. The square holes also cut in the rock may have supported stelae bringing to mind Gergas. The best example of the defence towers are in the west section of the lower town wall.

A number of **cisterns** dug in the rock have been identified on the acropolis, making it self-sufficient and an ideal refuge. In Roman times an **aqueduct** carried water into the town from the west; a number of arches are still standing beyond he acropolis. **Necropoleis** have been identified all around town, the largest to the north. They are mainly rock-cut Carian graves with a number of sarcophagi but no inscriptions.

MILAS

In the south of the area, not far from Bodrum airport, is Milas (*map B, 6*), sited on the plain, in a position that cannot be defended. The ancient Mylasa, a name with an Anatolian ring to it, was not originally where Milas is now. The site of Peçin Kale (*open 8–dusk; charge*), signposted 5km to the south of town, a flat-topped rock with a commanding view of the plain at a height of 213m, shows ancient occupation, with material from the Geometric Period and earlier. Artefact-based evidence comes, however, to an end around the 4th century BC. There are no traces of Hellenistic or Roman occupation. Interest resumes with the Byzantines and later the Menteşe in the 14th century, who both used the site purely for military purposes; the present fortifications (largely Ottoman with a recent makeover), beneath which a large marble structure, possibly a staircase, has been identified, incorporate a certain number of spolia.

MILAS: A SHORT HISTORY

The move to the plain is surprising but one has to consider the political situation at the time. In the early 4th century BC, Mylasa was in Persian hands, but Persian control functioned only up to a point. The satrap was not a Persian but a local warlord, the founder of the Hekatomnid dynasty. Hekatomnus, the son of Hyssaldomos (*see p. 182*) was the father of Mausolus, who eventually left Mylasa for Halicarnassus, signalling a desire to be by the sea and closer to the Greek world. Hekatomnus' elevation to the satrapy went hand in hand with a programme to beautify Mylasa and a bid to make Caria a place of cities, not villages, a foretaste of his son's great mission of Hellenisation. Quite how Hekatomnus achieved this is not clear, possibly by absorbing villages and moving the population around, as happened later in Halicarnassus.

In later times Mylasa, though no longer the capital of Caria, maintained prestige through the control of Labranda, by now expanded into a national sanctuary site. Its economic fortunes waxed and waned. There was the vexed question of access to the sea, which pitched it against Iasos and, later, there was the foundation of Stratonikeia. As a result, Mylasa found itself uncomfortably placed between Halicarnassus, then belonging to the Ptolemies, and Stratonikeia, in the hands of the Seleucids.

Roman Mylasa is little known. It was a judicial and administrative centre and seems to have been fully integrated into the Roman world. The Temple of Augustus and Rome that Richard Pockoke lovingly drew in 1745 was still complete at the time. By the time Richard Chandler visited about 20 years later, there were only six columns standing. A house had been built on the site but he could not get access to it because it was the harem of the owner. Other monuments, like the temples to Zeus Carios and Zeus Osogos (by a salt water spring according to sources), show a continuation of local cults. An aqueduct had been built along the top of the Baltalı Kapı (so called because of the relief of the double axe, *balta*, embedded in it on the outer north face) and on other arches that can be traced in town and in the countryside. Extravagant mausolea were built. The town had a bishop in the 5th century (though no church has been located), after which it slipped into obscurity, only to re-emerge as a centre of the Menteşe and later of the Ottomans.

Visiting Milas

At the moment there is not a lot to see in Milas. The chief attraction remains the **Gümüşkesen Mausoleum** (the 'Silver Purse' Mausoleum), west of the town centre on Hıdırlık Tepe in a small park. The structure, which is difficult to date (estimates fluctuate between the 2nd century BC and the 2nd century AD), is thought to have been inspired by the Mausoleum in Halicarnassus, though apparently there was not much left of the latter even by the earlier building date. The Gümüşkesen Mausoleum is a two-storey building with an open colonnade in the upper part, pilasters in the corners supporting a pyramidal roof painted red on the inside and a fine coffered ceiling with rosettes and foliage, which may originally also have been painted. The burial chamber below was accessed from the west. Libations were poured through the hole in the floor of the upper chamber supported by four square pillars, thus sharing with the dead the pleasures of a funerary banquet.

Milas, however, has a brighter future ahead of it. The aim is to create an archaeopark right in the middle of town and if things go according to plan, Milas will be on the prestigious UNESCO list of World Heritage Sites. This exciting state of affairs is the immediate consequence of illegal digging. It had been known for some time that the area between Belediye Cd. and Tabakhane Cd., known as the Uzun Yuva platform, was worth a thorough investigation. There was the landmark **Corinthian fluted column**, 8.2m tall that gives the site its name. Uzun Yuva means 'tall nest', a reference to the nesting storks on top of it. Antiquarians had described it since 1645, had read the inscription on it and correctly identified it as a 1st-century honorific monument to one Menandros, possibly originally topped with his statue. The column is still standing but without the inscription, which was erased in the 19th century by the owner of the nearby house, who disliked the idea of strangers climbing the steps to read it and in the process possibly seeing things they should not. The column sits on a 3m podium measuring 29m by 36m, which itself is supported by a huge terrace, 91m by110m, with monumental marble walls all around. The German archaeologist Frank Rumscheid, who had studied it in detail, had concluded that the construction, Hekatomnid in style and dated to the 4th century BC, was unfinished. He thought the podium could be the base of one of Mylasa's missing temples, possibly the one to Zeus Carios. As for the column, it was a later, secondary use.

At the time, early 2000s, the area, cut by a winding alleyway, was completely covered in housing. It was from a room in one of these very houses that illegal diggers drove a 10m long tunnel and reached the grave chamber of Hekatomnus. They found his sarcophagus in fine marble, with reliefs all around. There was a scene of him banqueting with his wife and others of him out hunting. It was encased in a chamber covered in wall-painting and accessed via a dromos constructed in fine, jointed, stone masonry. Portable finds were looted and when the thieves tried to sell them they were caught. Immediately there ensued a flurry of official activity, which had been conspicuously absent before, when the site could have been investigated according to accepted excavation protocols. Houses were expropriated and vast stretches of the platform were cleared. Now the talk is all of the archaeopark and a bright future with lots of tourists. The whole project has been carried out without the involvement of the local population; no survey or recording work has been undertaken prior to demolition of the area, which is at the heart of old Ottoman Milas. Information on progress is minimal and no completion date is set. This has raised a few eyebrows in heritage circles, prompting the Italian academic Anna Frascari to ask whether the authorities intended to obliterate the town in order to extract the monument.

LABRANDA

The sanctuary site of Labranda (*map B, 6*) is in fact one of a pair with Milas (*see above*), as the two were linked in antiquity by a sacred way. This is at least what the people of Mylasa (the ancient name of Milas) thought. The priests at Labranda viewed things differently and so did the rest of Caria, which saw Labranda as an expression not just of Mylasa's identity but of Carian identity as a whole. But the Sacred Way was there and so was the link, successfully fostered by the Mylasians. Today the paved road, 14km long, over 7m wide and largely built with the technique of cut and fill which allows it to run remarkably straight, starts around the Baltalı Kapı at the northeast end of Milas (the only remaining element of the Roman walls), in the direction of Kargecakköy. In recent years it has been largely tarmacked over to allow lorry traffic to the quarries. The layout, however, is roughly known, including a continuation north in the Alinda direction. The numerous spring houses and the forts dotting it have been studied. They suggest that beyond the religious dimension, there was a strategic aspect to the endeavour, quite apart from the logistics of supplying the building programme and the day-to-day running of the sanctuary.

The site, perched on the south slopes of the Çomakdağ, affords wide and distant views as far as the Datça peninsula on a clear day; it monitors the Milas plain, the road from Muğla to Stratonikeia, the west coast road and the access to Latmos. It is rich in water (indeed it supplies Milas with it), in wood and building stone, including marble form the nearby Sodra Mountains.

HISTORY OF LABRANDA

Labranda is not a settlement but a sacred site of the Carian people, who worshipped here a warrior god, protector of soldiers: Zeus Stratios later called Zeus Labrandynus because of his symbol, the labrys (the double axe). It has been put forward that the original deity was modelled on the Persian Ahura Mazda and that, according to Appian in his account of the Mithridatic Wars (66), was honoured with the burning of huge bonfires complete with sacrificial offerings of wine, oil, milk and honey. Certainly the remote location and the abundance of trees would have lent themselves to such practices. In appearance the god has an Oriental look, in a stiff stance, arms forward, a hand holding the double axe, a *polos* hat and things unspecified hanging on his breast, reminiscent of the Ephesian Artemis.

According to Herodotus (5,119), when Carian soldiers sought refuge here from the rampant Persians in 597 BC, there was a sacred precinct but no buildings, only a grove of plane trees. Evidence of some form of occupation goes back to the 7th century BC. According to some, activity was centred around the Split Rock, right at the top of the site where there is a spring. Building in Labranda was not for the faint-hearted. The land is very steep, it requires terracing and the place is totally isolated; even so it was a popular place of pilgrimage.

The first building to go up was a rather modest temple to Zeus, a simple temple in antis with an Archaic date. With the advent of the Hekatomnid dynasty in the early 4th century BC, things changed. These petty local lords, starting with Hekatomnus, made Labranda the focal point of national Carian identity, beautifying the place with impressive buildings in an eclectic style which appropriately demonstrated their appreciation of things Greek while at the same time paying homage to their Persians masters. Here Mausolus and his successors held court as kings, high priests and satraps rolled into one. Here the members of the Carian federation came together and worshipped their divine rulers while at the same time strengthening communal bonds with games and festivities. The building of a stadium c. 200m long on an artificial terrace to the west of the site—no mean feat given the steep topography—should be viewed in that perspective. It all lasted a mere 60 years, from the time of Hekatomnus who paved the road and made the terraces, to Mausolus, who built the first andron, and Idreus, who completed the programme with more magnificent structures. Clearly the purpose was political and no expense was spared.

When the Hekatomnids retired from the scene and Caria was contended by the successors of Alexander the Great, and later still when it became part of the Roman province of Asia, the sanctuary did not lose its pull. The sacred site was maintained and facilities for pilgrims were improved, with the addition of baths and another meeting house (Andron C), although of inferior quality in workmanship. However, while it remained a focal point of Carian identity, it also became a bone of contention between Mylasa, who claimed it for itself and eventually won, and the priests who wanted to run it independently.

As the cult of Zeus Labrandynus petered out in the 4th century, the site was maintained but the temple was not. Glass fragments found during excavation suggest that in late antiquity it was turned into a workshop for itinerant glass makers, producing some rather coarse goods. But though some churches went up, its main value became strategic. The acropolis hill, 100m to the north at a height of 795m, had already been fortified in the 4th century BC. Those commanding sights mentioned above were from this vantage point. At the time of the infighting after the death of Alexander the Great, the wall circuit was improved with the addition of a massive pentagonal tower, the latest in Hellenistic defence architecture. The forts along the Sacred Way were also brought up to date with the addition of catapult towers. When things became precarious for the Byzantines and defence became their main priority in the 13th century, the acropolis was apparently in the hands of a very select army unit, the *akritai*, in charge of a last-ditch defence. They occupied high points, held the territory and were practically independent of the Byzantine state, to which they paid no taxes. It is thought that the fortress was destroyed c. 1274 by the Turks fleeing the Mongols and pushing west. Beyond that, Labranda was lost until 1827, when it was visited by Anton Prokesch, an Austrian scholar but also a soldier, who was not deterred by talk of the bandits that were said to infest the area. Later, Alfred Laumonnier identified the location from an inscription but did not have the money to dig. In 1934, the then crown prince of Sweden, Gustav Adolf, a keen archaeologist, expressed to Atatürk the desire to work at Labranda, then a military zone, in order to investigate the possible link between the site and Crete, where the same labrys symbol occurs. Things began in earnest only after WW2 and the involvement of Swedish archaeologists continues.

Visiting Labranda

Labranda (*open 8–5; charge*) is due north from Milas signposted on the way to Alinda up a narrow, steep and wild road. You will be climbing from 50m to 700m in some 14km. Arm yourself with good shoes. The entrance is on the west side of the new parking area by the south terrace wall. To the west, the remains of a tetraconch structure, now under a metal roof, were originally part of a Late Antique private bath. It is thought that it was turned into a church because of the pulpit found in it and dated to the 5th–6th century.

The site is entered between the South and East Propylaea, where the Sacred Way ended. Only short sections of the temenos wall that defined the area of the Temple of Zeus are still visible at the back of the East Stoa. In the area of the monumental entrance, a single-aisled **church**, partly incorporating an earlier bath house, has a

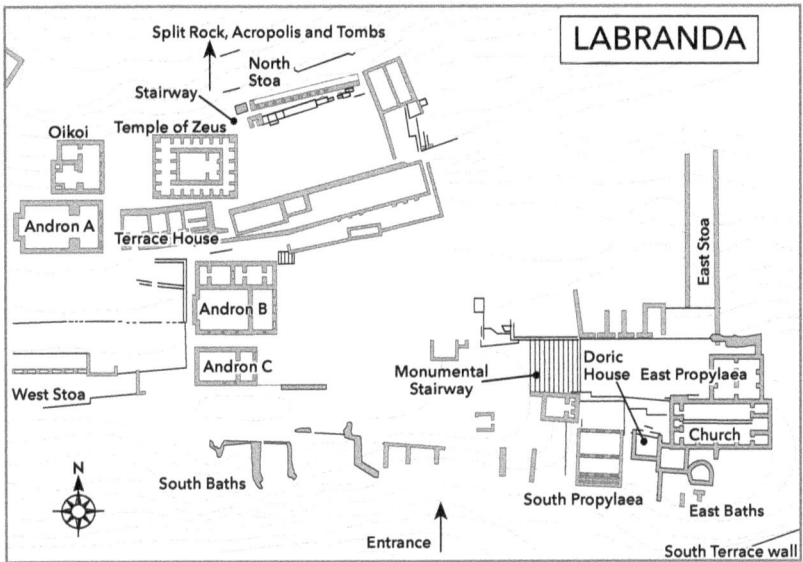

4th–5th-century date. The two towers on the west front and the engaged pilasters with blind arcades inside betray a Syrian, eastern Mediterranean influence. Later, when the building was in ruin, a small chapel was inserted in the northwest corner. The **Doric House**, not far from the church entrance, originally a 4th-century BC building of uncertain function, was at the time a fountain house serving the church for ritual ablutions, after a spell as the tepidarium of the earlier bath complex.

The well-preserved **Monumental Stairway**, 12m wide, is a fitting introduction to the heart of the sanctuary on a grand terrace. Here, centred around the Temple of Zeus, are a number of stoas for people to congregate and meeting houses for the select few, the so-called androne. The temple was developed by Idreus in the mid-4th century BC, with the addition of a Ionic colonnade. The space to the east was enclosed between two stoas. Note the staircase leading to the north. West of the temple the oikoi buildings, with Doric columns, housed the priests. The so-called **Terrace House**, immediately south of the temple, with four rooms joined by a corridor built in the 4th century BC, was presumably use for storage.

The two large buildings on the edge of the terrace, just inside the temenos in a prime location, with a view over the whole of Caria, represent what Labranda is all about: power. **Andron A**, willed by Mausolus, and **Andron B** by his brother Idreus (Andron C is later and not so grand), were built on the same plan, with a deep porch followed by a single room with huge windows with provisions for shutters, and a wide, elevated niche in the back wall presumably reserved for the king when he entertained selected guests at banquets. Reclining couches running along the walls have been identified in both buildings. One can imagine a seating hierarchy, with the most important spot close to the king and the least important close to the door. The *hoi polloi* feasted outside in the open air, being possibly served a different menu, but still enjoying the potlatch. Architecturally the androns were oversized and clearly built to impress; that much is obvious from the surviving sections of the walls. Add in your mind's eye some fine furniture, painted stucco decoration and whitewashing to disguise the locally-sourced gneiss, as well as, in the case of Andron B, a pair of male, bearded sphinxes as acroteria (just like those that guarded Darius' palace at Persepolis) and you have the complete picture.

Beyond to the north (just off the map) are the **Split Rock** and the acropolis and a number of tombs all around. The **Built Tomb**, not far from the acropolis, is quite spectacular. It consisted of a partially paved forecourt followed by two chambers with sarcophagi, one of which is too large to have fitted through the doorway, suggesting that the tomb chamber was built around it. The tomb was closed with a slab weighing six tons. Both chambers were roofed with stone corbelling skilfully cut away to make it look like a vault. Above both chambers a low room, entered from the forecourt, was covered with long stone slabs. The sherds found in the filling of the forecourt that sealed the tomb date to the 4th century BC and have suggested to some that this was the tomb of the satrap Idreus, brother of Mausolus.

PRACTICAL INFORMATION

TOURIST INFORMATION

For organised tours around the Latmos area and the Bafa Lake, consult Latmos Travel at their office in Kapıkırı Köyü or online (*latmos-travel.com*). Most hotels in the area will run organised tours. Do not miss the chance to explore the Latmos mountains on donkey back. (This type of tourism explains why out of season there are so many donkeys idling their time away around the village.)

GETTING AROUND

By air: Bodrum International Airport between Milas and Bodrum, with a national and an international terminal, is very busy in the summer, mainly with charter and budget airline flights. The Havaş Shuttle (*milas-bodrumairport. com*) is timed to coincide with domestic flights.

By bus: For Herakleia the bus on the Söke–Milas road will drop you at Bafa, 10km from your destination. A dolmuş might come past, though it would be wiser to arrange a pickup with your hotel in Kapıkırı. Stratonikeia is close to Route 330 (Milas–Yatağan). Lagina, being further away, will require private transport. In Milas the otogar is to the north on the Bodrum–Söke road. In the town centre is the small ilce otogar at the Köy Tabakhane Garajı; a dolmuş will take you to local destinations such as Bodrum and Iasos.

WHERE TO STAY

For **Herakleia and the Latmos region**, most accommodation is in Kapıkırı; the common language is German. The Selene Pansiyon (*selenespansion. com*), the Zeybek Pansiyon (*T: 252 543 54 41*), the Haus Yasemin Pansiyon (*bafa-see.de*) cater for tourists, offering organised treks; prices often include half board. It means you will live in a bit of a bubble but all of these are in Kapıkırı and there is nothing stopping you getting around in the village.

For the budget-conscious, the campsite (*T: 537 338 61 45*) on the shores of Lake Bafa, on the west side of Kapıkırı opposite the island, is a good choice. Its restaurant will do you well. Overlooking the lake on its south side and accessed from Route 525, the Hotel Silva (*hotelsilvaoliva.com*) offers splendid views, a great breakfast spread, a beach, and valuable advice on visiting the area.

In the **Lagina and Stratonikeia region** it is worth investigating inland locations like Yatağan, especially if you want to explore further east. In Yatağan the Sultan Otel (*otelsultan.com*) is not far from the otogar, which is in the centre of town. While you are there you may like to visit the recently restored home of a wealthy camel drover (ask for **Haci Ömerler Evi**) and get an idea of the local Ottoman architectural style. The camel stable has been converted into a meeting room. Nearby the cistern has also been restored and is open to the public. It is a rare chance to see from the inside those round buildings with a cupola that are so ubiquitous in Turkish towns.

LOCAL SPECIALITIES

Market day in Milas is Tuesday. Other villages and towns will have markets where you can sample a bewildering variety of olives and indulge in the most delicious fruits picked ripe and offered to you with a smile.

BODRUM & ITS PENINSULA

Before you visit Bodrum (*map B, 5*), see if you can climb up the hill to the north beyond the theatre and Route 330. The climb is steep and there are winding roads (making it longer and slower) but no paths, so some cross-country scrambling through the olive groves is needed. Once you achieve a good height, you can see the harbour, the Zephyrion Peninsula with the castle to your left (*see map on p. 197*), Salmakis to the right and Kara Ada (the ancient Arkonesos) guarding the entrance in the distance. If in your mind you edit out the moored boats and the urban sprawl, you can for one delicious moment savour the old Bodrum before it became the nightlife capital of Turkey.

Hampered by a rocky and poor hinterland, in a peninsula chronically short of water, Bodrum was a backwater for most of its life. Never on a crucial sea lane, never the final destination of a caravan trail, never a place of pilgrimage, Bodrum does not even figure on the portolans, the maritime maps of the 15th century. Between the 8th and the 15th centuries it appears to have been deserted. Bodrum's high points have always been willed. In the 4th century BC it was Mausolus, the star ruler of the Hekatomnid dynasty, who built one of the seven wonders of the ancient world here, ensuring the city's international fame well beyond the physical life of the monument itself. Then, from the late 1960s, it has been the Turkish government's plan to improve communications that has created the tourist boom.

When the first Danish archaeologists arrived in town in the 1960s, there was one choice of accommodation (Pansiyon Artemis). The road connecting the town to the rest of the world was all twists and turns and was not asphalted, it took six hours to get to İzmir by bus and households kept camels in their yards to shift heavy loads. Now there is a good road network and, more importantly, an airport. Bodrum, a town of some 35,000 residents according to the last census (2012), welcomes the bulk of the 3.5million that arrive at its airport (2014 figure). It is quite a change from the 1970s when Bodrum was a village of fishermen and sponge divers and a fair amount of the land that had access to the sea—in other words the beaches—was in the hands of the military. Even with their departure, Bodrum is still short of beaches within walking distance of the town. You will have to explore the peninsula or venture in the Gümbet direction for a good choice.

HISTORY OF BODRUM

Finds of characteristic pottery in necropoleis on the Bodrum Peninsula show Mycenaean connections but details are scarce. The number of tumuli suggests that this part of Caria was involved in the Aegean world from early on. Equally, on the Zephyrion Peninsula, the uninterrupted pottery sequence from the

Mycenaean to the Archaic periods suggests continuity of settlement, but more substantial information only comes around the 5th century BC. At the time, the town was called Halicarnassus and was under Persian rule. Here the historian Herodotus was born in 484 BC. His father was a Carian but he considers himself Greek and wrote his *Histories* in Ionian Greek. The settlement, originally a Dorian foundation, later Ionian, was turned towards the Aegean world and in particular towards the islands of Kos, Rhodes and Samos. It is only recently that this link has been severed. First by the Italian occupation of the Dodecanese following the dismemberment of the Ottoman Empire after WWI, and then by the international border separating Turkey and Greece.

Little is known about the early phase of Halicarnassus's history apart from the figure of Artemisia the Elder, who took part in the Battle of Salamis in 480 BC on the Persian side, making her the first known woman admiral. In the early 4th century BC Caria was still under Persian rule, although they governed with a light touch. The satrap was based in Milas until his son Mausolus moved to Halicarnassus with a plan to make the city a showcase of Ionian Renaissance in Caria. The short-lived Hekatomnid Dynasty left a lasting legacy in the town, beginning with a wall circuit and later including a palace and a temple on the Zephyrion Peninsula defended by a separate circuit, and of course the Mausoleum, a building hailed throughout antiquity and beyond as one of the Seven Wonders of the World; it was named after Mausolus, for whom it had been built. The term 'mausoleum' thereafter entered the language as a synonym for a large, stately tomb, which explains why Augustus's last resting place in Rome was called a mausoleum in his own times.

Later Halicarnassus is more subdued, slipping into insignificance. Alexander the Great cleared Anatolia of Persian rule and the city drifted in and out of the control of his warring successors. Roman rule brought peace and some civic buildings such as a theatre, a stadium, more temples, a synagogue close to the sea, and two gymnasia. There is evidence of prosperity to Late Antiquity, at least to judge by finds such as the House of Charidimos, a large establishment with a wealth of mosaics featuring the seasons, hunting scenes, centaurs and nereids. Beyond that things become blurred; no bishop is known after the 5th century; the remains of the Byzantine monastery show wealth but it was fortified. Arab raids up the coast in the 8th century probably hit the town badly, coming hard on the heels of the Persian invasion of 620. Certainly by the time one next hears of Halicarnassus, in the 15th century, there is no longer a town to speak of, possibly some squatters but possibly not even those. The lack of late Byzantine and medieval finds suggests abandonment.

At the beginning of the 15th century the map of Anatolia was redrawn once more. The Ottomans, the up-and-coming emirs from Bursa, suffered a serious setback at the Battle of Ankara (1402) at the hand of Timur (Tamerlane). The invading Mongols then proceeded to Smyrna where they razed the Castle of St Peter that belonged to the Knights of St John, a sovereign Catholic religious order, the ancestor of the Knights of Malta. When eventually the Ottomans regained the upper hand, they refused permission to the knights to rebuild in Smyrna. They suggested Halicarnassus, which did not belong to them, being in the hands of the Menteşe. It was crucial for the knights to have a presence on the Anatolian mainland to be able to drum up financial support in Europe as an outpost of Christianity in the land of the infidels, able to offer refuge to persecuted Christians waiting to be ransomed. The Castrum Sancti Petri, later called Petronium, that in due course became Bodrum, was a small affair to start with. It consisted of a wall with four bastions cutting off the Zephyrion Peninsula from the mainland, of a tower (the French Tower on the highest point), of the Naillac building west of it, and a few houses. Building supplies mainly came by sea from Rhodes and Crete (a large consignment of cypress timber). Locally there were apparently no forays into town for spolia. Some cut stone may have been available on the spot from the crumbling antiquities.

In the second half of the 15th century, with increased Ottoman sea power and possibly facing hostility from a growing Turkish population in town (a town that the knights never controlled), new defences were needed. Incidentally, the presence of a town or settlement of some sort can be inferred by the fact that the Venetians sacked and destroyed it in 1472. On the peninsula more space was enclosed; the English and the Italian towers went up. The 28 Ionic column drums embedded in the Italian Tower and believed to belong to the Archaic Temple of Apollo built by Mausolus, suggest that there was still building material available on the peninsula, though forays into town now became necessary.

It was the during last wave of building activity in the early 1500s when, with the increasing use of gunpowder weapons, existing walls had to be strengthened with heavy gun ports and interior passages and a new, massive curtain wall facing town went up, that the fate of the ancient remains in town was sealed. This chronology, painstakingly reconstructed by the meticulous work of the Danish archaeologists, is based mainly on the sequence of the shields and of the coats of arms embedded in the walls and in the towers, on tracking down the characteristic green lava-cut stone of the Mausoleum's foundation, and on scarce written sources and limited excavation. In 1523 the knights left for Rhodes; and when the Ottomans conquered that island they moved on to Malta.

As part of the Ottoman Empire, Bodrum, as it then became known, sank into oblivion, though not entirely. The proximity to the sea made it liable to further losses: 172 marble column drums were at some point shipped to Rhodes, while much of the theatre was stripped by 1811.

The fate of the Mausoleum

While it had been thought that the Mausoleum was recognised by the knights as early as 1497, a time when the invention of the printing press had made Classical texts more widely available, this was probably not the case. According to the knights' account, in 1522 when they stumbled upon an underground chamber (later recognised as the funerary chamber) while digging for stone through the foundations, they were unable to make any further investigations. It was getting dark and they had to retreat to the safety of the castle. The locals did the digging and the plundering. When the knights came back a few days later, they stripped away the marble and the stucco for lime, suggesting a blissful state of ignorance. Round about the same time, Friar Sabba Castiglione paid a surprise visit, hunting for sculptures for Isabella d'Este, a keen collector. He did not leave empty-handed but he took no notice of the Mausoleum, suggesting that there was not much to see. Antiquarians and travellers seem to have given Bodrum a wide berth in later times. They either went to Rhodes or to the Levant. It seems therefore that even if the ancient writings about the Mausoleum were known, its remains were not recognised.

In the early 1840s, the then British consul in Mytilene, Sir Charles Newton, was able to secure 13 relief slabs from the castle walls as a personal gift of the sultan to Ambassador Canning. This is how the British Museum comes to have part of the Amazon Frieze from the Mausoleum (a couple more slabs ended up in Genoa and Rhodes). A firman for excavations followed. Sir Charles worked in Bodrum in 1857–8, identifying precisely the site of the Mausoleum and pinpointing the entrance, surveying the town and the castle for spolia, which he duly forwarded to the British Museum. Later, another British official, Alfred Biliotti (the discoverer of Satala), made additional investigations in 1865.

When eventually the team of Danish archaeologists started work in 1966, they feared there would be no Mausoleum left to investigate. It is their painstaking work, which is still ongoing in Bodrum as well as on the Bodrum peninsula, that has pieced together the evidence and created a coherent narrative charting the development of Halicarnassus and of its monuments.

EXPLORING BODRUM: THE CASTLE

Bodrum is home to the Castle of the Knights of St John (*open Mon–Sun 8.30–6.30; shorter hours in winter; charge*) and inside it is of one of the best museums in Turkey in terms the setting and the quality of the exhibits. The **Museum of Underwater Archaeology** houses much of the material excavated in the Aegean and in the Mediterranean by the Institute of Nautical Archaeology affiliated to Texas A&M University, as well as other local finds. The sprawling setup of the museum, making the best use of old and purpose-built new structures, is particularly suitable to the layout of the interior of the castle, where culture mingles with strutting peacocks, fine flowers, shady plants and cafés. Give it time and enjoy the views.

After the entrance to the castle, not far from the Information Kiosk on the Zephyrion Peninsula on the east side of the harbour, past a number of gates and coats of arms, you will arrive in the lower courtyard with the chapel. Have a look inside at the replica of late Roman Yassıada Ship and at the amphorae strewn around, and then take the steps to the east. You are now standing on the terrace erected by Mausolus for his palace, a construction in brick and marble, covered with a shiny stucco that made it glitter like glass and was much admired by Vitruvius (*2,8,10*).

A section of the retaining wall running north and at right angle to the chapel, has been identified. This area of the Castle is mainly devoted to glass artefacts (**Glass Gallery and Glass Wreck Hall**) with exhibits spanning several centuries from the Mycenaean material to the Fatimid vessels (c. end of 1st millennium AD). Of particular interest is the Serçe Limanı Wreck that sunk off the south coast of Turkey opposite Rhodes c. 1025 loaded with three tons of broken glass items from Syria ready to be recycled somewhere up north, possibly in the Black Sea area. A careful examination of the ship's remains has enabled archaeologist to construct the replica you see here, some 16m long and 5m wide.

Past the **Italian Tower**, with the unfluted column drums thought to belong to the 5th-century BC Temple of Apollo known from inscriptions (*see above*) and believed to be under the French Tower, the **Carian Princess** beckons in a purpose-built-hall looking like Andron B at Labranda. Her monolithic sarcophagus was found during building work northeast of town in 1989. She was certainly a woman of substance to judge by the jewellery. According to forensic examination she was in her mid-40s when she died. Speculation about her identity has been rife, since the dating of the associated material falls towards the tail end of the Hekatomnid period. The best candidate so far would be Aphneis, the Cappadocian wife of Pixidarus. In the display, the princess has been fleshed out by the same team from Manchester University who reconstructed the physical appearance of Philip II of Macedon with his blinded eye. The piped music and the subdued lighting make the whole experience a trifle sinister.

Follow the trail to the **Uluburun Wreck Hall** to see the replica of the ship that sank off the south coast of Turkey near Kaş c. 1300 BC. The display shows how the five-ton cargo was stowed, including the vegetable padding that was found in the excavation. Its load included numerous bronze ingots, jewellery, daggers, ivory cosmetic boxes and a very rare instance of a hinged wooden tablet. The discovery of this trading ship, which was hugging the coast anticlockwise from the Levant, picking up merchandise on the way, has revolutionised our understanding of Bronze Age trading patterns. It was not the Mycenaeans who controlled the ancient sea routes but rather the Near Eastern seafarers. It confirms the conclusions drawn from the analysis of the Cape Gelidonya Wreck, also exhibited here, which was excavated in the 1960s and which is younger by some 130 years.

End your tour with a visit to the **English Tower**, built with English financial contributions in exchange for indulgences with the full blessing of the then pope in Rome. Fully restored after the French bombed it in WWI, it is now a medieval theme restaurant complete with communal table, suits of armour, standards and appropriate music as well as stag trophies alternating with stuffed animal heads on the walls.

BODRUM: THE TOWN

For the rest of Bodrum beyond the castle, you need some imagination to piece together the limited, visible archaeology. A lot has been lost over the centuries; the rest has been concreted over. However, on paper one can see a fair amount of Hekatomnid Halicarnassus, whose layout Vitruvius (*2,8,10–13*) compared to that of a theatre, with the closed harbour as the orchestra. The earlier Dorian city is more

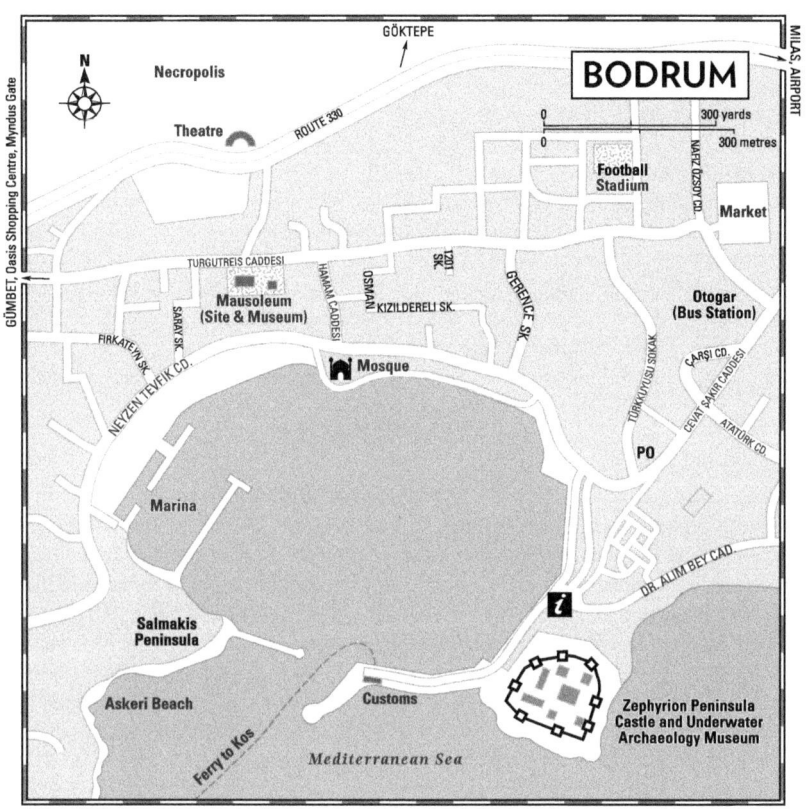

elusive. Some fragmentary remains, with the Archaic lotus and palmette motif, have been spotted built into a local mosque. They may belong with the stray Archaic capitals exhibited in the grounds of the castle.

When Mausolus moved his capital here, he increased his demographic capital by transferring population more or less forcibly from at least six surrounding villages. This process of synoecism was meant to urbanise the Carians, reduce the number of small settlements that could not be defended and at the same time boost the manpower available for public works. He enclosed the area with a very long defensive wall, in limestone and andesite, hugging the heights for some 6.5km to defeat siege engines, making the best of steep escarpments and deep rock-cut ditches. With regularly spaced towers and four integrated fortresses (one on the Salmakis peninsula to the west, two to the north on top of the hills overlooking the town and a fourth one on the Zephyrion peninsula) all built to last, the wall was pierced by five gates: it proved unable to withstand the first serious challenge when Alexander the Great successfully besieged the town in 334 BC. The best surviving traces of wall can be seen to the north, well beyond the built-up area.

The town was laid out on a grid, with today's Turgut Reis Cd. as the main east–

west axis. The Mausoleum, the theatre on the slopes of Göktepe to the north and the Roman Temple of Mars represented by a massive platform east of it, as well as the stadium uncovered during road works in the 1980s close to the east section of the town wall, are aligned to it.

The Myndus Gate
To the west of town the Myndus Gate (*just off the map to the west*) stands forlorn, with the usual complement of flags, in a patch of green to the south of Turgut Reis Cd., roughly where it meets Büyük İskender Cd. The two towers have recently been restored but the wall either side is lost. The towers marked the western corners of a paved gateyard integrated iton the curtain wall and measuring 26m by 23m, protected by a rock-cut ditch to the west. If enemy forces broke in, they could be controlled and contained in a confined space and attacked from the battlements.

THE MAUSOLEUM

Halicarnassus has sailed through antiquity and modern times on the wings of the fame of its most important monument, the Mausoleum, willed by its most famous ruler, Mausolus, as his tomb and perpetual reminder of his presence at the heart of the city, well beyond his death, a bit like the embalmed Lenin in the Kremlin. This was not a very Greek thing to do. The Greeks celebrated their heroes with monuments but the body of the deceased was buried out of town in the necropolis. Clearly Mausolus' love of things Greek had its limits. It is possible to visit the site where the Mausoleum stood (*open Tues–Sun 8–5, longer hours in summer; charge*) on the south side of Turgut Reis Cd. where it meets Hamam Sk. However, what one can see (mainly remains of vaulted structures preceding the mausoleum itself) is a poor substitute for the whole story as pieced together over years of meticulous investigations.

The building process
Mausolus placed his final resting place at the heart of the city, just as his father Hekatomnus had done in Mylasa, but Mausolus set his sights higher. The construction was to stand prominently, some 50m high, on a purpose-built terrace 241m by 100m overlooking the agora to the east and connected to it by a monumental propylon with a staircase of comparable size to that at Labranda. His references were varied, inspired equally by East and West; technically his work at Labranda shows that he had mastered the art of building huge terraces pioneered by the Lydians. The building work dates from between 360 and 350 BC and was never completed.

Investigation of the structures preceding the building of the terrace, revealing a complex of chambers, corridors and water features, has been inconclusive. The chosen site on the lower slopes of Göktepe was edged by ravines on either side. In the terrace now filled and paved, the rocky eminence to the northeast was cut back to construct the foundations for the Mausoleum building, measuring 32.5m by 38.5m and over 6m deep, known, after Newton, as 'the quadrangle'. Previous features were filled in and a marble drainage system was installed. The funerary chamber, with marble flooring and painted stucco decoration all around, was built underground to the west and off centre; in the centre of it a pit contained precious offerings. It was preceded by two smaller anterooms separated by a pair of marble doors and sealed to the west by a stone plug (2m tall, 1.23m wide and 1.45m thick) fixed top and bottom with bronze clamps, which Newton found in place in the 19th century.

The exterior courtyard in front of the stone plug was paved with marble and was connected to the surface of the terrace by a monumental staircase. In this space the archaeologist identified the funerary offering to the spirit of the dead ruler. The rest of the body of the Mausoleum was of solid, well-cut green lava blocks, most of them 90cm by 90cm and 30cm thick, held together sideways with copper clamps to a height of c. 50m. The structure was topped with a stepped, pyramidal roof. The exterior of the Mausoleum was clad in marble with a couple of friezes running all the way around and a profusion of Ionic columns. On top of the roof a small platform accommodated a marble quadriga driven by Mausolus on his way to heaven in the same way that Herakles, from whom he claimed ancestry, had ascended to Olympus after his demise. Pairs of heraldic lions completed the roof decoration. A number outsize statues belonging to the building and to the platform were found, some bearing traces of polychrome paint.

With such a grand tomb came an equally grand funeral, which is known in some detail through the written sources. Artemisia the Younger, Mausolus' wife and sister, was so distraught at his death that after the cremation, by some accounts, she mingled her husband's ashes with spices and wine and drank the cocktail, so that she could be his living tomb. That may be the reason why Mausolos' remains themselves have proved elusive; on the other hand, there could have been an upper chamber. The widow organised funeral contests in true Greek fashion. Theodectes the rhetorician, from Phaselis in Lycia, submitted a tragedy, *Mausolus*, but the victor was the historian Theopompos from Chios. There were also games and horse and warship races.

Artemisia died shortly after, leaving the work unfinished. She was probably buried in the huge sarcophagus that the knights found in the anteroom when they stumbled on the funerary chamber while digging for stone from above. After Artemisia was laid to rest, the plug was positioned in place on metal rollers. The entrance in the well of the monumental staircase mentioned above was sealed with a huge one-off deposit of fresh victuals intended to assist the dead in the afterlife. Examinations of the bones and other remains concluded that five oxen, two calves, 25 sheep, eight lambs, three colts, one chicken, eight pigeons and ten other fowl had been slaughtered. Ten hen eggs were added for good measure. The cuts of meat (no legs and no heads) had been sorted and covered with huge stones. They had not been burnt, as was customary in sacrifices, but had been deposited raw.

The afterlife

At this point the building began its extraordinary afterlife. Already by the 3rd century BC it was numbered among the Seven Wonders of the World. This was a time when listmania was gripping the Hellenistic world. One should not assume from this that the monument itself had survived intact up to this time, though its memory obviously had.

According to the latest research, deterioration started pretty soon. Within a short time the Hekatomnids were no longer around to take care of it and when Alexander the Great besieged the town in 334, he caused substantial damage. Moreover, the outer shell of the monument, if not the solid core, was certainly liable to suffer from earthquakes and this is a risk zone. Columns, quadriga, lions and statues may have come tumbling down. There is evidence of neglect in the late 2nd century BC, when a 106m by18m wide industrial structure in the northwest corner of the platform was erected. Clearly the temenos was no longer sacred. The hill to the north, now Göktepe, was steadily eroding and depositing layers of silt on the terrace and on the fallen statues and friezes. It is unlikely that the monument was scavenged for material, though fallen blocks may have come in handy. By the time Pliny the Elder was enthusing about the building in the 1st century AD, giving a detailed description and listing the illustrious Greek sculptors that had worked there (36,5–9), it is not clear what state the monument was in. Probably Pliny never came this far to have a look. It is possible that beyond losing some elements and gently crumbling, it was slowly covered with vegetation. As Halicarnassus faded from the scene, the memory of the monument endured, though not that of its precise location. After the Knights arrived in Halicarnassus, it took them a long time to make sense of the stump that they could see in the distance, under a blanket of silt, vegetation and possibly lean-to houses, across the harbour from the battlements of their castle. That is, if they ever did make sense of it.

THE BODRUM PENINSULA: TORBA, MYNDUS, STROBYLOS, GARA & ALAZEYTİN

A beautiful collection of bays, shelters and creeks, the volcanic peninsula west of Bodrum is undergoing the very same tourism-led transformation that has changed Bodrum beyond recognition in recent years. Ancient remains must fit into that plan, so archaeological investigation is patchy and limited. A barren land with a few arable pockets, the peninsula has been historically poor, with settlement on the heights for security. Tumuli and Mycenaean pottery in the necropoleis show Aegean connections. Later, Mausolus emptied six of its villages to populate the refounded Halicarnassus. The city of Myndus (now Gümüşlük) in the west was moved from the interior to the sea, where it did not prosper beyond Roman times. Perhaps the one success story is Strobylos, a strategic settlement on the south coast with an occupation from the 8th–16th centuries. Otherwise, the peninsula is a land of windmills, tangerines and figs (the latter more profitable as they travel easily in the dried state), good stone and the occasional silver mine. The andesite for the Mausoleum was quarried at Koyunbaba near Myndus, not far from the silver mines that gave the town its modern name and were exploited to comparatively recent times. The windmills, some still functioning in the 1970s, in the traditional Aegean style with a cylindrical body, a roof of metal sheeting and a wooden mechanism, required a fair amount of maintenance. They could grind 320kg of wheat on a good day. A few sites of interest, most requiring private transport, are detailed below.

TORBA

Torba (*map B, 5*) was an ecclesiastical complex on the north coast, east of the village of the same name. The place is also known as Manastır, suggesting the presence of a monastery, a possible interpretation for the ruins on the eastern end of the bay. The complex includes a mausoleum, a large residence, baths, a basilica and a sturdy, rectangular building that could either be a depot or a cistern. The oldest feature, dated to the 2nd century AD, is the mausoleum, the small apsidal structure nearest to the water. Built in rubble and mortar, it had a porch with two columns, a marble lintel at the entrance and a vaulted roof. Later in the 4th–5th century it was reused as a chapel. Nearby the so-called bishop's palace, immediately to the south, some 22m by 16m, contained several rooms and is roughly contemporary with the chapel and the nearby baths, which have the standard features. The large basilica, measuring 34m by 22m, appears to have been an afterthought, at least to judge by its awkward shape, having to fit between the baths, the palace and a rocky hill. It had a baptistery attached to the outside of the apse to the south, with a cross-shaped marble pool. All four buildings have remains of polychrome mosaic floors (the workmanship is cruder in the baths) with geometric patterns and elegant tendrils and volutes.

Overlooking the village Torba, on a platform to the west, is the misnamed Gebe Kilise, not a church at all but a grave built by the Lelegians, the native people of Caria about whom little is known. The round structure some 13m in diameter, dated to the 7th century BC, is built of solid stone slabs with a rounded roof. Inside, the tomb chamber, accessed via a dromos, has a pyramidal vault.

MYNDUS

Myndus, on the west coast (*map B, 5*), has recently been in the news. Excavations have been taking place on Tavşan Adası, the small island overlooking the pretty harbour, that was once connected to the mainland by a causeway now barely submerged as sea levels have risen. Here remains of a temple dated to the early 2nd century AD, of a theatre, a 5th-century church and burials and a 13th-century tower have been exposed. The island will be turned into an archaeopark and the rabbit population that gave it its name will be allowed to flourish again undisturbed. Unfortunately, however important these finds are, they will not shed much light on the history of the settlement on the mainland, as anyone taking a walk on the rising ground overlooking the harbour can see from the odd remains strewn around. The history of Myndus, from its heyday as an important harbour, well protected against the northern wind behind a sturdy wall circuit, to its decline in late antique and Byzantine times, remains to be unveiled. It looks as if the job is being left to private initiative, such as the clandestine excavations that were going on for three months in 2017, within the town walls, before officials intervened.

STROBYLOS

The site of Strobylos on the south coast is one of the few settlements that could shed light on the so-called Dark Ages, the troubled period from the 7th to the 9th century when written sources dry up. The place is on a barren, conical hill (Strobylos means 'pine cone' in Greek) near the holiday village of Aspat, east of Akyarlar (*map B, 5*). Presently it is scheduled to become an archaeological park, an elegant adjunct to the tourist resort. That means that some ruins will be rebuilt, as has already happened to the Byzantine baths tentatively dated to the 13th century, now stark white and looking brand new. It does not necessarily mean that much archaeology will be done to recover the plan of the settlement and its sequence. The highlighting of the odd feature is probably the most we can expect.

Fortunately, we have the work of Clive Foss to fall back on. He has been able, by piecing together evidence from archival sources, to present a coherent history of the settlement. Strobylos must be considered in its geographical setting, located as it is opposite the island of Kos, which lies less than 8km to the south. It therefore owes its importance to the control of a maritime lane from the east up into the Aegean while at the same time being quite difficult of access by land. It is first mentioned in the sources in AD 724. Whether it had an earlier history only excavation will tell. As a naval station it was hardly a city as it never had a bishop. It was, however, an important military and administrative point for collecting customs dues. It doubled as a place of exile and refuge. Bishop Theophylact of Nicomedia was confined here for 30 years for opposing Emperor Leo's iconoclasm, while St Andrew the Fool-for-Christ, at about the same time, thought it would be a good place to be when the end of the world that he had prophesied overtook the Earth.

After the Battle of Manzikert, Strobylos was sacked by the Seljuk Turks in 1080, but recovery was quick under the Comneni and Lascarids. When the Byzantines gave up the south coast, Strobylos became a nest of Turkish pirates conducting a flourishing slave trade. Later, as part of the Menteşe Emirate, one hears of a strong presence of Venetian traders and of a substantial Jewish colony, reflected in a the alternative appellation of the site as Çıfıt Kalesi (Castle of the Jews). When it was raided by the combined action of the King of Cyprus and the Grand Master of Rhodes in 1472, four hundred houses were torched, suggesting a sizeable settlement. It still appears on portolans in Ottoman times but when Evliya Çelebi visited in the 17th century he found it deserted.

In 1857 Charles Newton made a number of observations. He described a square citadel on the highest point with projecting towers and cisterns. He found evidence of a walled civilian settlement, terraced on the landward side of the hill overlooking the clear stream at the bottom and its watermills. Scattered remains of marble and inscriptions suggested a church and a monastery.

GARA AND ALAZEYTİN

Just west of Bodrum, the village of Bitez may be worth a stop just to check if the church at Gara is accessible. The building, signposted 'Chapel' with a yellow sign, has not yet been investigated. It has been suggested that the building and the mosaic floor do not belong together, which does not detract in any way from the beauty of the mosaic, which features some very fine fish.

The ruins of Alazeytin are east of Bodrum facing the Orak Körfezi. They can be accessed via Çiftlik (it is about an hour's walk to the west among the olive trees) or from Kızılağac, where they are signposted but not all the way. Presently Alazeytin, even in its remote location, is beginning to attract visitors as part of a more adventurous Bodrum peninsula trail; it is on offer from some local tourist operators. It is advisable to get a guide locally or to join an organised tour.

The name of the place is modern. Although it is frequently identified with one of the two Lelegian settlements in the area mentioned in the written sources, either Theangela or Syangela, there is nothing to prove that it is either. It is certainly a native settlement, not Greek or Carian, which by default makes it Lelegian. It is situated on a knoll at an altitude of 300m overlooked from the west by the Koca Dağ, where a smaller fortified settlement has been identified as a refuge. From its vantage point, Alazeytin has a view of the gulf and of the access along a valley. Wolfgang Radt made an exhaustive survey of the site in the 1970s, beyond that not much work has been done.

In his survey Radt identified a walled citadel entered from the west at the centre of the settlement with a secluded compound arranged around a rock-cut cistern in the middle. The balance of the walled space was occupied by a large sanctuary. The watchtower with the different masonry, situated on the highest point, is of a later date. To the east an open space was identified as an agora and at its edges a number of single-room structures with tiled roofs, too large to be dwellings, have been identified as public buildings or temples. A 10m-long seating arrangement made of large blocks looks like a rudimentary theatre or viewing area. The style of these limestone constructions, with roughly cut, large, irregular blocks and the occasional small stones to fill the gaps, differs markedly from the later, beautiful Carian stonework that you can see at the Myndus Gate in Bodrum, for example. It is no more than functional. The civilian settlement clustered around the citadel was also walled. It looks unplanned, with small square rooms tightly packed in an agglutinative architectural style with no axial alignment. It had been thought that the Lelegians build round structures, but these are now known to be animal pens. Indeed a few have been identified at Küçük Kalesi, 300m to the south of the walled settlement.

The most intriguing feature of the site is the presence of Aeolic capitals in the public buildings of the citadel with the characteristic palmettes and volutes that do not look quite Lelegian; they have been dated to the second half of the 6th century BC, though judging by the pottery the buildings themselves are later. They remain unexplained. According to Radt the settlement started in the 7th century BC or earlier, suffered great damage at the hands of the Persian Harpagos in the 540s and declined in the 4th century BC. At that point it was minting coins.

PRACTICAL INFORMATION

TOURIST INFORMATION

Bodrum Tourist Information Office (*open daily May–Sept 8–5.30*) is just north of the castle.

GETTING AROUND

By air: Bodrum International Airport between Milas and Bodrum, with a national and an international terminal, is very busy in the summer mainly with charter and budget airline flights. The Havaş Shuttle (*milas-bodrumairport. com*) is timed to coincide with internal flights.

By bus: The Bodrum Otogar, conveniently still in the centre of town, now welcomes buses from anywhere in Turkey. In the old days the bus route use to bypass this area, going straight from Aydın to Muğla. That was before Bodrum became a major holiday resort. For some locations on the Bodrum peninsula you will be able to get a dolmuş (look out for the turquoise ones). The other colours serve town (orange) and Gümbet (green).

By ferry: You can reach Bodrum by ferry from Kos, Rhodes and from the Datça peninsula. Other ferries operating from Bodrum to local destinations can be unreliable. You may be able to find a departure time but it is not clear when you will be able to get back or how long the trip will take.

WHERE TO STAY

Bodrum is well provided with accommodation. Some large hotels have sprung up recently, while anyone who could lay hands on a house has turned it into a pansiyon. If you arrive on a late bus you may find pansiyon managers prospecting for clients at the otogar.

The new hotels all have swimming pools and beautiful views—which come at a price and in a location outside the city centre. The smaller outfits delight you with shady courtyards and are likely to be more central. At the luxury end of the spectrum, consider the Marmara Hotel (*themarmarahotels.com*) which is part of a chain, or the Aegean Gate Hotel (*aegeangatehotel.com*). In the heart of town you can try the Anfora Pansiyon (*anforapansiyon.com*) on Dere Sk in the Omurca district (off Atatürk Cd.,; *east of the area shown on the map*) or the Hotel Güleç nearby (*hotelgulec.com*). There is also the very pleasant Hotel Su (*suhotelbodrum.com*) on 1201 Sk.

Some of these central pansiyons come with car parking but not all. Do check. Driving and parking in Bodrum can be challenging. The one-way street system is baffling to the uninitiated.

If you want to to be sure of a good night's sleep away from the noise of the nightlife, the Butterfly B&B (*T: 252 313 83 58*), between Bodrum and Gümbet, high up on Ünlü Cd. with a fine view, is the place for you. Run by an American couple, it only has six rooms, so you will need to book.

Finally, on Atatürk Cd., Bodrum Backpackers (*bodrumbackpackers.net*) will give you the use of a bed and a laundrette.

WHERE TO EAT

As one might expect, fast food reigns supreme; indeed Gümbet, the beach resort north of Bodrum, used to offer nothing else when it was first developed. However, these days Bodrum has a more varied menu. Bearing in mind that the price sometimes goes with the view, it may be best to forgo the latter for a moment and indulge in mezes, fresh fish and sample some exotic cuisine. While it is possible to enjoy good Turkish fare at the Urfa Diyarı, where the locals go (in the Oasis shopping centre on Turgut Reis Cd.; *just beyond the map to the west*), one should not miss the chance to try Spanish at La Pasión on Atatürk Cd., east of the castle in an old stone house (quite a rarity here since Bodrum up until comparatively recently was just a village; the only stone buildings were the castle, the mosques and the cisterns). Alternatively, you can eat Argentinian at the Tango Restaurant in the Marina Vista Hotel on Neyzen Tevfik Cd.

For the catch of the day go the Fish Market on Çarşı Sk, along Cevat Şakir Cd., past the post office going towards the mountains. When you reach the crossing with Atatürk Cd., look for a narrow opening to your left between a fishmonger and a greengrocer. You will find a large hall with a number of restaurants. The best eating places will be the busiest. (A word of warning: because the hall is large and the ceiling very high, the smoking ban is not strictly applied in spite of the numerous 'No Smoking' signs.) Alternatively, try the Gemibaşı on Neyzen Tevfik Cd. For a good spread of mezes, the Orfoz on Zeki Müren Cd. (east of the castle) is a good choice.

WHAT TO DO

Spend time at the market. It is a feast of colours. Bodrum has one every day of the week.

GENERAL PRACTICAL TIPS

WHEN TO GO

The Aegean coast of Turkey was firmly on the tourist map before Turkey or a Turkish state existed. Pilgrims to the Holy Land would make landfall on the coast and continue their long journey inland. Later, antiquarians also made the journey. The ruins in those days were quite spectacular and news of still-standing Classical buildings was not slow to reach Europe. Mass tourism also came early to the Aegean coast, as holidaymakers flocked to the beaches after WW2, looking for sun and fun. The cultural side has developed alongside this, but in a more muted fashion.

If you want to avoid the crowds and are prepared to forego the swimming and the nightlife, the best seasons to choose are spring (April–May) and autumn (late Sept–Oct). Winter has its attractions too and temperatures can be mild (as long as you do not go too far inland).

GETTING AROUND

The Troy to Bodrum region is well served in terms of transport facilities.

BY AIR
You can fly directly to Bodrum in the summer from a number of locations in Europe. İzmir Airport has scheduled non-stop connections to Europe all year round. Both regional airports have good connections to the city centre either by bus (Bodrum) or by train and bus (İzmir and Bodrum). Alternatively there will be local flights from Sabiha Gökçen International Airport on the Asian shore of Istanbul. If you are travelling onward from Istanbul by coach, try to arrive in Turkey on a flight that gets in to Atatürk Airport. From there there is a good metro connection to the otogar, where you will find a number of coach operators.

BY BUS AND COACH
The coach network is quite comprehensive: you can get to most destinations. If you arrive in Istanbul, it is best to make a start from the main otogar. It is pointless to try and find a coach from the Asian side. Local people all know where to go, but for the uninitiated, encumbered with luggage, it can be trying. Competition is fierce but shopping around is probably a waste of time. It is easiest simply to go for the first available bus. As a foreigner you will be quickly spotted and the staff at the ticket

office will offer you the help you need. If you are at the wrong booth, they will bodily take you to a colleague covering the area you want.

When you have a ticket, note that it has a *koltuk numarası*, an allocated seat number. These are assigned so that women do not sit next to men who are not relatives. The rule is not as strict as it used to be, but it is still implemented; so do not take a different seat unless you wish to start a minor diplomatic incident. The other thing to note on the ticket is the *peron* number. That is the bay your coach goes from. Some coaches leave from unexpected places, outside the coach station. It is a good idea to look as clueless as possible. The staff in the ticket office will help you to get on the right coach.

Coach stations have waiting rooms, shops and eateries to while the time away; if you do not wish to be encumbered with your luggage, ask your ticket office if you can leave it there. It is a good idea to hang around the ticket office anyway, to remind the staff of your presence. When you board, your luggage goes in the hold and, these days, you are normally given a token with a number so you can reclaim it. Serious valuables should always stay with you.

Coaches tend to be full. There is a lot of supply but also a lot of demand. Turks take long coach journeys in their stride from an early age (which may explain why the children are so quiet and well behaved).

Coaches have no toilets on board. There will be comfort stops at huge roadside cafés every three hours or so. Stops normally last in the region of 20–30mins. The driver will make an announcement containing the word *dakika* (minute); the number preceding it tells you how long you have. Memorise which coach is yours; there will easily be a dozen or so other buses around, all looking very similar. Head for the toilet queue (do so without delay if you are a woman; the queues for the female toilets are always longer as all the children are there) and have some small change ready. The roadside cafés have everything from self-service restaurants to shops with fresh fruit. Look out for the stalls selling frothy *ayran*, a healthy yoghurt-based drink, and fresh *poğaça* or *börek*. The coach will leave at the appointed time or thereabouts: it will not wait. There is no head count and no one will notice your absence if you are not back on board.

On board some of the coaches there are free cups of sealed chilled water as well as the occasional cup of tea, coffee, orange or Cola.

BY DOLMUŞ
For local destinations you will travel by dolmuş. These can also be flagged down on the road and if there is room they will let you on. Note that in a dolmuş, seating restrictions do not apply and fares are paid to the driver. Pass your cash down the bus and the change will be returned to you by the same route. Dolmuşes may depart from somewhere in town, from the ilce otogar or from the main coach station. Enquire at your hotel.

BY TRAIN
Travelling by train is another possibility. The development of rail transport in Anatolia goes back to 1856, when the Ottoman government built the first track from İzmir to

Aydın in the west of the country, a total of 130km. Since then, expansion of the network has been muted. Road transport has until recently been given priority. Considering that the area covered by this section of the guide is comparatively a not very large one, you might find that railway routes are of little help. Buses are likely to be more efficient.

BY CAR

Travelling by car is of course the best option if you want to visit a number of out-of-the-way places. Only the very brave would choose to hire a car in Istanbul, which entails negotiating the city's hectic traffic. Car rental is in any case widely available. You can arrange to pick up a vehicle at the airport or at your hotel or a destination close by (ask your hotel to arrange the delivery). You will be able then to return the car at the hotel. The staff will be happy to help. Avoid driving in town if you can and leave early in the morning.

Some car rental companies may have familiar names, but the Turkish branches of these firms do apply their own standards. Make sure when you pick up your car to check the basics such as the presence of a spare wheel in the boot and a jack (every piece of it); check the windscreen for cracks, note the various dents and scratches and so on, and take a few pictures.

Travelling with your own transport affords great freedom and pleasure but it comes at a price. While the road network is good, roads can be very busy, especially between Bergama and İzmir, where there is a lot of heavy industry (which explains all the lorry traffic).

Car hire in itself is not expensive but petrol is. Petrol is available near and in towns and on main trunk roads. The countryside away from the main roads can be pretty empty and there is nothing much in the villages; note that occasionally petrol stations may have run out of the sort petrol your car takes. Do not leave it too late. Cars are normally delivered with a full tank and are expected to be returned with a full tank. It is also worth tidying up the interior of your car and giving it a wash before you return it, to avoid an extra, irritating charge.

MAPS

On the whole the choice of maps is limited and those that are available are poor in detail compared to the standard motoring maps you find in Europe, for example. The biggest scale you can get is 1:700,000 (meaning that 1cm corresponds to 7km). It might be worth hiring a SatNav loaded with the maps covering your destination before you leave home. It will certainly be useful in the towns. Rural areas will not be covered in so much detail.

On the whole, destinations are well signposted along the main traffic axes. Beyond that, on the smaller roads, there is plenty of scope for adventure. It is best to explore with plenty of time ahead of you and a full tank.

The Turkish Aegean coastline is dotted with beaches. Normally if a beach has some tourist facilities (deckchairs etc.), environmental standards will be higher. Venturing along an unmarked lane towards the sea can result in the discovery of a beach but also of a lot of unwelcome rubbish.

PRONUNCIATION GUIDE

Turkish was originally written in Arabic script. Atatürk, in a drive to modernise the country, introduced a modified Latin alphabet in 1928. It uses a total of 29 letters, to take into account the specific requirements of the language. Unlike English, Turkish is a phonetic language, so it is easy to read it in order to ask for directions.

A	as in <u>a</u>damant	İ	as in <u>I</u>taly
E	as in <u>e</u>lephant	I	as in mantr<u>a</u>
Ç	as in <u>ch</u>arming	O	as in p<u>o</u>nd
C	a soft g, as in <u>G</u>eneva	Ö	as in b<u>ir</u>d
G	a hard g, as in <u>G</u>anges	Ş	as in di<u>sh</u>
Ğ	a consonant that is not voiced. It occurs between two vowels, separating them and lengthening the first one.	U	as in l<u>u</u>minous
		Ü	as in Z<u>ü</u>rich
		Y	as in <u>y</u>eti

ACCOMMODATION

Accommodation is plentiful in Aegean Turkey but you do need to book in the summer. Bear in mind also that out of season, small pansiyons (and even some hotels) may be closed. The very basic accommodation that is normally available in the east or in Anatolia is rarer here because the hospitality industry is older. Standards (and prices) tend to be higher. If you are visiting destinations inland and you have your own transport, it will pay to explore what is available in the towns there. Do the usual check on the quality of the mattress, the performance of the shower, and the reliability of the hot water.

Half-board can sometimes not be avoided. Breakfast is normally included, but do check. It can be very variable and is not always terribly exciting. Coffee (not Turkish coffee unfortunately) will be available but you may have to ask for milk. The choice of food is normally rather thin and uninspiring.

The answer is to look out for a *kahvaltı salonu* (a breakfast salon) or an *un mamulleri* (a place where they sell flour-based products, a pâtisserie). Check that they have tables: it means they will serve coffee and tea; in any case there will be hot water available: if you like, you can bring your own coffee granules. Go for böreks, baklava, biscuits that come in sweet (but not too sweet) and savoury varieties and buns (*poğaça*). If you spot a MADO, a branch of the smart catering chain that is now spreading across Turkey, take the plunge and breakfast on ice-cream, *salep* (a traditional Ottoman warm milky drink) and any sweet that takes your fancy. Some of the branches offer dinner as well, so you can come back later.

TIMELINE

PALAEOLITHIC

Limited research and limited evidence (e.g. in the Çeşme Peninsula)
6th millennium BC: Beginning of the Cretan Neolithic. If, as it is thought, settlers came via Rhodes and the Karpathos islands, the Aegean coast was already inhabited by people able to take to the sea with their domesticated cattle

BRONZE AGE

Mid-4th millennium BC: Settlement evidence in Troy (Troy 0)
2nd millennium BC: Diffuse Mycenaean presence on the west Aegean coast and up the Meander Valley. Limited Hittite presence.
1200 BC: Trojan War

IRON AGE

1100 BC: The Aeolians. The earliest migration wave from the Greek mainland followed by the Ionians and the Dorians (the coast becomes known as Ionia)

ARCHAIC AND CLASSICAL PERIODS (900–323 BC)

Mid-6th century BC **to 332** BC: The Persians, mainland Greeks and local powers fight for supremacy
546 BC: The Persians overthrow the Lydian kingdom of Croesus
494 BC: Battle of Lade. Miletus is defeated by the Persians
480 BC: End of the Persian threat. The Persians retreat home
480–c. 400 BC: Athenian supremacy. The Delian League
387–332 BC: The King's Peace: return of the Persians. A peaceful period Ionian Renaissance. Mausolus builds his Mausoleum

HELLENISTIC PERIOD (334–167 BC)

Alexander the Great conquers Asia Minor. The map of Ionia and its hinterland is redrawn by his successors

ROMAN PERIOD (167 BC–AD 337) AND BEYOND

133 BC: Pergamene bequest. Setting up of the Roman Province of Asia.

88–83 BC: Mithridatic wars

13 BC: Battle of Actium sealing the power struggle in Rome and bringing peace to its empire. A time of prosperity begins. The major upsets at this time are geological, from earthquakes

260: The Goths: a taste of troubled times to come

337: Death of Constantine. The empire is now Byzantine with its capital in Constantinople

7th–9th centuries: Arab incursions from the south by land and by sea. Raids, no settlements

9th century: Beginning of infiltration of nomadic Turks form the East. Raids and settlement

1071: Battle of Manzikert. The Byzantine Empire is under serious threat. The Byzantine-imposed security in the east Mediterranean crumbles. The Levant becomes a land of opportunities for pirates and warlords

1204–61: The Byzantine Empire is divided into four. In Asia Minor the Nicaean Empire brings a measure of stability to coastal and some inland regions

1243: At Köşedağ the Mongols defeat the Seljuks. The Sultanate of Rum is reduced to vassalage. By the turn of the century it will break up into several emirates that will eventually dislodge the Byzantines from the Aegean coast and attack the islands

1299–1923: The Ottomans, from small beginnings, build an empire which eventually unifies Anatolia and extends into the Middle East, Europe and North Africa

1923: The Republic of Turkey is founded.

GLOSSARY

Acrolithic A statue where the exposed extremities are made of stone or other durable material while the (originally draped) body is made of something cheaper and less fine

Acroterion A decorative element, normally in fired clay, mounted on the roof apex of an ancient public building

Adyton The inner part of the cella of a temple, a place of restricted access

Aedicula An architectural feature looking like a small temple

Ağa The landowner in a Turkish village

Alevi Refers to the followers of a branch of Islam

Analemma The retaining wall on the outer edge of a Greek or Roman theatre

Anta A pillar or a post on either side of the doorway of an ancient temple. When these project forward to create a porch, with columns between the projections, the columns are said to be 'in antis'

Apotropaic With the power to ward off evil

Arcuate Of a lintel, arched

Bekçi The Turkish word for the guardian of an archaeological site

Belediye A Turkish municipality or Town Hall

Bothros A pit into which libations and offerings to the gods are poured or placed

Bucranium (pl. bucrania) An element of Classical decoration featuring an ox skull draped with garlands

Bouleuterion A public building in the Classical Greek world, where the council of citizens (the *boule*) met

Boustrophedon System of writing where lines go in alternate directions, left to right and right to left; the term refers to how a team of oxen would plough a field

Börek A baked savoury flaky pastry with a meat or cheese filling, a mainstay of Turkish cuisine. Not to be confused with *su böreği*, which resembles macaroni cheese

Chalcolithic Period The very beginning of the Bronze Age, when copper was worked unalloyed

Caravanserai, Caravansaray A large building used for trade and storage in both town and countryside in the East. A safe place for pilgrims and merchants

Castellum aquae In the Roman era, a building functioning as a holding tank from which water brought by an aqueduct was directed to the pipes supplying the town

Cavea The semicircular seating bowl of a Classical theatre, frequently built against the natural slope of a hill

Cella Inner part of a Classical temple

Clerestory The upper part of a church nave, pierced with windows intended to add light to its central portion

Colonia In the ancient Roman world, an outpost in a newly subjected land, normally implying an input of citizens from the conquering power

Crepidoma The stepped platform of a Greek temple

Diazoma In a Greek theatre, the

passage dividing the upper from the lower rows of seats

Dipteros A temple surrounded by a double row of columns

Dodecanese A group of islands in the southeast Aegean, of which Rhodes is the largest

Dolmuş A cheap and cheerful form of Turkish public transport, a bus that makes unofficial stops and pick-ups, not normally used for long-distance travel

Dromos The entrance passage to an ancient tomb

Dipylon A monumental gate

Emir A Turkish chief, one level below a sultan

Ephebe An adolescent boy of the upper classes brought up in Classical society to be a leader

Ephebeum A large hall in an ancient gymnasium for young people to exercise, socialise and learn the civic values of their city

Episcopeion The bishop's residence

Euergetism A practice mainly known from ancient Greek and Roman times, whereby wealthy citizens financed high-status public buildings and facilities

Exedra A semicircular recess or alcove in a building

Firman Document conveying the sultan's orders in an Islamic context

Gigantomachy Scene of a battle between gods and giants, the opposing forces of order and chaos

Graben a depressed segment of land flanked by two parallel faults (*see Horst*)

Hamam A Turkish bath

Heroön A sepulchral monument dedicated to the memory of a hero

Horst The raised ridges of land on either side of a graben (*qv*)

Hüyük A man-made elevation, the result of a long sequence of occupations, usually found in conjunction with mud-brick architecture; also called a tell or a mound

Hypogeum In Classical architecture, an underground feature

İlce otogar A minor bus station in a Turkish town, for local travel using a minibus rather than a coach

İmaret A soup kitchen in a Turkish context

In antis The term describes a Classical temple with a recessed porch in front framed by an extension of the side walls and by columns

Insula The basic unit of Classical town planning; a block of housing

Ionian Renaissance The flourishing of art and culture that took place on the shores of the eastern Aegean in the 6th–5th centuries

Isodomic A construction technique using masonry blocks of uniform sizes with the joints placed at the centre of the blocks above and below.

İwan A recess closed on three sides in a colonnaded courtyard of a large

TYPES OF MASONRY

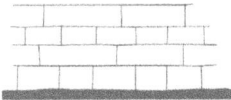

Isodomic

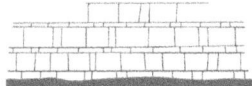

Pseudo-isodomic

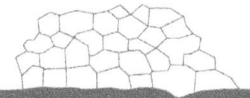

Polygonal

Islamic public building

Kışla *See Yayla*

Kouros A sculpture of a Greek youth of the Archaic Period, in a standardised frontal pose

Lokanta A restaurant in Turkey

Luwian An extinct Indoeuropean language of Anatolia, written either in cuneiform or hieroglyphs and spoken from the 2nd and 1st millennia until c. 600 BC by people about whom little is known

Kastron A Byzantine stronghold

Külliye A complex of buildings centred around a mosque and managed as a single institution; it may include a caravanserai, a mausoleum, a school, a hospital and baths

Macellum In antiquity, a covered (indoor) retail market

Megaron The large room of a well-appointed ancient Greek dwelling; the term is used also in non-Greek contexts

Menteşe Medieval Turkish dynasty from the Aegean region, who came to prominence with the decline of the Seljuks (13th century)

Meze A Turkish appetizer

Metope An element of the frieze of a temple of the Doric Order

Mimber In a mosque, the pulpit from which sermons are delivered

Medrese/Madrasa An Islamic school for teenage boys

Naiskos A small secluded space, shaped like a mini temple, with columns and a pediment

Neokorate Originally a neokoros was the warden of a temple but around the 1st century AD the title started to be attributed to whole communities as guardians of a local cult. Soon it became an honour bestowed on cities devoted to the Roman imperial cult, mainly in Asia, and as such was a source of immense prestige and expense

Nymphaeum In the Classical world, a natural feature or built monument sacred to the nymphs and associated with water

Oculus In Latin 'the eye'. The opening in a dome allowing the light (and the rain) in

Odeion A small Classical roofed theatre

Opus sectile A wall or floor cladding made of pieces of different types of coloured stone, cut to shape

Otogar In Turkish, the main coach station of a town (though often located some way from the centre)

Palaestra The exercise yard in a Classical gymnasium or baths complex

Pansiyon (spelled in various ways) A small Turkish hotel, a guest house

Paradeisos The Greek name for Persian parks and gardens; the term evokes something grand and prestigious bordering on the otherwordly, hence our 'paradise'

Paşa A high ranking official in the Ottoman administration and army

Pediment A low-pitched gable above a portico, doorway or window

Pekmez A sort of molasses made in Turkey out of condensed grape juice

Peripteros A temple completely surrounded by a colonnade

Peristyle Inner space of a house open to the skies and edged by columns

Pithoi Very large vessels used for storage

Poğaça A savoury bun

Polygonal Construction technique using irregularly laid large blocks

Pronaos The vestibule at the front of a classical temple

Prostyle A temple with a full row of

TYPES OF COLUMN

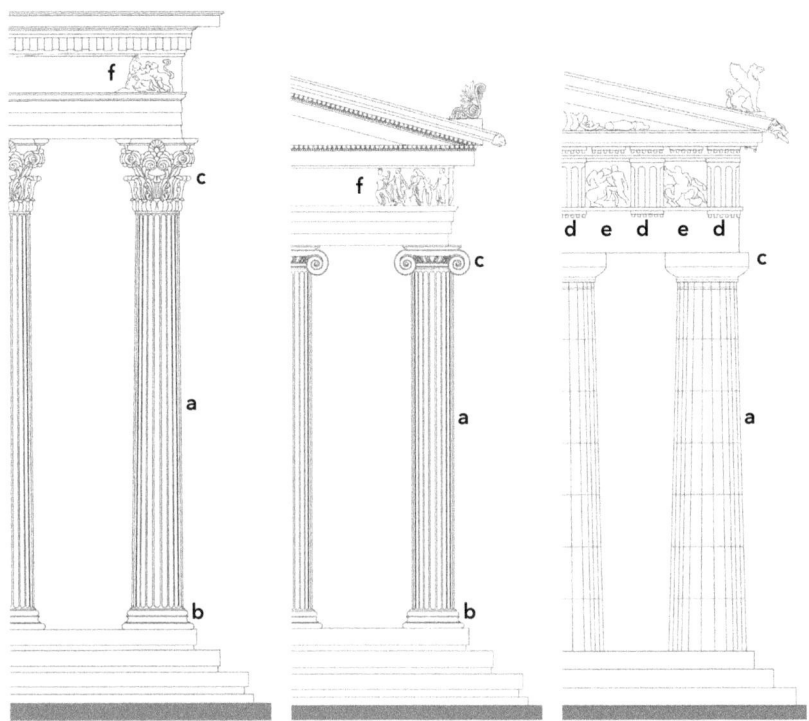

Right: Section of a temple portico in the Doric order. The column shaft **(a)** is stout, made of fluted stone rings placed one on top of another. The shaft stands directly on the temple platform, without a base. The capital **(c)** is plain. Above it, the entablature is decorated with triglyphs **(d)** alternating with carved metopes **(e)**.

Centre: Section of a temple portico in the Ionic order. The column shaft **(a)** is slender and fluted and stands on a base **(b)**. The capital **(c)** is distinguished by its scrolls, known as volutes. Above a stepped architrave, the entablature is decorated with a continuous carved frieze **(f)**.

Left: Section of a temple portico in the Corinthian order. The column shaft **(a)** is very tall, slender and fluted and stands on a base **(b)**. The capital **(c)** is distinguished by its decoration of acanthus leaves. The entablature is decorated with a continuous carved frieze **(f)**.

columns at the front

Prytaneion The heart and hearth of the city, where the sacred fire, symbol of its vitality, was kept, together with the official weights and measures

Propylon A monumental gateway

Pseudo-dipteros The term refers to a temple on the same plan as a dipteros but instead of being surrounded by two rows of columns, there is only an outer row. As a result, in the space which would be occupied by the second, inner row, a large space is created, an ambulatory between the columns and the cella wall

Pseudo-isodomic Construction technique where the core of the wall is rubble masonry and the facing is made of uniform blocks of ashlar, in courses of alternating taller and narrower blocks (*see illustration on p. 213*)

Şadırvan The fountain in the centre of a mosque courtyard used for ritual ablutions

Satrap Under Persian rule, a governor or proconsul

Sebasteion A sanctuary of the Roman imperial cult

Skene, Scaena The stage building of a Classical theatre

Società dei Dilettanti A London club whose members had been on the Grand Tour and wished to promote things Classical

Spolia Elements of Classical monuments reused as building material or ornaments in later buildings. The practice flourished from late antiquity onward

Stoa In Classical architecture, a covered portico for public, civic use

Stylobate The continuous base on which a row of columns stands

Synthronon Semicircular structure behind the high altar in early churches, with a throne for the bishop and benches for the clergy

Temenos A defined piece of land marked off for religious use; a temple precinct

Tetraconch A building with four apses

Tetrastyle A building with four pillars

Thermae An ancient Roman public baths complex

Topos A traditional theme in literature

Tholos A small circular building in Classical architecture

Triconch A building with three apses

Türbe A Turkish monumental tomb

Türkmen A controversial term used in this guide to indicate the nomads who infiltrated Asia Minor from the 10th century; also called Yürüks (those who walk). According to some, the term should only be applied to the descendants of specific Turkish tribes from Central Asia who moved west and remained faithful to their original nomadic lifestyle. These are considered the real Turks of pure blood. More restrictively still, the term is applied only to those who were Muslim

Velarium The awning stretching over the seating area of a Roman theatre

Xoanon A cult image made of wood

Yayla/Kışla Terms indicating summer and winter pastures in Turkish

INDEX

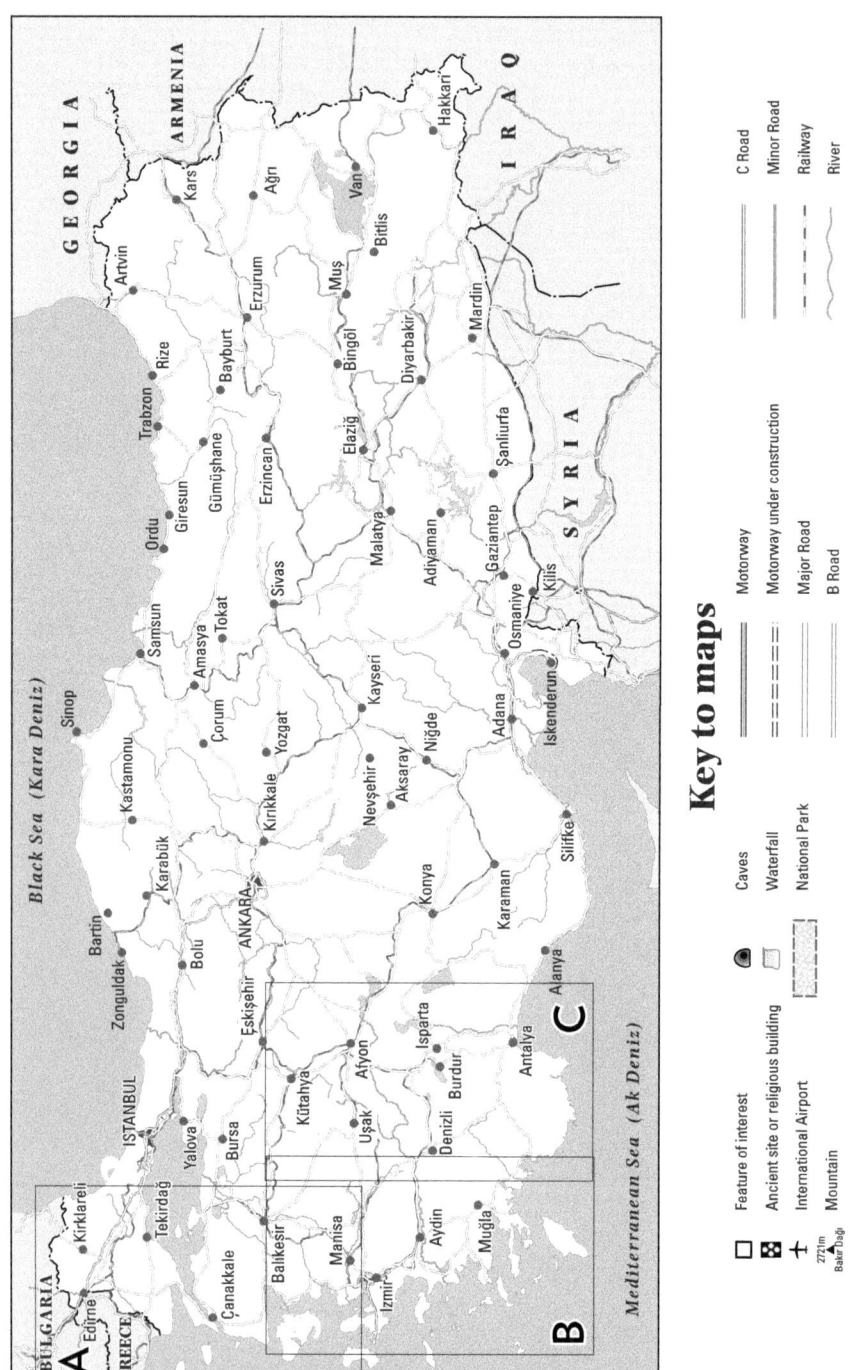

Key to maps

□ Feature of interest	══ Motorway
✠ Ancient site or religious building	═ ═ ═ Motorway under construction
✈ International Airport	══ Major Road
▲ 2721 m Baba Dağı Mountain	══ B Road
◉ Caves	══ C Road
▢ Waterfall	══ Minor Road
▦ National Park	～ Railway
	～ River

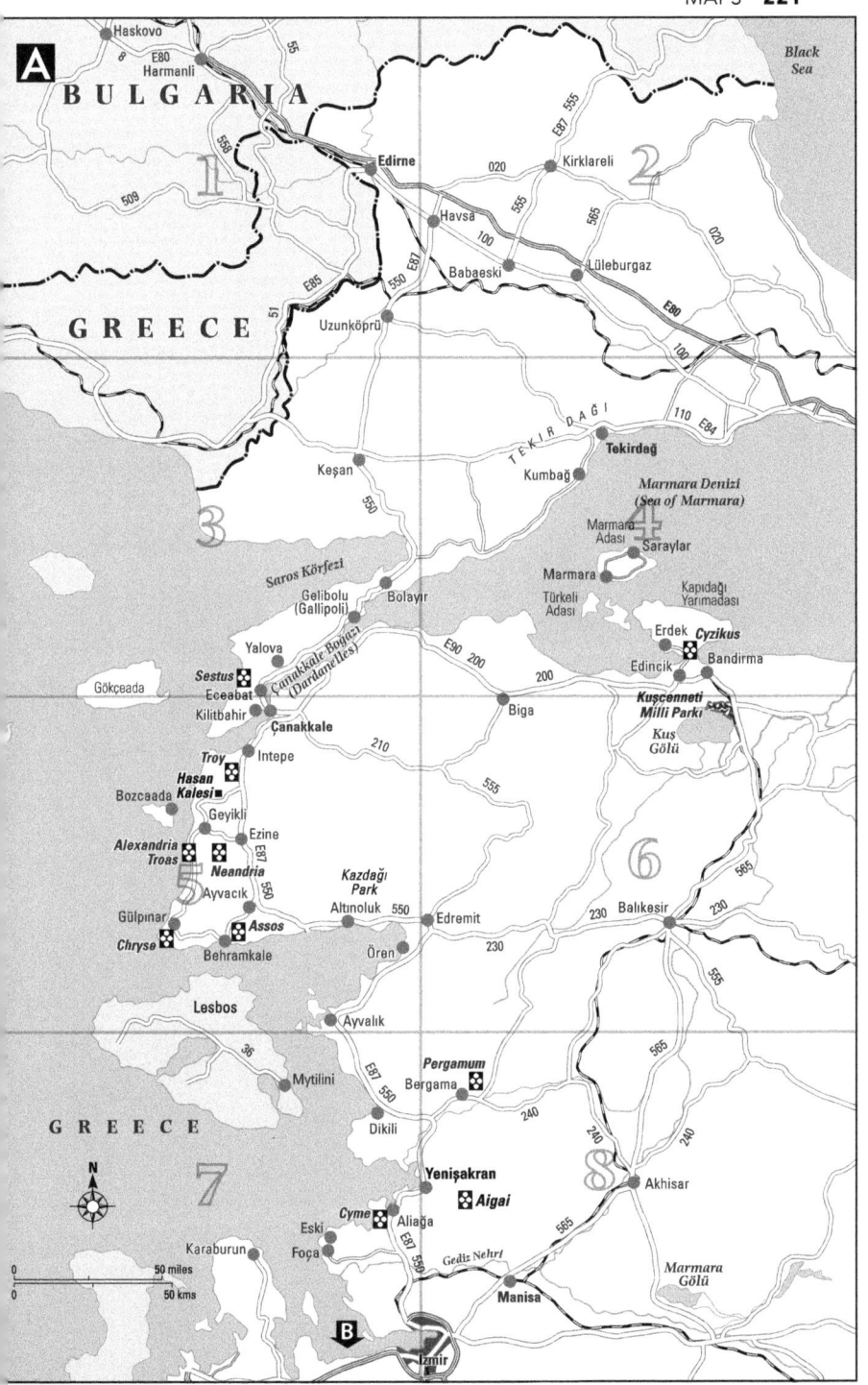

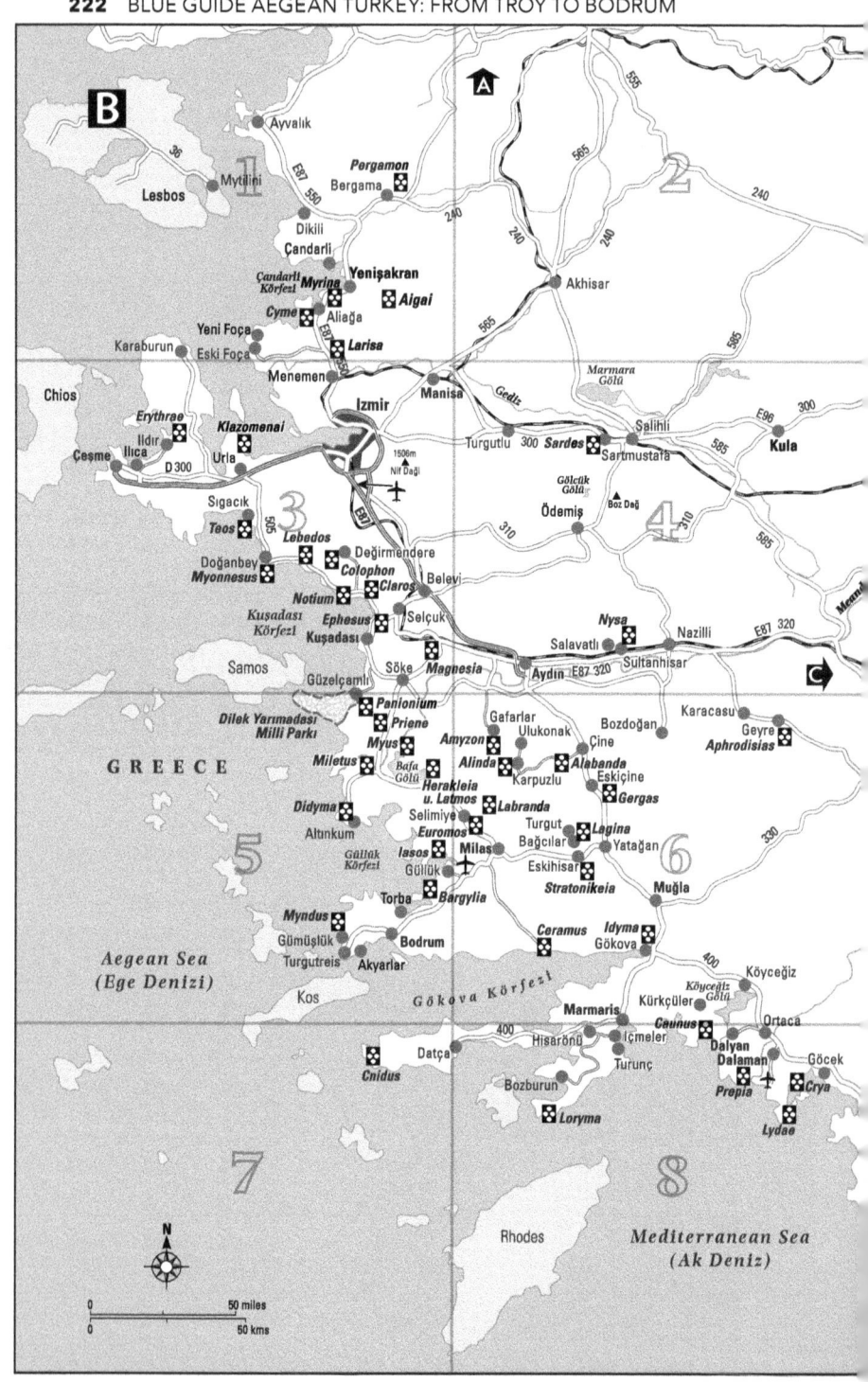

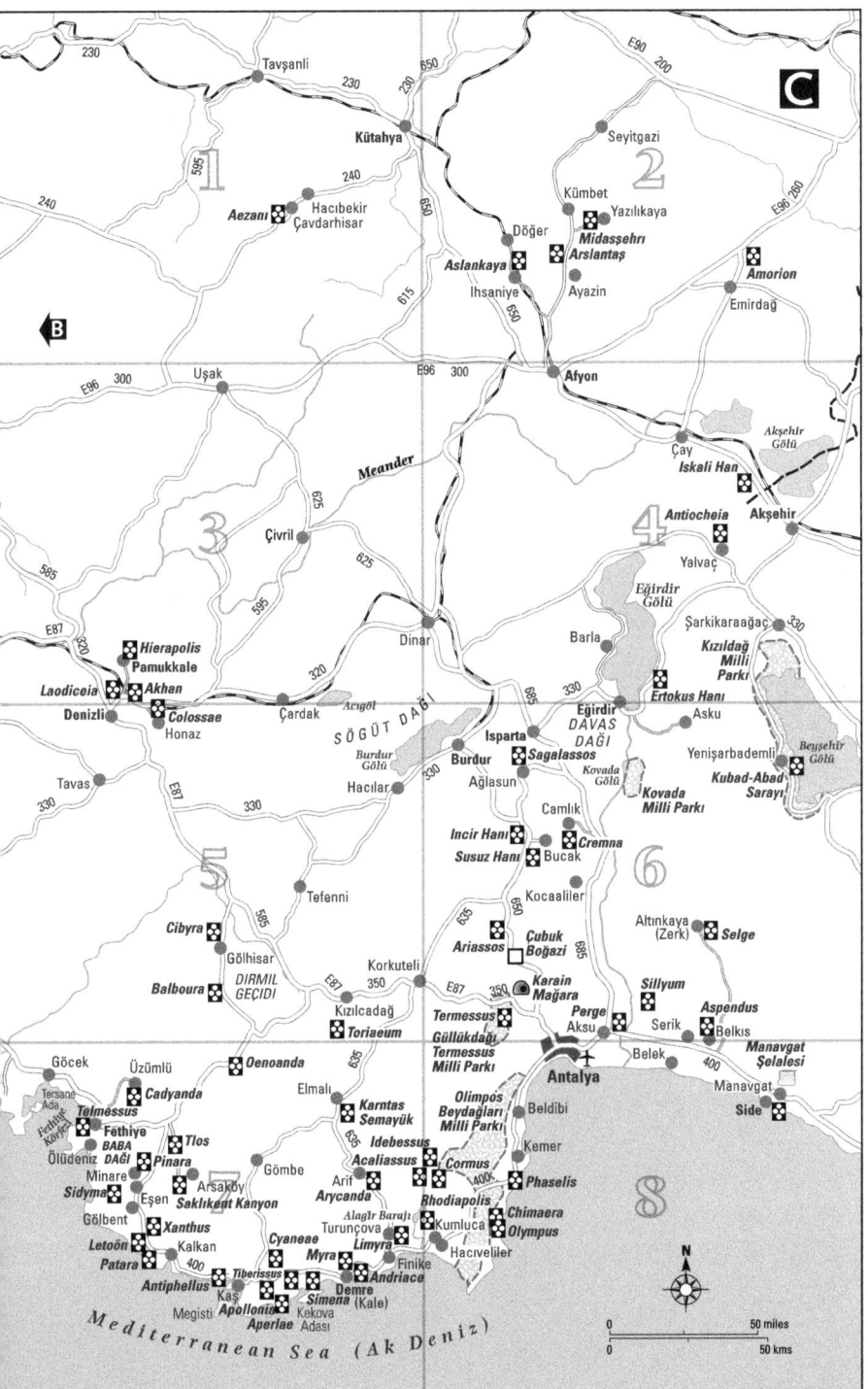

Milton Keynes UK
Ingram Content Group UK Ltd.
UKHW022224180823
427047UK00009B/176

9 781916 568006